Who Let the Dogs Out?

'The times they are a - changing.'
Bob Dylan

'In Xanadu did Kubla Khan a stately pleasure dome decree.'
Samuel Taylor Coleridge

Who Let the Dogs Out?

The Revival of Newport Rugby

Steve Lewis

Vertical Editions

First published in the United Kingdom in 2002 by Vertical Editions,
18-20 Blackwood Hall Lane, Luddendenfoot, Halifax HX2 6HD

Editor, Valerie Rice

ISBN 1-904091-01-6

Jacket design and typeset by HBA, York

Printed and bound by CPI Bookcraft, Midsomer Norton

Contents

Acknowledgments

Writing a book is a lonely occupation. Many a time I had to ask myself why I had undertaken this mammoth task and what the recriminations would be if toes were trodden on, noses put out of joint and egos tampered with. When I sat down with Keith Grainger to discuss the concept of the book his prime concern was that it should tell the truth and, eighteen months later, looking back over the finished work I feel that this criteria has been satisfied. There may well be factual inaccuracies, which will be my sole responsibility, similarly there will certainly be opinions which the reader will disagree with and I must stress that such opinion is mine and mine alone unless otherwise indicated.

While the book is ultimately accredited to one person there are many whose contribution and encouragement cannot go unrecognised. Firstly, Tony Brown was enthusiastic about the project and readily made himself available from the outset. I hope his commitment is justified. On a day-to-day basis Keith Grainger gave of his time much more freely and copiously than I had any right to expect. Not only did he answer my many questions but contributed with anecdotes which I feel add to the content. Neither was he slow in correcting any error found when reading draft copies and this contribution is much appreciated. Likewise all the staff at Rodney Parade were generous with their time and opinions and they are all to be thanked.

I decided early on that to get a players perspective of the events of the last seven years I would rely on the input of three individuals; Rod Snow, Gary Teichmann and Andrew Powell. These players were chosen because I felt that between them they were able to view Newport firstly from the stance of a player who has been at the club throughout the professional era, secondly from one who came at the time when the revival began in earnest and finally from one who represents the future. All three offered an invaluable insight into the playing side but all who have pulled on the famous jersey during the period covered by the book have contributed to the story and my thanks also goes out to them.

Coaches Allan Lewis and Ian MacIntosh were an education to sit and listen to. These are men who really are at the sharp end of the game and the buck will inevitably stop with them and their like. Although they are there to be shot at, I hope my comments fairly reflect their valuable contribution.

Paul Williams and Dennis Bennett, past and present chairmen of Newport Rugby Supporters Club, helped put into perspective the animal that is a Newport supporter and helped identify this beast that was saved from the threat of extinction by the skin of its teeth.

A special thanks goes to Kevin Ward, Deputy Editor of the South Wales Argus who allowed me unlimited access to the papers excellent catalogue of photographs. All the photographic content of the book came from this source and I am grateful to Chief Photographer, Steve Phillips for his assistance in selecting the best. In addition to Steve the photographers are Peter Dash, Mark Lewis, Mike Lewis, Pendre Sims, Betina Skovbro and Adrian White.

Karl Waddicor, Managing Director of Vertical Editions, showed complete commitment to the project and even if he didn`t know that 'that try scored by the Barbarians' needed no further explanation, his general guidance was much appreciated.

Peter Owens read the manuscript and his comments were readily taken on board while John Billot kept telling me to write it. Whether he is to be thanked or not, others will decide.

Finally thanks must go to Mr Smudge and the Mouse. They cajoled, encouraged and pestered me into seeing the project through to the end. They know who they are but readers will have to guess.

Steve Lewis
Newport, September 2002.

Introduction

'Always make the audience suffer as much as possible.'
Alfred Hitchcock

It rained at Caerphilly on Saturday, 8 May 1999. The heavens opened and it rained. This was not your common or garden rain, this was the stuff of monsoons.

Watching from the shelter of the clubhouse at Caerphilly Rugby Football Club, expectant supporters looked on as ground staff worked to get a surface ready that would please referee Nigel Williams and allow the match to proceed as scheduled at 2.30 pm. Armed with forks and buckets of sand, and, looking more like fishermen digging for worms on the Gower Peninsula, they succeeded. In a few short hours the Black and Amber faithful, who had travelled the short distance up the A468 from Newport, would wish that they hadn't. For them this was to be their Armageddon, but why an end of season game that had no bearing on any promotion or relegation issue should merit the attention this encounter did needs explaining.

The 1998-99 season in Wales had started in chaos and had proceeded through the winter months into spring reeling from one crisis to the next. Newport Rugby Football Club had been in the thick of it from day one. More accurately, Newport RFC had been in the thick of it from day one minus five. Confused? So was everybody else.

The previous season had ended with Newport propping up the Premier Division and duly relegated. Politics at the highest level saw Cardiff and Swansea withdrawing from the league thereby handing Newport a lifeline, a fast track back to the top flight. Joined by Division One runners-up Aberavon, Newport had five days' notice that they would be playing against the top sides. Five days to prepare for the visit of Neath.

Fast forward to 8 May and the rain at Caerphilly. This was the fifth time the two clubs had met during the season. Caerphilly and

Newport had first played as recently as 1987 when Newport visited Virginia Park for a match to mark Caerphilly's Centenary .They next met in the seventh round of the SWALEC sponsored Welsh Cup, Newport winning 16-10. Now, three years later, the two clubs were meeting for the fifth time in a season. Why?

The Premier Division was made up of eight clubs and consequently there were only fourteen matches to be played. The WRU decided that after these matches had been completed the league would be divided into two groups. The four clubs in the top and bottom halves of the table would play each other home and away - a further six matches. Only then would the final league placings be decided. After the initial fourteen matches, Caerphilly and Newport were both in the bottom half of the table which resulted in two further fixtures bringing the total to four. Ironically, both clubs were in the same Pool in the European Shield competition which produced their fifth meeting of the season. Yes, the 1998-99 season was different.

This then was the scenario. On the one hand, Newport RFC, a club steeped in rugby history, victorious against the three major touring nations from the Southern Hemisphere - Australia, New Zealand and South Africa - and cradle for many Welsh international players and British Lions. Caerphilly RFC on the other hand, had spent over one hundred years in district league and cup competitions. Then, in 1992-93, the club won the Mid-District Tennants League and gained promotion to the big time - Welsh League, Division Four. Comfortable with its new status in the game the club gained further promotion in each of the following three seasons, arriving in Division One for the 1996-97 campaign. The following season saw the introduction of an eight team Premier Division. Newport were among the eight while Caerphilly were one of sixteen clubs in a new Division One. Newport ended the season propping up the Premier Division while Caerphilly, on the other hand, were Division One champions. The clubs should have passed as ships in the night, but fate took a hand, Cardiff and Swansea opting for cross-border competition, hence the five matches.

Now here comes the crunch, the reason the game at Caerphilly on that wet and miserable afternoon was of such significance. Caerphilly hadn't run out winners in one of the previous four matches played, nor indeed two. Caerphilly RFC had won all four previous encounters and, almost inevitably, they won the fifth. For the record the clubs met at Newport on 9 September and 7 November in the league and European Shield respectively, the visitors winning 28-20 and 35-30. The second league match at Caerphilly on 27 March ended 40-25 and the two play-off matches, at Newport on 28 April and finally at Caerphilly on 8 May finished with 35-16 and 36-20 scorelines. Not good reading if you're a Black and Amber supporter. Times were bad. Not even Cardiff had beaten Newport five times in a season. Four times yes, on four occasions with Newport failing to return the compliment. But five times, never! No team beats another five times in a season does it? Well, Caerphilly did and Newport are reminded of it every time the two clubs meet!

Sections on Caerphilly in local travel guides, in addition to informing tourists about the town's castle and the famous cheese, now relate tales of the locals' great sense of humour. Comic genius Tommy Cooper was born there on 22 March 1922 and the town's rugby club beat Newport five times in a season. Funny or not, it was probably the kick in the backside, the rude awakening, that Newport RFC needed.

This book attempts to explain, starting from August 1995, firstly how Newport RFC had plummeted to previously unimagined depths and secondly the events that raised the club back to the top of the domestic game in Wales. Over the seven-year period two stories unfold, one dependent on the other. The first tells how the reorganisation and restructuring of the club led to one of the great marketing successes the game has seen and the second relates the on-field events which saw the club challenging for senior honours once again.

The journey begins with a meeting in Paris and ends with another in Cardiff. The first, arguably the most important in the game's history, and the second, of equal importance to the future of the game in Wales. And more meetings. Meetings at airports, in hotels, overseas and in the boardroom at Rodney Parade. Then there are the on the field meetings. Those involving Newport's oldest and greatest rivals and those against new opponents, the best sides in Europe among them.

Many questions are asked. How good a club is Newport? Is its off-the-field marketing success matched by its on-the-field performances? And what of the new band of supporters that the club has attracted. What are they looking for from the club and the game? Then there are those that have followed Newport through thick and thin, mostly thin, in the recent past. Recent past? More like twenty five years - a not so recent past! What do they think of the turnaround and all that has changed in its wake? Finally, there are the broader issues. Is the game financially viable at club level? Will supporters still turn out to watch matches when they are being played at 3.30 am on a Tuesday because television rights decree it?

Not all these questions are easily answered. The subject, the game of rugby union as viewed from the stance of Newport RFC, is continually changing. Win a few important games or lose the very same games and the whole balance of the equation is affected.

It's all about success and it will be for the reader to decide if the levels of success reached by Newport RFC are acceptable and also, if there is good reason to be optimistic about an uncertain future.

However, one thing is certain. From the day the dogs were first let out at Rodney Parade things would never be the same again.

From Brown Envelopes to Blank Cheques

'The only true amateurs in sport these days are those who are no good at it.'

Chris Brasher - 1968

It was inevitable. It was always going to happen. The only question that remained unanswered was when? When would rugby union, the only major sport that retained an amateur ethos, bow to the pressures that were increasing day by day and become, like many before it, professional?

Whether in 1823, William Webb Ellis really did pick up a football and run with it or, whether the union game evolved from less fanciful events, for all its one hundred and seventy two years it had remained an amateur pursuit. That was the official line. Of course it was a nonsense. Everybody connected with the sport knew that the laws relating to amateurism were being regularly flouted throughout the rugby playing world. There was denial upon denial and no proof, but everybody knew. And everybody involved knew that everybody knew!

1995 witnessed a sequence of events that would lay to rest the days of brown envelopes and the other trappings of 'Shamateurism'. As with everything else the game had come to expect, the rumblings began in the Southern Hemisphere and grew to an almighty crescendo as the leading countries gathered in South Africa for the third Rugby World Cup. By the end of the tournament Australia, New Zealand and South Africa had signed a ten-year television deal that would see them playing each other on a home and away basis in a Tri-Nations tournament to rival the Northern Hemispheres' Five Nations. A provincial Super 12 tournament would also be launched in 1996 expanding the Super 10s which had been growing in popularity since its inception in 1993. The deal with Rupert Murdoch's Australian News Corporation was reputed to be in excess of £350 million over the ten-year period. The revenue generated would, in part, be filtered through to the players but not on a 'pay for play' basis. This coup by the three Unions managed to stave off proposals of a World Rugby Corporation bankrolled by Australian entrepreneur Kerry Packer who wanted to establish franchises on a global basis. WRC had held negotiations with the game's leading players from both hemispheres which left those in the north out on a limb when the players in the south made a commitment to remain within the auspices of their respective Unions.

The International Rugby Board had to act - and act it did. The Ambassador Hotel is located on Boulevard Haussmann in the 9th Arrondissement of Paris. It was here that the IRB met over the last weekend of August 1995 to discuss the current turmoil and, ultimately, the future of the game. On Sunday 27 August IRB Chairman, Vernon Pugh QC, faced the rugby press and media. His statement, while not unexpected, was nevertheless one of mind-blowing proportion. Rugby union would no longer be an amateur sport. It would become open, i.e. professional - with immediate effect.

'There has been a great deal of hypocrisy in the game, players have been paid for a number of years now, at club, state, province and international level,' said Mr Pugh. 'The system of trust funds that we had in place at international level was nothing more than a sham and we needed some honesty. We needed to demonstrate that rugby union was our game, the International Board's game and not a game that the media giants and others could suddenly seek to acquire.'

A few days later, in his capacity as Chairman of the Welsh Rugby Union, Mr Pugh viewed the development from the clubs' point of view and expressed 'concern that clubs will launch themselves into the transfer market and become involved in the highest bidding'. However it was felt that 'clubs have sufficient experience to know that there is no more money and that their budgets are fully extended. The answer lies in contracts. The commitment will be relatively modest, the clubs will proceed on what they can afford and what the product is worth.'

As we know, hindsight is a wonderful thing, but suffice to say that after seven seasons of professional rugby, many clubs in Wales have been shown not to have the experience necessary nor has the commitment proved to be relatively modest and clubs certainly didn't proceed on what they could afford or, indeed, on what the product was worth.

But, enough of generalising. This isn't about the IRB or the WRU or Cardiff RFC or Llanelli RFC or Pontypridd RFC or any other club in the make-up of the WRU or any other Union. This is about Newport RFC. Where the club was in August 1995 in terms of success or otherwise, and where it is now, seven years later.

Immediate reaction to the announcement by the IRB came from the chairman of Newport RFC, David Watkins. 'It's a minefield and a real can of worms. Where do we start? Who do we pay? Contracts will have to be drawn up and solicitors will have to be involved. It is an horrendous task. Where does the money come from? Who pays? Do you demand transfer fees ? Who does the negotiating? Who sits on tribunals? And there's a million other things to do.' All valid points, particularly coming from Watkins who was one club chairman who could speak from experience. An ex-Newport player he had turned professional in 1967, signing for Salford Rugby League Club, and would have had first-hand dealings with contracts, transfer fees, solicitors etc. Together with the pessimism, Watkins continued optimistically. 'Internationally it will be no problem at all. And it certainly cements the argument of the Heineken League First Division clubs in Wales, that all sponsorship money should go to them and be equally distributed so that the best players go to the best clubs.' Unfortunately, for the Welsh clubs Watkins' comments would be proven both justifiably pessimistic and falsely optimistic.

So what exactly was the state of affairs at Newport RFC in August 1995? The 1994-95 season had seen the club finish in eighth position in Division One. Led by Richard Goodey, Newport had won nine of the twenty-two league matches played and were followed in the final placings by Newbridge, Abertillery, Dunvant and Pontypool. The league had already been won by Cardiff when Newport travelled to the Arms Park for the last match of the season. While coming away with the spoils the gloss was taken off the result when Cardiff coach Alex Evans was heavily criticised for selecting a below strength team preferring to rest several players who would shortly be travelling to South Africa for the Rugby World Cup.

Enter the professional era and Newport's first match in this brave new world. Aberavon were the visitors to Rodney Parade the match ending in a 30-9 victory for the home side. For this landmark match the Newport XV saw Mark Yendle at full back, a three-quarter line made up of Richard Rees, Duncan Hughes, Shane Webley and Paul Hopkins with Gareth Rees and Jason Hewlett at half back. Up front Damion Thomas and Sean Duggan propped alongside hooker Andrew Peacock. Neil Jones and Kevin Moseley were in the second row with Goodey, again leading the side, flanked by Mark Workman and David Grey. The first team fielded by Newport in the new era was, if nothing else, a competent looking one but, at the same time, one never likely to sweep all before it. The season would end with the club consolidating the previous campaigns effort of eighth position in the league. While this may have been acceptable before, things were changing rapidly and there was a feeling that it wouldn't be good enough. Just like the IRB before them, now it was the clubs that had to act, and quickly, or they would be in danger of being overtaken by events.

Played six days after the IRB's announcement, the programme for the Aberavon match makes interesting reading. Newport supporter Mrs Myra Lewis had won the WRU's Lottery and her prize, a Volvo car, was presented by international prop, Spencer John. The club had made fourteen new signings in the close season, and was about to launch the Newport Rugby Credit Card. Jeff Cranton, a wing three-quarter in the 1970s, looked back on his playing days with the team. The coach taking supporters to the first away match of the season at Newbridge would leave the club at 1.00 pm and return at 6.00 pm. The cost for adults £4.00 and £3.00 for OAPs and children. All very interesting, but surely something's missing? Six days after the most momentous decision in the history of the game and the only references to it are a couple of paragraphs found in articles by Willis Huntley, writing on the new season and John Billot commenting on the problems with the league structure in Wales. This is not to suggest that the powers that be at Rodney Parade were in any way apathetic in the light of recent events. To be fair to them they had increased the cost of match programmes from 80p to £1.00. The money problems now facing clubs were huge. The need to generate income over and above anything previously perceived was paramount and adding twenty pence to the price of a match day programme wasn't ever going to be enough.

Joking apart, while all the clubs were faced with the same problems, the weighting of the problems varied considerably. Common sense suggests that clubs at the top of the league had the better players and the bigger gates while those at the bottom were experiencing the reverse. Obviously, the financial demands on the clubs by the players would be greater at the top than the bottom but the fact remained that clubs were not going to start the new era on an equal footing. For those at the bottom of the table here was the granddaddy of vicious circles. To get the quality players, clubs had to get money. To get the money they had to get the crowds. To get the crowds the clubs would almost certainly have to win matches and to win matches they had to have the players. This certainly wasn't rocket science. There was only one commodity that would make the professional game work - money.

Hot on the heels of the IRB's announcement, Rugby World magazine conducted a survey of the top clubs in Britain. Forty-one, including the twelve that made up the Heineken First Division in Wales, were asked ten questions and, seven years on, the responses make fascinating reading. The majority of clubs polled were happy with the decision but all ten English clubs and the eleven Irish clubs questioned felt they would not be able to pay players. The feeling among the Welsh clubs, however, was slightly different. Five of the twelve involved were positive and felt comfortable with the issue while north of the border there was also a degree of optimism with two out of eight clubs also replying in the affirmative. Whether this was naivety or just plain stupidity on behalf of those seven clubs is no longer relevant but

when asked if they felt they would be in a better position in five years'
time 73% of the clubs polled said yes which begs the question: How?
Most clubs, 83% in fact, agreed they couldn't afford to pay players,
but 73% saw a brighter future. They were in for a rude awakening
that wouldn't be long in arriving.

The finances of a rugby club in the summer of 1995 were fairly
straightforward. Income was generated from season tickets and gate
receipts together with other matchday activities which would include
programme sales and bar takings. Added to this would be sponsorship
income. Local businesses like to be involved and see their name and
logo on team jerseys, pitchside hoardings and in the matchday
programme. Throw in a bit of fundraising, the odd sportsman's dinner
or social function and you have a fair reflection of the sum total of a
club's revenue potential. On the other side of the balance sheet
you find the costs of running the team or teams: maintenance and
administration expenses, salaries, rent and rates, in fact normal,
everyday business expenditure. But wait a minute - surely rugby clubs
weren't businesses in 1995, this would come later. True, but in reality
that's exactly what they were - businesses! The only problem was
nobody had told them.

Off the field circa 1995 Newport RFC had a lot going for it. First
and foremost it owned its ground. More accurately Rodney Parade
was owned by Newport Athletic Club of which the Rugby Club was
one of several playing and non-playing sections. The income earned
through the rugby section undoubtedly supported the other activities
and in time the constitution would be changed to reflect this.

The clubhouse was bigger and better than most clubs could boast.
Two large bars on the ground floor could cater for the crowds on the
biggest match days and on the first floor was the hallowed members'
bar which would soon become a bone of contention. Add changing
rooms, tearoom and the offices and you have the foundations for a
club going into the new professional era.

It was all very well having a stadium and a team, regardless of its
success or otherwise, but if the product was not deemed to be attractive,
if it didn't appeal to the new breed of supporters the game was going

to have to find, then it would flounder, it wouldn't get out of the starting blocks. Rugby union had its support base and had always been popular with the public, but as the twentieth century drew to a close the competition for the public's leisure time and money was greater than ever. Club rugby was not going to survive the new demands professionalism would bring, if it failed to reach a wider audience.

If the television networks were to be included in the promotion of the game, and it was essential that they were on board, then change was inevitable. The laws would need to be addressed. The game needed speeding up was the thinking behind this, the accent had to be placed on the scoring of tries. Also, the game of rugby would have to be seen as a good diversion by parents of young, aspiring athletes looking for a sport in which to indulge themselves. These were demands that would have to be addressed with regard to the on the field activities. Off the field, the need for improvement would be equally, if not more demanding, if a new audience was to be introduced to the game and, more importantly, retained.

And then there was Jonah. The 1995 Rugby Word Cup had unearthed a superstar, the biggest name the game had ever seen. Jonah Lomu had exploded onto the rugby stage on 11 June 1995 and as a result of his exploits during eighty minutes of rugby he was made for life. Newlands, Cape Town, was the venue for the New Zealand/England semi-final and a huge global television audience watched in awe as the big man tore England apart. He scored four tries in a 45-29 New Zealand victory. From his position out on the left wing he devastated the English defence. He ran inside opponents, outside opponents, over opponents and he ran through opponents. He was beautiful. If the television moguls worldwide needed any convincing of the game's marketability then here it was. One man had changed the game's public persona in a few short weeks. Dramatic as this undoubtedly sounds, it was true, and the entrepreneurs quickly realised it. Jonah Lomu was a marketing manager's dream. A fax received at the New Zealand team hotel summed up public reaction. From a youngster back home it read 'I know it's a team game but you other fourteen, just make sure you get the ball to Jonah!' Lomu was exactly what the game needed. The summer of 1995 saw rugby union on the front pages of the world's press - the time for change had arrived.

From the early 1950s the British Broadcasting Corporation had shown rugby union matches live on television. The Five Nations Championship was the game's flagship and rapidly gained a high profile among televised sporting events. Alongside the FA Cup Final, Wimbledon, the Grand National and the Boat Race it was seen to be an event that should be in the public domain, an issue that would one day be raised on the floor of the House of Commons. A weekly magazine programme eventually appeared and the coverage of the game reached club level. By the 1980s rival television companies were fighting for the right to broadcast the game. The BBC had covered the first Rugby World Cup in 1987 but made such a pig's ear of it that when the Five Nations hosted the second tournament in 1991, ITV were given an opportunity which was gladly accepted, and commercial television continues to cover the tournament, a situation that must surely be under threat when one considers the fact that ITV broadcasts no other live rugby.

The arrival of satellite television with its huge coverage of sport was one of the prime reasons behind rugby union becoming professional; certainly the timing was in response to the threat of the game being hijacked by the networks. While television was prepared to pay handsomely for the right to cover the game, slowly but surely its demands would have a great effect on the very infrastructure of it. A more attractive game was wanted. No more 3-0 results thank you very much. If the game was to be sold to a wider audience it would have to take a close look at itself.

Then there would be the not insignificant matter of kick-off times. These would have to be varied to accommodate the television networks, much to the irritation of supporters who were used to their Saturday afternoons being spent watching their local club with the occasional midweek match being played under floodlights. This would change and nowhere more so than in Wales where matches would be played on Friday nights and early Saturday evenings to appease the schedulers at BBC Wales and the Welsh speaking channel S4C. A few years into the professional era would see this live coverage and, more so, the timing of the matches, blamed for the declining lack of interest that would creep into the game at club level. This would be a ready-made excuse for a decline in attendances but there would be clubs that would show that it was possible to have home matches shown live on television at irregular times and still attract the public through the turnstiles; and in big numbers.

Generally speaking, by 1995 attendances at club matches had fallen to a woefully low level. Games between the top clubs attracted sensible crowds but for the remainder, while not exactly at the one man and a dog depths, attendances were disappointing. It had long been assumed that rugby union was solely dependent on the scoring of tries for its public appeal, the value of the try had been increased on two occasions in an effort to reflect this, while efforts to open up the field of play had received generous assistance from the law makers. And in Wales there were the bonus points!

The bonus points had been introduced for the start of the 1995-96 season and were awarded over and above the league points earned for winning a game and the point gained from a draw. Score three tries and one bonus point was awarded, five tries merited two points and in the event of seven tries being scored, then three bonus points were on offer. Win or lose, it didn't matter, the points were there to be won. The system threw up ridiculous anomalies. In losing 95-25 at Cardiff, Abertillery won two bonus points by virtue of scoring five tries. On another occasion, Newport, although winning away at Cardiff 22-18, found themselves dropping a place in the league table due to the number of bonus points picked up by other clubs. Ridiculous!

However, come the end of the season, the final league positions were much the same as they would have been under the traditional system seen in previous years, with just one exception. Neath were champions ahead of Cardiff who, although ending on the same number of points, in fact winning one more match, scored two fewer tries and had to settle with the runners-up spot. No other league position was affected.

Bonus points remained for a further three seasons. The system was overhauled in 1996-97 to such an extent that leading mathematicians would be left scratching their heads. Points for tries over and above those scored by opponents, points awarded to losing teams scoring three tries and points for losing teams beaten by fifteen points or less - complicated to say the least. But did the introduction of bonus points achieve anything? There were certainly more tries on offer. In 1994-95, the twelve First Division clubs scored a total of 573, while in the following season the same number of clubs produced 842. Again, in 1996-97, a further increase was seen with 966 tries. With the league then reduced to eight clubs, further comparison is not possible. Bonus points were laid to rest after four years but their legacy lives on. In 1999-2000, the first season of the Welsh-Scottish league, 855 tries were scored. The league once again had twelve clubs, no bonus points were on offer and yet almost three hundred more tries were scored than in 1994-95.

With this new-found plethora of scoring, this end-to-end rugby, one can be forgiven for thinking that a pretty quick fix had been found, that the turnstiles were ticking and the coffers were bursting. Of course this was far from the reality.

Welsh rugby was in a poor state of health in August 1995. In truth, the game turning professional could not have come at a worse time. The national side had returned from the RWC with little credit and the public were fed up with the same old chestnuts: learning curves, back to basics and the structure of the game in the Principality. There were very few people brave enough to suggest publicly that the players may not be good enough, that maybe there was far to much accent on the social side of the game. With the sport about to go professional these and other factors would shortly be cruelly exposed.

Care has to be taken when generalising, obviously there were exceptions, players who looked after themselves and would cope in the new era, but they were very much in a minority. When it arrived professionalism meant just one thing to most players in Wales: money in the bank. Seven years on the same can still be said; many players haven't grasped the ethos of professional sport and are content to sit back, take the money and damn the consequences.

The WRU weren't doing much to help the process of change get under way. The sums of money that were paid to the clubs fell way short of what was required. The leading clubs formed First Division Ltd, their main contention being that they should receive all revenue earned from television coverage and sponsorship of the club game, with the Union retaining all the income from the international game. This seemed a reasonable argument to take to the table but it fell on deaf ears. The WRU were about to get involved in the development of a new stadium which would host the 1999 RWC and it seemed that all else was of secondary importance once the project was up and running.

With little or no guidance from the WRU, the clubs were also slow to react to the change. Compared to their English counterparts time would suggest they fell two or three years behind in grasping what was happening to the game. What gave English clubs a distinct advantage was the apparent wealth that members or interested outsiders made available to them. Within a matter of weeks, cheque books to the fore, money men appeared at Newcastle, Richmond and Saracens and more would follow at Bath, Gloucester and Northampton. While these were seriously rich individuals who could take a financial knock if it came their way, they were also hard-nosed businessmen who had not made their way in the world backing losers. There were varying levels of success, short term to long term, with Richmond destined to become the game's first serious casualty. Whatever the outcome, there was no doubt that the English clubs had stolen a march on the clubs in Wales and a game of catchup had begun.

The only Welsh club that looked capable of taking professionalism on board was Cardiff. In Peter Thomas they had a man who had played for the club and whose interests didn't go beyond wanting Cardiff RFC to succeed at the highest level. There was no suggestion of a hidden agenda with Thomas, in addition to which he was very wealthy and was prepared to help the club find its feet in the new world. There weren't many individuals like Peter Thomas in Welsh rugby circles in 1995 and this shortage of people who were able to offer stability during this period of transition would result in many clubs in Wales falling into serious financial difficulties while the professional game was still in its infancy.

This then was the state of affairs in the 1995-96 season. The IRB had responded to outside pressures and created what in effect was a new game. There was still an oval ball, thirty players and a referee but everything else was about to change. Instead of a sensible moratorium that would allow time to take stock, it was open season and it would be the survival of the fittest, sink or swim. The buck was then passed downwards. Rather like a hot potato the IRB handed it to the Unions who in turn dropped it down to the clubs. In Wales nobody was ready, neither the WRU or the clubs. That's not quite true actually. Certainly the WRU and the clubs weren't ready but one faction within the game was ready and waiting - the players. They had their hands out before the planes bringing the officials back from Paris had left Charles de Gaulle airport. That was the problem - and the game in Wales didn't have a chance.

Living in the Past

'History is more or less bunk.'

Henry Ford

There are the corridors of power, corridors full of photographs of teams and players, photographs of days gone by on wood panelled walls that lead to the committee room, the inner sanctum where entrance is forbidden to all but the honoured few: the secretary, the treasurer, Mr Committee Man and all he stands for. The blazer, the club tie, the portraits of past chairmen, presidents even, the trophy cabinet that nobody outside the inner sanctum is allowed to see. It is from such corridors, rooms and individuals that professionalism would meet with the greatest resistance. In a word - tradition. Rugby football in Wales was steeped in tradition and breaking down the barriers it presented was the first hurdle to be overcome.

The demands of the professional era against the conservatism of the traditionalists would tear Welsh rugby apart. This wasn't a battle that would be resolved in a few months. This would rage on for years and the longer it continued the bigger the problems that riddled the game in Wales would become. Self-interest, greed and ignorance would all spring to mind when observing the situation from the out-side. Two hundred and thirty-nine clubs make up the membership of the WRU and, regardless of size, each has the same voting power when it comes to the passing or otherwise of proposals. Even in the years leading up to 1995 this was a ridiculous parity that was long since outdated, but the only people who could seemingly do anything about it were the member clubs themselves. With such self interest - the match tickets, the dinners, the jollies for Mr and Mrs Committee Man at stake - to expect rational reform was like, well, like turkeys voting for Christmas.

Newport RFC was steeped in history and tradition. It was committee-driven in 1995, as it always had been, and although it was a big club within the club structure in Wales, it had lost its way over the last twenty years or so and was, more than any other club, living on past glories. Now it was threatened. Threatened because in August 1995 nobody on the planet gave a toss about Newport RFC, its past achievements, its excellent facilities or its tradition. Nobody except the eight or nine hundred members who would blindly follow the Black and Ambers to the precipice and beyond if duty called.

Rugby Football had first been played in Newport in 1875. The game was introduced to the town by Thomas Phillips, a brewery owner who hailed from the West Midlands. Phillips had bought the Dock Road Brewery and, when he and his family arrived at their new home, among their possessions was a rugby ball. Keen to be involved in the town's sporting activities, Phillips invited leading businessmen and luminaries to a meeting held at the brewery in September 1874. The outcome was the formation of a football club with the intention that the Association game be played. Unable to arrange any fixtures, it was decided that the club would play the Union game and the following year saw Newport's first recorded rugby match. Played in Cardiff on 5 April, the match against Glamorgan Rugby Football Club ended in a draw. For the first full season, fixtures were arranged with Glamorgan, Cardiff, Swansea, Pontypool, Vale of Usk and Panteg. It was from such humble beginnings that the game of rugby union took root in Newport and the club that would become known wherever the game was played first saw the light of day.

Originally known as Newport Cricket, Athletic and Football Club, home fixtures were played at the Marshes. This was a parcel of land located on the west bank of the River Usk, now known as Shaftesbury Park. Early matches attracted some public interest and crowds of three to four hundred would be in attendance.

The Rt Hon Lord Tredegar was a staunch supporter of the town's sporting activities and he owned large areas of land both in the town and its surrounding districts. In 1877 Lord Tredegar offered the club the use of a piece of land located on the other side of the river. His generosity offered improved facilities at what can only be described as a 'peppercorn rent' and, of course, the move to Rodney Parade took place.

Why Rodney Parade? In the 1820s the most popular form of transport with those wanting to cross the Bristol Channel was steamship. Operating twelve times a week in summer and six in winter, the crossing took four and a half hours to complete. A vessel named the 'Lady Rodney' made the first trip to the distant shoreline in 1823 and would continue to do so for the next thirty-one years. The point of departure was a wharf on the east of the river, adjacent to the old town bridge, and in time this came to be known as Rodney Wharf. One thing led to another. A short distance from the wharf was a stretch of land and a hall which the militia had taken over as a depot and parade ground; this would become known as Rodney Parade. Today, Rodney Parade is a walkway along the bank of the River Usk while its namesake is found a matter of a hundred yards inland. Rodney Road will lead the visitor to the Memorial Gates which were hung in 1923 in honour of those club members who gave their lives in the First World War.

The playing area in use today was not included in the land originally allocated but added on when a twenty-one year lease was signed in 1889. The 'Salt Pool', as it was then known, needed a lot of preparation before it could be used for rugby. Matches were played inside a cycle track, this practice continuing until 1891 when the new pitch was finally ready, Newport defeating Cardiff at the official opening on 21 November. At the expiry of the lease Newport Athletic Club, as it had been renamed, had the chance to purchase the freehold of Rodney Parade. Lord Tredegar had passed away in 1912 and the trustees of the estate offered the sale of the land for £7,026, well beneath its market value and an offer that could not be passed up. To this day Newport is one of only a handful of clubs that own their ground. This then was Rodney Parade in 1995.

Until recently the ground looked much the same as it had done for, well, nigh on one hundred years really. The only significant changes had been brought about by the Safety of Sports Grounds Act 1975, seats acquired from the National Stadium which replaced the benches in the main stand, and a paint brush. And that was how people liked it. Remember, in 1995 Rodney Parade was owned by Newport Athletic Club and not Newport RFC, an important distinction. In addition to rugby the Athletic Club had incorporated several other sports under its umbrella. There were, or had been, cricket and hockey sections, tennis, bowls, badminton and netball. Table tennis and bridge enthusiasts were catered for and way back, archery, athletics and gymnastics had been included. The club was a members' club and after paying an annual subscription, for an additional fee, members could then join the section or sections of their choice. The rugby section had playing and non playing members and there was never any doubt that the revenue generated by it heavily subsidised the lesser supported sections.

How did it all work? How, in the days before the dog eat dog world of professionalism, did Newport Athletic Club function? Obviously, a club of its size had to employ people to manage its everyday affairs: office staff, groundsmen and a club steward. Each of the sections would then have a committee that looked after the internal affairs pertaining to it and the club had a general committee that controlled the broader picture. And, silly as this may now seem, these committee members gave freely of their services. Each would have his or her responsibility, duties to be carried out for which they would get nothing in return. Neither did they want or expect anything, it just went with the territory.

Okay, those involved with the rugby section had certain perks. In addition to the routine committee meetings that had to be attended there were matchday duties; programmes to be sold, turnstiles to be manned and a car park to control. For carrying out these duties there would be food and refreshments after the match, committee men would probably be taken to away matches and then there was the international ticket. These were valuable bits of paper in years gone by and committee members would have first choice before the rest of the members got a look in. But nobody complained, nobody rational anyway, and it worked. What is now viewed as an archaic, outdated system, worked. And why did it work? It worked because the players weren't being paid and because nobody was that concerned with profit; providing there wasn't a loss it was OK. That, and because there were enough people who were prepared to give up their time to make sure it worked.

It wasn't only off the field that services were being given gratis. The players were doing it for the love of the game, most of them anyway. The talk of boot money and brown envelopes had haunted the amateur game for many years and, while there was ample reason to believe these practices existed, we aren't talking big money here. If that were the case why did all those players go north and play the thirteen man game? No, in real terms what we are talking about here is pocket money, and not every club elected to pay it. Whether Newport RFC got involved in under the table payments to players is a matter for conjecture. There are plenty of ex players who will deny it vehemently but they mostly hail from the 50s and 60s. More recently, in the lead-up to the game going open, there has to be a doubt about the integrity of most clubs and players and it would be naive not to include Newport in this. The payment of players may have become a lot more sophisticated, perhaps they worked for a sponsor or even the club in some public relations role, but it is highly unlikely that the big names in Welsh club rugby were going unrewarded during the 1980s and the early 1990s.

We have seen the way in which the game of rugby was introduced to the town and the events that followed with regard to the development of the ground at Rodney Parade. But what of the playing side? Success had been plentiful in the early years. Five invincible seasons before the turn of the century, a sixth would follow in 1922-23, and five times winners of the South Wales Challenge Cup had established the club among the best in Wales. Many of its players gained international honours and, indeed, it was down to one of the club's early administrators that there was a national side to play for. Richard Mullock was Newport's secretary and it was Mullock who organised what has become recognised as the first international match played by Wales. This was against England on 19 February 1881and the following month saw the formation of a Welsh Football Union, Mullock becoming the first Secretary and Treasurer.

The first player to score a try for Wales was Newport's Tom Baker

Jones and the first Welsh Triple Crown came under the captaincy of another Newport player, Arthur Gould. Gould was the Gareth Edwards of his day and at the end of his glittering career would become the centre of the first major crisis to hit the game. Ironically, this was an issue that was money, or more accurately property, related. It had been decided to recognise Arthur Gould's contribution to the game by setting up a testimonial. The public were invited to contribute and sufficient money was raised to enable the deeds of his house to be acquired and given to Gould. This was seen to be in contravention of the amateur standing of the game and the RFU and the Scottish Rugby Union made their feelings known. Fixtures were cancelled and the argument raged on. This did not prevent Arthur Gould receiving his testimonial at a dinner held at the Albert Hall, Newport, on Easter Monday, 19 April 1897. Matters eventually returned to normal, but not before Gould had agreed to retire from international rugby.

The turn of the century saw the advent of the major tours from the Southern Hemisphere rugby playing nations. Australia, New Zealand and South Africa started to undertake long tours, playing as many as thirty-five or more matches, a great feature of the amateur game that would sadly disappear with the arrival of professionalism. Newport enjoyed a lot of success against these visitors, one of the early high-lights being the victory over the South African Springboks in 1912, a victory that earned them the springbok head awarded to the first club side to defeat the tourists. In time Newport would defeat the 'Boks again and add memorable victories over Australia and New Zealand, the latter in 1963, being widely regarded as the club's finest hour.

This then was no ordinary rugby club. The 1950s saw Newport's best extended period of success and it was during this era that the crowds were the biggest seen at Rodney Parade. Attendances in excess of twenty thousand were not uncommon and it was estimated that some thirty thousand spectators filled the terraces when the South Africans arrived in 1952.

However, by the 1990s success was something followers of Newport RFC tended to read about rather than experience first hand. There had been an unofficial Welsh Championship in 1968-69 and the SWALEC Cup spent a year in the trophy cabinet after the club's victory over Cardiff in the final in 1977, but generally speaking the club had fallen into decline when results were compared to years gone by. And the players? There had been a paucity of international representatives at the club for twenty years. A handful of players had won a handful of caps but the days when there was a Newport player ever present in the Welsh team were long gone. No Newport player had toured with the British Lions since 1977, a trait that would continue into the twenty first century. And yet it would be true to say that Newport RFC had everything going for it in August 1995 - everything, that is, except a team that people wanted to come and watch.

Despite being Welsh club champions in 1968-69 and cup winners in 1977 the fortunes of Newport RFC had taken a slow, but continual decline in both performance on the field and public interest off it. That is not to suggest that there were no highs during the period leading up to the professional era, far from it, but plotting results and attendances over the period 1968-95 would show the graph dropping from left to right on the paper with the occasional peak threatening a recovery but quickly falling dramatically away to continue the downward trend.

The 1970s were a period of great success for the Welsh national side and this was reflected in the interest shown in the game at club level. The third 'Golden Era' of Welsh rugby saw the likes of Gareth Edwards, Barry John, Phil Bennett, Gerald Davies and JPR Williams performing deeds behind the scrum that would go down in the annals of history, while in the forwards the Pontypool front row - Graham Price, Bobby Windsor and Charlie Faulkner - laid a platform that Mervyn Davies, John Taylor and Dai Morris could work off in the back row. These were great players by any measurement and when you are able to add John Dawes, JJ Williams, Delme Thomas and Geoff Wheel to the list it is not difficult to believe that the quality of player produced by Wales during this period has never been bettered.

What these players did for the club game in Wales was attract those members of the public who had no previous interest in the sport to go and watch them perform. For most people not connected with the game on a regular basis there would be no opportunity to see these stars perform on the international stage. Television would whet the appetite and when the chance to see the greats at a local club arose, many would go along. Fathers would take their children to see Gareth or Barry, Gerald or JPR; these guys didn't need reference to their surnames. When these players came to visit the turnstiles would click but, had the public come to see the game or the stars? One by one these great players announced their retirement from the game and much of the public interest disappeared resulting in a decline in match attendances. Another story it may be but the twenty-five year wait for home-grown superstars to spark the club game in Wales continues. This would not go unrecognised when Newport RFC went in search of players who would generate that additional public interest.

When trying to plan a future in the professional era, clubs would have done well to consider the amateur years and in particular the periods where match attendances were at their highest. The reasons for the high attendances are fairly obvious: a winning team and a smattering of top class players. The argument that the public respond best to a successful club and the star players in the game is well illustrated by London Welsh. Here was a team that played all the leading Welsh clubs, was included in the Championship table but was based at least 150 miles away from the leading clubs. In the early 1970s many of the stars of the international team were London Welsh players: JPR, John Dawes, Gerald and Mervyn Davies, John Taylor, Mike Roberts, Geoff Evans, Jim Shanklin and Clive Rees. Easter would see the club tour South Wales playing three clubs in four days, among them Newport on Easter Monday. Travelling support was minimal so the 10,000 plus that would attend these matches were largely from the town and its immediate environs. These would not all be Newport supporters, a high percentage being followers of the game attracted by the big names in the London Welsh team. The last Easter Monday visit by the Exiles was in April 1995. This time the crowd could be counted in the hundreds, the low hundreds at that. What was the difference? The two clubs were the same and it was the same Bank Holiday. The difference this time was the absence of star players and the fact that neither club was enjoying the success of earlier years. The first lesson to be taken on board when the game turned professional could be learnt from comparisons such as this or any one of the many other traditional fixtures that told the same story. When was the last time that the ground had been full for a Cardiff/Newport match, or a Llanelli/Swansea derby. These were the big games in the season for the clubs involved and yet there was always room on the terraces. And we're not talking about grounds with large capacities; none of these clubs can cater for more than 15,000 people. If there was a lack of interest in such famous derbies then what hope did the clubs have of attracting sufficient numbers to their other home matches, numbers that would be essential if there was to be any hope of balancing the books at the end of the season.

It was clear that rugby union at club level was not the game it perceived itself to be, or rather, it was not the game that the people involved in the running of it perceived it to be. International matches would spark more than sufficient interest to ensure full stadia but elsewhere the story was very different. Professionalism would see fresh demands identified, winning teams and big names may have satisfied the public in the game's amateur days but there would have to be more on offer now.

This leads us to the very essence of the problems that plague the game in Wales today. When the game became professional it effected the whole Welsh rugby structure and that meant forty-six year old Dai Jones playing for Abercwmgraig in Division 16 of the Central League wanted his cut of the action. And those running Abercwmgraig made sure he got it! Of course, this Dai Jones, Abercwmgraig and the Central League don't exist, but many clubs do that let the Dai Jones's of this world have their way. Where was the governing body when it was most needed? Where were the men of vision who would steer the ship through the storm that was about to break? When the game went open nobody, certainly nobody in the Northern Hemisphere, was prepared for it and nowhere was this more apparent than in Wales.

To this day, after seven seasons of professional rugby, the situation in Wales is no better. The English clubs finally achieved a working relationship with the RFU which is clearly a success as shown by the results at both club and international level. The Scottish Rugby Union upset the clubs north of the border with their Regional teams but they are sticking with the change of direction and it may yet prove to be the right policy. In Ireland, where the Provincial set up had long been in place, the Union has taken a strong grip of the system controlling the international players, their salaries and the number of games they play in a season. And in Wales, this self styled home of rugby, this land of song and fly half factories, Ponty and Pop, Groggs and Gareth - nothing! Unless you can call seven years of meetings, debate, argument and disillusionment an achievement to be proud of.

To hell with professional rugby, the clubs can look after themselves, there's a stadium to be built. To listen to Glanmor Griffiths and his cronies at the WRU one could be forgiven for thinking they had put on the hard hats and built the Millennium Stadium themselves. For all the time that was seemingly devoted to the domestic game in Wales they may well have done just that. So Welsh rugby was allowed to go from crisis to crisis. Blame the schools, blame the pit closures, blame the coaches, blame the players, get a 'Messiah' from the Southern Hemisphere and then blame him, and best of all, blame the structure. In fact blame anything except the fucking boogie and that's what we're supposed to blame isn't it?

Sadly, there was nobody with anything resembling vision who could guide, point the way, foresee the pitfalls. We're not talking Nostradamus here, just somebody who could add up, see what most of the clubs obviously couldn't, that two and two make four. What was it Dickens' Mr Micawber said? 'Annual income twenty pounds, annual expenditure nineteen, nineteen and six, result happiness. Annual income twenty pounds, annual expenditure twenty pounds, ought and six, result misery.' Staying with the great man, Dickens that is, here's another one - 'It was the best of times, it was the worst of times, it was the age of wisdom, it was the age of foolishness, it was the epoch of belief, it was the epoch of incredulity, it was the season of Light, it was the season of Darkness, it was the spring of hope it was the winter of despair, we had everything before us, we had nothing before us, we were all going direct to Heaven, we were all going direct the other way.' This, about another revolution - the French Revolution. Pity then that nobody in Welsh rugby was a reader of Charles Dickens.

What club rugby in Wales needed in 1995 and still needs seven years later is a two tiered structure, the upper tier to be fully professional and the lower to accommodate the game as an amateur pastime. Where the dividing line should appear is a matter for debate but no lower than the top two divisions would seem sensible, if not downright generous. Then the talented player would have something to aspire to if a career in the game was his ambition. Australia has ninety professional rugby players. These are divided equally among the three Super 12 sides - ACT, New South Wales and Queensland - the Brumbies, the Warratahs and the Reds. Three provincial sides, ninety players and World Champions - twice. The game isn't even that popular Down Under, Aussie Rules and Rugby League are both bigger each generating much greater public interest than union. But outside the three Super 12 franchises rugby union is an amateur sport, this in a country that has been the most successful in the professional era. New Zealand and South Africa have similar policies and, though rugby union is the number one sport in both, the game is two-tiered and the number of full time professional players is relatively small. Why then should Wales, a country starved of any sustained period of international success, believe it can support a fully professional game? Obviously it can't, but try telling that to the clubs.

Few clubs can claim to have entered the professional era with their eyes open. Few can, hand on heart, claim to have maintained a financial policy that saw them firstly testing the water. Most dived in with both feet regardless of any repercussions and remarkably, some might even say unfairly, survived to tell the tale. Llanelli and Neath should have gone under; they were insolvent, both needing to be bailed out of their respective crises by an over-generous WRU. Llanelli sold Stradey Park to the Union and now lease the ground, while Neath ran up debts in excess of £600,000 prompting the Union to put in place a new management board effectively buying the club in the process. Things weren't much better at Bridgend where players had to take a cut in wages and at Ebbw Vale where leading players had to be sold in an effort to balance the books. In England, Richmond were the first major casualty. Taken over by wealthy businessman Ashley Levett the club had seemingly landed on its feet. Then, after relocating to Reading, Levett pulled the plug, and Richmond RFC went into voluntary receivership. A founder club of the RFU Richmond may have been, but in their hour of need the men down the road at HQ were nowhere to be seen. And at Newport, even allowing for a prudent approach to the new era, sitting in the wings was a financial crisis waiting to happen.

While sponsorship at rugby clubs was far from being a new innovation having generated much valued revenue over many years, this was now, unfortunately, going to fall well short of what would be required. The main sponsor at Newport for the 1995-96 season was Robert Price, Builders Merchants, and Carlsberg-Tetley were the club's brewery sponsor, which meant members with an aversion to Carlsberg Lager or Tetley Bitter had a problem when it came to the after-match festivities. The team's kit was sponsored by manufacturers, Le Coq Sportif providing the jerseys and Mizuno the boots, while the club's junior teams benefited from the generosity of local businesses. The matchday programme was full of adverts featuring local companies some of which had been involved since time immemorial: Wildings, a large department store in the town, the Monmouthshire Building Society, DH Bowkett and Sons and Chez Giovannis restaurant among them. However, clubs had to face up to the reality that, commendable as it most certainly was, this level of support would not be sufficient to ensure their survival in the professional era.

Local businessman Martin Hazell is the club's President and he in particular had been generous with his financial support going as far back as the introduction of leagues in 1990-91. Newport had found themselves in what was the second division even though it was called Division One. There was a Premier Division which Newport had not been included in and it was therefore imperative that the club gain promotion at the first attempt. Ironically, when they duly did they still found themselves in Division One, the Premier tag having been dropped, for the time being anyway.

Martin Hazell recalls putting some £12,000 into Newport RFC at this time which, ten years on may seem an insignificant amount, but it was obviously put to good use as promotion was secured with the loss of only one league game. In Gareth Rees' first season with the club Hazell paid the princely sum of £100 per week to cover the players' travelling expenses. This increased to £400 at the start of the 1995-96 season but once players had come to terms with their apparent worth in the game the price went up and Rees' demand of £80,000 per season did not come within the budget.

Come the 1998-99 season and Martin Hazell was backing Newport with a £200,000 loan secured by the title deeds to Rodney Parade, making his overall investment in the club something in the region of £400,000. No small sum, which all of a sudden made the club's major asset, the ground, look very threatened indeed. Developments during the summer of 1999 would see the whole financial structure of the club change and Martin Hazell hand back the title deeds of the club in return for shares in a newly formed limited company. But that's a long way off and is preceded by a four-year journey that nobody who experienced it first hand will ever want to see repeated.

Going Nowhere - Slowly! 1995-99

'Well balanced, impresses with strength and activity. Massive bone throughout, but not giving heavy, inactive appearance. Noble, majestic and powerful.'

The Newfoundland - from the Kennel Club's Illustrated Breed Standards

Newfoundland is Canada's ninth province in terms of both size and population. It is divided into two regions by the Strait of Belle Isle: mainland Labrador and, lying off the eastern seaboard, the Island of Newfoundland. Located between latitudes 47-60 degrees north, Newfoundland covers an area in excess of 156,000 sq miles and is the home of approximately 500,000 Canadians, a quarter of whom live in the capital, St John's.

Well known for its fishing industry, the hydroelectric scheme at Churchill Falls and the large dog that bears its name, one thing that Newfoundland is not immediately associated with is the game of rugby union. Certainly, the Memorial University of Newfoundland in St John's fields a team and the city is home to three clubs, the Dogs, the Swilers, and the Vandals but you are more likely to see somebody carrying a hockey stick than a rugby ball. However, it is from this unlikely background that Newport RFC secured one of its first professional signings.

The Boet Erasmus Stadium, (now Telkom Park) in Port Elizabeth, South Africa, has seen more than its share of battles. It was here in 1974 that the Lions won the third test match and thereby the series, but not before Willie John McBride's infamous 99 call had been brought into action on two occasions resulting in mass brawls involving most of the players on the field. On 3 June 1995 the stadium witnessed another pitched battle as players from South Africa and Canada stood up to each other. This was the final Pool A match in the Rugby World Cup. The hosts were leading 20-0 with less than ten minutes remaining on the clock when wings Pieter Hendricks and Winstone Stanley got into a private confrontation that quickly developed into a free for all. Springbok lock forward Hannes Strydom was forced to leave the field with a severe gash to his forehead and, after consulting with his touch judges, referee David McHugh of Ireland sent three players off. James Dalton, the South African hooker, saw the referee's action prevent him from taking any further part in the tournament thereby denying him a place in the final and a winner's medal while Canadian captain Gareth Rees was dismissed together with tight head prop Rod Snow.

For Canada the World Cup was over but both players, along with Dalton, received 30-day suspensions. It wasn't quite that straightforward for Snow, however, as there had been a suggestion of eye gouging, a charge that he strongly denied. 'While I was prepared to put my hand up for the fighting, the idea that I could be thought of as a gouger sickened me. I was embarrassed by the accusation and contested it. Sure, there are always going to be punches thrown and you have to take any punishment handed out, but there's a stigma about eye gouging that tends to stick with a player and I wasn't going to be tarred with that brush. It's a totally unacceptable part of the game and fortunately I managed to convince the officials of my innocence.' Snow went home to Newfoundland and sat out his suspension before returning to South Africa to join Eastern Province for its campaign in the country's major domestic tournament - the Currie Cup.

At the end of the domestic season in South Africa Rod Snow again headed for home. Enjoying some well earned R and R back in St John's he received a telephone call from his good friend Rees who told him that his club, Newport, could be looking for a front row forward and, if so, would Snow be interested. After giving the matter some thought he decided to go for it. The deal was put in place, £250 a week during the season, and he packed his bags. At the bottom of one bag, in his 'secret compartment', Rod Snow hid his contract - big mistake!

'Anything to declare sir?' This is the last thing anybody wants to hear on arriving in a foreign land at 8.00 am after spending the night on a plane. Snow can laugh at it now but it was far from funny at the time. 'The Customs officer had been flicking through my passport and came across the stamp marking my entry into South Africa as a competitor in the World Cup. He asked if I intended playing rugby while I was in the UK. I must have sounded a bit vague because the next thing he's emptied my bags and found the hidden evidence - the contract. I needed a work permit, hadn't got one and was in the proverbial up to the neck and sinking fast.'

Newport Secretary, Campbell Black, together with Committee member Martyn Kirtland had driven to Heathrow Airport to meet Snow and take him to his new home. They knew the plane had landed so where was the player? He was a front row forward for goodness sake, you couldn't miss him even in a busy arrivals hall! Well they hadn't missed him because he hadn't come through, and he wouldn't come through until 6.00 pm, ten hours after arriving, and then it would only be for a couple of days. Without a work permit Rod Snow was effectively refused entry into the UK. He would have to return to Canada, acquire the necessary documents and try again.

Snow spent a couple of days at Eton, a stone's throw away from Heathrow, at the home of Gareth Rees who was a master at the famous old Public School. Two days later he was winging his way back across the Atlantic to obtain the documents that would enable him to gain authorised entry into the UK and ply his trade.

At this time Rod kept a journal. The following extract was written at 1.15 am on 17 November. 'It's been two very trying days but at this moment I'm lying in bed at Eton School, England, writing by candle light and it's relaxing. Through the window I can see Windsor Castle. Hopefully, things will get better tomorrow, though I feel very good right now.' Earlier that day his troubles had started. The journal entry continues: 'I was in an immigration holding room with my bags awaiting the decision on what was to happen to me. I now know that I have to report to British Immigration at Heathrow at 10.00 am on Saturday morning and leave for Newfoundland on the midday flight. Neither I or Newport RFC can do anything about it. I have to leave the country in order to have the chance to return with a proper work permit, my work will be rugby. Hopefully I will be able to return on Tuesday of next week. I'll stay with Gareth as he lives within half an hour's drive of the airport and tomorrow I'll help him do some coaching at the school and check out the town. I may get to teach Lady Di's kid, William!' Some humour in what was obviously a trying time.

But who was Rod Snow? Followers of Newport only knew him as the other guy sent off with club outside half Gareth Rees at the World Cup. The club certainly needed a prop, Sean Duggan and Sven Cronk were the established first team players but the back-up was not perceived to be adequate. What better then than a player, an international player at that, who was comfortable on both sides of the scrum.

Rod Snow had been introduced to the game at an early age. Doug Hammond, a supply teacher, had brought a rugby ball to twelve-year-old Snow's school and taught the kids the basics of the game. At this stage the only sporting aspiration in the young man's mind was to play for his beloved Montreal Canadians, one of the top sides in the National Hockey League but he soon realised that he didn't have what it would take to play this fastest of team sports at the highest level. At sixteen he joined the Dogs club in St John's and soon made an impression with the national selectors. It was in the back row that Snow won international recognition, firstly at Under 21 level and then with the Under 23 team. At this stage in his career Snow weighed in at less than sixteen stone so when it was suggested that a move to the front row was where his future lay he was a little taken aback, but if this was where the selectors saw him playing then so be it.

While he accepted the change of position, getting games and match experience was not easy. Bigger and more experienced men dominated the front row at provincial level and getting any opportunity proved difficult. In 1994, after a handful of games, Rod Snow had his first chance with the full Canadian squad. On a European tour that took in Italy, England and France he made two appearances for the mid-week team but it wasn't until March the following year that he made his international debut against Argentina in Buenos Aires. The Pumas were renowned as powerful scrummagers and Snow was put in at the deep end, chosen to play hooker. During the match both Canadian props were injured and Snow ended up playing all three front row positions in his first capped appearance for his country. In a close match Argentina ran out 29-26 winners but the visitors outscored them four tries to one. Then followed the Rugby World Cup, the sending off and the refusal of entry into the UK.

While Rod Snow was home in Newfoundland kicking his heels waiting for a work permit Newport were quietly going about the business of club rugby in this first season of professionalism. The opening month had started with four wins in the league before the away game at Pontypridd brought the run to an end, the home side recording a comfortable 38-3 victory. October saw the club at both its best and its worst. On the last Saturday of the month a fine 21-8 defeat of Llanelli at Rodney Parade helped restore a little faith after what had happened earlier. A far from star-studded Barbarians side had romped to a 59-28 victory which was followed by a hard earned draw in a league match at home to Neath. But it was away at St Helens, Swansea, that the warning signs started to flash. Warning signs that Newport were perhaps far too reliant on one player to keep the scoreboard ticking over with his reliable place kicking. Gareth Rees had joined the club midway through the previous season and in his short time there, he would break many of the points scoring records previously held by black and amber players. However, Swansea in October 1995 saw only one record broken - Newport's biggest league defeat.

Surprisingly, the half time score showed the home side enjoying a narrow 14-6 lead but after the break Newport imploded. Swansea scored a further 64 points, including ten tries, while Newport didn't trouble the scoreboard operator again. Before the end of the year four more league matches would be won, including a creditable away victory at Cardiff, but it would be a long time before the enormity of the defeat at St Helens would be forgotten.

This then was the state of affairs at Rodney Parade when Rod Snow finally arrived there. Fourteen out of twenty-two league matches had been played with nine victories and a draw to the club's credit. The weather started to have its say and matches were postponed or indeed cancelled if they were only friendlies.

Snow made his debut for his new club on 6 January 1996. High-flying Pontypridd were the visitors and the debutant was to play tight head which would see him pack down against Ponty captain Nigel Bezani, one of the most experienced and respected props in the game. Welcome to Wales! The match saw the home side have one of their better days although the spoils went to the visitors who won a thrilling encounter 30-29. Yet again, Gareth Rees was prominent on the score sheet recording all his side's points. Snow's next two appearances saw him at loose head and hooker, achieving in three games for Newport what had only taken him one for Canada - playing in all three front row positions.

In his second game, a cup match at Ystradgynlais, Snow recalls the match as 'an intense and heated affair that had one explosive brawl. I was involved but only on the receiving end taking one to the jaw which dazed me for a few seconds and I was unable to throw any back. I think the big second row that hit me might have hit me again but he seemed a bit amazed that the first shot I walked into hadn't put me down. Nevertheless, it was all broken up with one of the opposition sent off and no one any worse for wear.'

Two things stand out when reading the pages of Rod Snow's journal written at the outset of his career with Newport. These are his ability to be self-critical and an awareness of his limitations. 'Training was tough this week though I must admit that I need the fitness training as I am not near the top of my game. The funny thing is that while I'm not confident about my own fitness I'm still much fitter than the other front row forwards here. But when it comes to scrummaging I always struggle. I believe that I'm far stronger physically than the other props but I can't make up for their experience. I will stick with it as it is the one part of my game that limits my progress. I need a big game for the club, for my own confidence, and to gain the confidence of the people around me: players, coaches, management and fans.' This entry smacks of somebody starting to get to grips with what being a professional rugby player meant.

By the end of the season Snow must have had plenty of occasions when he questioned what on earth he had let himself in for. If ever a club experienced the highs and lows of the game in a season it was Newport in 1995-96. Having suffered the humiliation at St Helens, what happens in the return fixture five months later? Newport win 27-16. And after beating Llanelli at home the away match ends in a 56-22 defeat. Then in a home game against Treorchy, a side struggling at the bottom end of the division, Newport are seemingly coasting at 25-5 only to fall apart and lose 36-30. Similarly at Neath, leading 20-3, in a remarkable fifteen minutes Newport give away four interception tries and finally lose the game 65-23.

This last result was particularly concerning as the teams were due to meet two weeks later in the semi-final of the SWALEC Cup. The match, played at Cardiff Arms Park, would further compound Newport's inconsistency. After three comfortable victories in the early rounds of the competition, at home against Tumble and Ystradgynlais followed by an away tie at Llandovery, Newport won a closely contested quarter-final with Caerphilly at Rodney Parade. And now it was crunch time.

Newport's record in the cup was not very impressive. Winners back in 1977, when they spoilt Cardiff's centenary celebrations, they had only appeared in two other finals, losing to Swansea in 1978 and Cardiff in 1986. A chance to appear in a fourth final was now up for grabs.

When Neath kicked off the Newport contingent must have been fearing the worst. Within a minute their side was leading 7-0. With what must be one of the quickest tries on record, Newport right wing Richard Rees had fielded the ball, brushed off a tackle and ran seventy metres to score. The try was recorded at fifteen seconds and Newport had their dream start. After almost eighty minutes of nail biting cup rugby the team was protecting a 22-21 lead when everything fell apart. A Newport forward was judged offside at a ruck some forty metres out and Neath scrum half Patrick Horgan stepped up to kick the match winning goal, which just about summed up Newport's season.

With nothing to play for Newport lost their four remaining league matches. The final game of the season, at home against Cardiff, did however, go down in the record books for witnessing an achievement that in the new era of professional rugby will never happen again. David 'Muddy' Waters, a towering lock forward, had first played for the club way back in 1973 and here he was twenty-three years later playing his 700th game. A player in the game today can expect to appear in a maximum of thirty matches in a season if he stays clear of injury. Ten years at a club is a realistic period which will make 300 appearances the stuff of folk lore in years to come. Rod Snow had played a few games for Newport United, the clubs second side, prior to his first team debut and this brought him into close contact with Waters. 'What amused me,' said Snow, 'was the fact that he didn't want to be lifted in the line-out. The laws had recently been amended to allow this but he wasn't having any of it. He got up there under his own steam.'

If Welsh clubs had treated this first season of professionalism with some caution, their English counterparts had seen a great deal of interest from wealthy individuals prepared to put money on the table, but no such 'sugar daddies' had come forward in Wales. This saw the inevitable happen - a player drain from the Welsh clubs to greener pastures on the other side of Offa's Dyke. Most clubs were affected. Cardiff lost their half backs Adrian Davies and Andy Moore to Richmond, Llanelli saw Phil Davies and Colin Stephens head to Leeds and Newport suffered a huge blow when Gareth Rees decided to accept an offer and move to London-based club, Wasps. When international lock forward Kevin Moseley was tempted away to that stronghold of rugby in the north east - West Hartlepool - then it really was time to take stock. The threat that Rugby League clubs had previously held over their union counterparts, certainly in Wales, was now being replaced by a greater threat from within. Players didn't have to worry about learning the new code, all they had to do was head in the direction of the biggest cheque book.

Not content with the signatures of Rees and Moseley, Wasps and West Hartlepool both showed a serious interest in Rod Snow as, indeed did Sale. 'I'd certainly started to feel at home at Newport.

Although Gareth was no longer at the club I had got myself settled and I enjoyed the way of life that I had fallen into. Sure there were offers on the table, better offers, but I didn't think too long about them. If Newport were prepared to put something sensible together then I was going to stay.'

And stay he did. Snow signed a new three-year contract that would keep him at Rodney Parade until the end of the 1998-99 season. Unfortunately, in addition to Rees and Moseley, players who went in search of pastures new included Richard Rees (Swansea), Jason Hewlett (Cardiff), Andrew Peacock (West Hartlepool) and Mike Voyle (Llanelli). Also leaving Newport in this fall out was Alan Carter. Carter had spent six seasons with the club during which time his outstanding play in the back row had brought him international honours with two caps in 1991. While he admitted to having enjoyed his time at Newport he felt the club lacked a structure that would take them forward. This was particularly pertinent coming from someone who had given the club such dedicated service, but time would prove his comments had some foundation. On the plus side Newport had attracted the services of half backs Shaun Connor and Nicky Lloyd together with Czech Republic back row forward Jan Machacek. Youth product Ian Gough would also make his mark in the senior side in the coming season.

The WRU had decided that at the end of the 1996-97 campaign the number of teams in Division One would be reduced from twelve to eight with no club eligible for promotion from Division Two. The previous two seasons had seen Newport finish in eighth position so there was going to be no margin for error this time round. In addition to the twenty-two league matches a further eleven were on the fixture list, matches that were included in two new competitions. Firstly, a European Conference was introduced based on the success of the previous season's European Cup. This put Newport in a pool of six clubs that would play each other once with the top two teams progressing to the knock out stages of the competition. An Anglo-Welsh competition also appeared on the fixture list which brought

Newport up against three English clubs who they would play on a home and away basis, a further six matches. By the end of the campaign the club would have a good idea as to its standing, not only in Welsh rugby, but also on the playing fields of Europe.

Remarkably, Newport ended the 1996-97 season in sixth position in Division One thereby ensuring their participation in the top division in the following season. Of the twenty-two matches played, twelve were won, two drawn and eight lost. But when they lost, Newport certainly did it with some style. Pontypridd 54-32 and 54-20. Llanelli 55-5 and Swansea - remember that record score in the previous season? - well, it was broken. This time the scoreline read 82-18. And, if that wasn't bad enough, the Barbarians in what would be their last game at Rodney Parade, piled up more points in an 86-33 victory.

Things weren't much better in the new competitions. Although winning two games in the Conference, defeats against Sale 52-22 and Montferrand 55-14 added to the misery. While in the ill fated Anglo-Welsh tournament, Northampton recorded two emphatic victories, 67-19 and 53-7. In nine matches Newport RFC had conceded a total of 558 points, a staggering average of 62 points per match. But the record books will always show that in the 1996-97 season Newport were the sixth best club in Wales, a statistic that really does beggar belief.

With the WRU having decided that Division One clubs would enter the SWALEC Cup in the sixth round Newport's first match saw Cardiff visiting Rodney Parade. The home side gave the season's eventual cup winners plenty to think about but were eventually beaten 44-30. A season of contrasting fortunes then. A season that saw the club retain its place in a reduced Division One but a season that had asked many questions, questions that most supporters doubted could be answered by the personnel both on and off the field.

When Rod Snow signed a new contract with Newport he could not have envisaged the depths to which the club would fall. It was obvious that a player showing some promise would be easily tempted by pastures new and, sure enough, over a couple of seasons Newport lost enough quality players to make supporters wonder why they bothered. The main reason Newport were not attracting the big names and, at the same time not able to hold on to many top players, was money. The committee had adopted a policy which meant working within fixed budgets thereby trying to avoid the club getting into a financial situation that it would struggle with. Without doubt, this was a sensible and prudent approach but at the same time it left the shop window looking decidedly bare. It was also a policy that would take the club to the very brink of disaster. There is no justification in trying to blame off-field policies for the demise of the club on the field and in many ways, particularly with the benefit of hindsight, the decision makers should be applauded for their firm stance on matters financial. One could even argue, strongly argue, that if all Welsh clubs had adopted similar stringencies the game in Wales would not have ended up in the mess it found itself in at the turn of the century.

A new season and a new captain. Hooker Ian Jones was in his eighth season with the club and it seemed fitting that this senior player should have his chance to captain the team. Nobody would argue with that, but by the end of the season Jones must have pondered his decision to accept the responsibility. Like many before him, and certainly most since, Ian Jones suffered from, putting it mildly, great inconsistency when throwing the ball into the line-out. What, from the touchlines appears to be the simplest of tasks, obviously isn't and a player regularly seen messing it up quickly gets the crowd on his back. Ian Jones was captain of a side that was again failing to perform and he needed broad shoulders.

Alex Lawson, Matthew Robinson and a young Richard Parks were notable among the new crop of players at Rodney Parade but their time with the club would be short-lived, each would eventually move to a more successful club. And, lest we forget, there was Paul Cooke.

Many clubs had looked to the Southern Hemisphere to bolster their squads. Providing certain parameters were observed there was room to include these overseas players and, not to miss out, Newport signed up New Zealander Paul Cooke. Cooke had shown a lot of promise in his early career. He was a member of the New Zealand Colts in 1986, a team led by Zinzan Brooke, and he became a regular in the Hawkes Bay provincial side in the late 1980s and early 1990s. On paper this appeared to be a pedigree of some distinction, but the player that turned up at Rodney Parade in 1997-98 certainly didn't match the profile. There was a suggestion that Cooke had misled Newport regarding his date of birth, records show this to be 9 January 1967, but surely at 30 years of age a player should not be consigned to the scrap heap. No, it was more down to the fact that Paul Cooke just wasn't good enough that saw club and player part company. Whether Paul Cooke couldn't hack it or whether he just couldn't be bothered we shall never know. However, there was a salutary lesson to be taken on board here, not only by Newport RFC but by all clubs thinking of casting a wide net in their search for players.

1997-98 was a landmark season in the history of Newport RFC. In a reduced and renamed Premier Division, now consisting of eight clubs, Newport lost all fourteen league matches played. Compared to the previous season most matches were much more evenly contested. Bridgend 27-19 and 24-13, Ebbw Vale 24-19 and 18-10, while single point defeats at the hands of Cardiff 26-25 and Neath 23-22 added to the frustration. After a mighty effort in the quarter-final of the SWALEC Cup the defeats, once again, registered on the Richter Scale: 61-24 at Cardiff, 66-10 at Llanelli and, in the last match of the season, 41-17 at home to Neath.

The European Conference had been restructured into eight groups of four, the clubs playing each other twice on a home and away basis. Newport were in Pool B with Sale and French clubs Montferrand and Montpellier. Though winning three matches, including a notable away victory at Montpellier, the club failed to reach the knock-out stages of the competition but there was still the Challenge Trophy to look forward to!

With the demise of the Anglo-Welsh tournament and the reduction in the number of clubs in the league, the WRU decided to launch a Challenge Trophy. If ever a tournament was concocted to test the patience of rugby followers in Wales to the utmost then this was it.

The eight Welsh Premier Division clubs were included together with Argentinian provinces, Cordoba, Rosario and Tucuman, Northern Transvaal from South Africa and national representation seen by the inclusion of Namibia, Spain and Rugby Canada. The structure of the tournament saw the fifteen teams divided into two pools. Pool A was made up of six teams and Pool B seven, thirteen teams in total but weren't there fifteen teams in the tournament? There were, and just to complicate matters, two teams, Cordoba and Northern Transvaal, would play in both Pools! The Welsh clubs had already played an opening round of matches by the time the overseas teams arrived in the new year for the second stage of the tournament, but what made the whole event ridiculous was that the overseas competitors were not able to progress to the final stages. The teams that had travelled from far and wide to take part in this nonsense couldn't win it! All right, they knew this before they left home, but this was the new age of professional rugby and it seemed that the powers that be in Wales had their heads well and truly stuck up their collective arses. When Pontypridd beat Cardiff 15-10 in the final held at Sardis Road, 5,000 spectators were in attendance, but throughout the competition as a whole, the public had voted - with their feet!

With the dearth of league matches the Premier Division clubs were drafted into the SWALEC Cup in the fourth round. Pwllheli, South Wales Police and UWIC had all been comfortably accounted for before the draw for the quarter-final saw Newport paired with Pontypridd, the match to be played at Rodney Parade. Since the inception of leagues Newport had only recorded one victory against Pontypridd, that in the very first encounter between the clubs in November 1991.They had also lost a cup match in 1994-95 by an embarrassing 56-0 scoreline. When prolific points scorer Neil Jenkins led out his team few of the home supporters could have held out much hope of a place in the semi-final. How wrong can you get? Rod Snow remembers this match as 'the best performance and the most rewarding result in the first three seasons I was at the club. Ponty had been a real thorn in our sides since I arrived at Newport and to beat them in the Cup was payback time.' With less than five minutes remaining on the clock Pontypridd were hanging on to a 27-26 lead. Two tries by Ian Gough and Matthew J Watkins, the latter a seventy-yard run in following an interception, had put the home side 17-10 in front but tries by Gareth Wyatt and Dafydd James saw the visitors in the driving seat at 27-17. Outside half Shaun Connor kicked three penalties to bring Newport to within a point and then, with time running out, dropped the match-winning goal. A nail-biting final few minutes saw the Black and Ambers hold on for a 29-27 win. This was the only high in a season remembered for the many lows it produced. The semi-final took Newport to Sardis Road and a tie with Ebbw Vale. It wasn't to be, the Gwent Valley club winning in convincing style 44-10. The season ended with Newport at the bottom of the league table and duly relegated - or were they?

As the 1997-98 season drew to a close off-field events were starting to steal the headlines. The Premier Division clubs received £400,000 per annum from the WRU and wanted more. Some were reported to be heading for financial ruin if more funding was not available and the demand was for an extra £350,000. Earlier, the clubs had been asked to sign a ten-year loyalty agreement with the Union but Cardiff had refused, causing the WRU to withhold all monies due, while Swansea were watching events unfold from a distance; for the time being anyhow. Without any other form of backing the remaining clubs, Newport among them, had signed the loyalty agreement. At an extraordinary meeting called by the WRU on 24 May the member clubs unanimously voted that Premier Division clubs had to sign the ten-year loyalty agreement. Cardiff dug their heels in. The legal fees started mounting up and the issue was heading for the High Court. As the new season approached Swansea joined ranks with Cardiff in the battle with the Union and an impasse was arrived at.

In the vain hope that the matter would be amicably resolved, i.e. the Union would get its way, a series of deadlines came and passed. 5.00 pm 12 August became 1.00pm 17 August but to no avail. Cardiff and Swansea would take no part in the Welsh League in the new season, instead they would play a series of friendly matches against the leading English clubs, much to the chagrin of the RFU.

Therefore, a week before it was due to kick off, the Premier Division in Wales found itself two clubs short. Division One champions, Caerphilly, had been promoted and the decision was made that runners-up, Aberavon, should join them, and that the club relegated from the Premiership should be given a reprieve and remain in the top flight - Newport.

During the close season Newport had appointed a new Director of Rugby, Allan Lewis. He'd had a few short months to prepare the squad for Division One rugby which meant a fixture list that included old Gwent rivals Abertillery, Cross Keys, Newbridge and Pontypool with, among others, Blackwood, Bonymaen, Llandovery and Merthyr. Familiar names but not clubs previously played on a regular basis. A 30-match season beckoned with no such thing as an early return to the Premier Division guaranteed. Instead it's Bridgend, Llanelli, Pontypridd etc with Neath first up at Rodney Parade on the opening day.

By the summer of 1998 Rod Snow had played rugby, virtually without a break, for the best part of three years. Although in the Northern Hemisphere, Canada played most of its rugby during the summer. Now a regular in the national side, for Snow this meant that no sooner had he finished a season with Newport than it was home to take part in the Pan America and Pacific Rim tournaments together with any matches scheduled against touring sides. Add to this any overseas tours that the Canadians made and you have a very full agenda. The domestic season in the UK used to be rigidly controlled; no rugby before 1 September and none after 30 April. Nowadays these restrictions are history and the season will start in mid-August and probably run through to the last weekend in May. When players do manage to get a summer break away from the game it is rarely for longer than a month, pre-season training starting in July.

Rod Snow accepts that his unusual circumstances mean that he is a professional rugby player in every way - seven days a week, fifty-two weeks of the year. Returning to Newport for the start of the 1998-99 season the player had mixed feelings. This was the last season he was contracted to the club and he was going to have to give his future serious thought. 'While I was still enjoying playing the game you can only take so many hidings and Newport had been on the receiving end of plenty in the last couple of years. Now, with barely a week's notice and totally unprepared, the club was expected to play another season of Premier Division football. Of course the committee had no choice other than to grab the chance to stay in the top flight but it wasn't going to be much fun if the previous two seasons' results were anything to go by. I had been desperate to get out of my contract with Newport, particularly as they were heading for the lower division. Swansea, then coached by John Plumtree, had expressed an interest and were prepared to pay a £20,000 transfer fee. I'd also received a call from the Canterbury Crusaders coach, Wayne Smith, asking if I would consider a move to New Zealand to play in the Super 12 competition. The Crusaders won it that year, the first of three consecutive victories, and I sometimes regret not having taken the chance to experience that high profile tournament.' In the end Rod Snow stayed at Rodney Parade and saw out the final year of his contract but a move to a new club was still uppermost in his mind.

One month before the start of the new season, and still expecting to play Division One rugby, the committee had called an extraordinary meeting to consider one proposal - that Newport Athletic Club change its constitution and become incorporated as a limited liability company. It is doubtful if any previous meeting in the club's long history had received as much interest from its members. Only those producing current membership cards were admitted but Rodney Hall was packed to the rafters when the meeting was opened. On the top table there were the familiar faces, among them David Watkins, Martin Hazell, Bob Atkins and Christopher Hill but most people in the room were interested in the quiet, unassuming character who also took his place at the table. The members had heard the name before but for most of them this was the first opportunity to put a face to it. This was Tony Brown who would shortly become the Chief Executive of the club and take it on a roller coaster ride beyond the wildest imaginings of those present.

The proposal to become a limited liability company was passed almost unanimously and when the new season kicked off on 29 August the club had a Board of Directors which had replaced the previous season's committee. There was a Finance Director, a Commercial Director, a Company Secretary, unfamiliar names on the Board, and of course, the new Chief Executive. This all looked very official and businesslike but there were still the on-field problems that were in need of urgent attention and drastic action if the club was to go forward.

When Rod Snow returned for what he was beginning to think would be his last season with Newport he found a club with a new purpose, a vision even. Recognising that it had been through the door of the 'last chance saloon' it appeared the many problems that had bedevilled the club were going to be addressed and quickly. However, while it was certainly a step in the right direction, changing the off field structure and introducing new ideas and personnel, in the short term this would not help performances on the field. At the end of the day a team has to stand up and be counted by its results and here was a problem that a show of hands wasn't going to change in an instant.

The first blow dealt Allan Lewis was the departure of promising second row forward Ian Gough to Pontypridd. Gough had gone on the ill-fated Welsh tour to South Africa in the summer, playing in the embarrassing 96-13 defeat against the Springboks at Pretoria. It may have been suggested to the young man that he would not do his international prospects any good if he stayed at Newport and that perhaps he should consider a change of club. Whatever, Ian Gough departed Rodney Parade, but only on loan - he would return to Newport two years later.

While Gough moved out several new names appeared in the matchday programmes. Not totally put off by the Paul Cooke experience, the club brought in two more New Zealanders. Brad Clarke, a back row forward, hailed from the Central Vikings, a Second Division outfit formed in 1997 with the amalgamation of Hawkes Bay and

Manawatu, while Matt Cardey, a wing/full back had been on the books of First Division team North Harbour. More familiar were Andrew Gibbs, Alan Harris, and Stuart Roy while Dale Burn, Scott Mitchell, Ceri Jones, Gareth Taylor, Joe Powell and Alix Popham would all figure prominently as the season developed and would become key players in the future. Sven Cronk was given the poisoned chalice, appointed to succeed Ian Jones as captain, and first up it was the Welsh All Blacks.

Disappointingly, the 1998-99 season was a case of more of the same for the Black and Ambers. Of twenty league matches played, fourteen plus the additional six in the second phase which saw the league split into a top and bottom half, only five were won and three of these against Aberavon who would prop up the table at the end of the season. A narrow 30-29 home win against Ebbw Vale and a surprising 33-0 defeat of visiting Bridgend (did they turn up?) were the only other reasons to be cheerful. Five defeats out of six in the renamed European Shield and a 60-38 hammering at Swansea in the SWALEC Cup completed a story that was becoming all to familiar. The Challenge Trophy reared its head again, tweaked to give all competing teams a chance to win it, but Newport failed to make the latter stages which saw Llanelli defeat Pontypridd in the final. And of course, in among those defeats were the five by Caerphilly. No matter what had happened off the field in the build-up to the season the Rodney Parade club was still failing to perform where it mattered, on the field.

It should come as no surprise to learn that Rod Snow, now out of contract, had decided to look elsewhere. There would be no difficulty in finding a new club. During his time at Newport, Snow had earned quite a reputation for his all-round play and top of the list of interested parties were Newport's greatest rivals, Cardiff. The directors knew that I was likely to be moving on at the end of the season. Allan Lewis had even sounded me out about taking over the captaincy. I never saw myself as a club captain. I was quite happy to lead from the front but didn't enjoy the added responsibilities that came with the job. I'd captained both Canada and Newport on the odd occasion when the regular guy was rested or injured, but I didn't want to know beyond that really. Allan insisted I think about it and I agreed, but privately my mind was made up - I was going to sign for Cardiff. I'd had meetings with Cardiff Chief Executive, Gareth Davies, and everything was in place, all I had to do was sign on the dotted line. I can remember practising some chipping and putting in front of the clubhouse when Tony Brown came up to me and said how things were going to change at Newport and that he wanted me to stay. I'd heard it all before and to be honest, my mind was made up, I was going to Cardiff.'

Back home in Newfoundland, enjoying a well-earned break before the new season and the Rugby World Cup, Snow had two important phone calls. The first came from Peter O'Flaherty, an old friend, who handled his business affairs. Newport were making an offer of a new three-year contract to which he was going to have to give serious consideration. The second was from Allan Lewis. Newport had signed Shane Howarth, the Welsh full back, and he was going to captain the side in the new season.

The Autograph Collector

'Develop the business around the people; build it, don't buy it; and then, be the best.'

Richard Branson

Tony Brown is a wealthy man. No, Tony Brown isn't a wealthy man, Tony Brown is a very wealthy, indeed, seriously wealthy man. This is a statement born out by his inclusion in the annually produced Sunday Times Rich List, the latest of which shows him at equal 375th among the wealthiest thousand individuals in the country. With an estimated wealth of £95 million the list places Brown alongside the likes of Sir Terence Conran, ex Pink Floyd member Roger Waters and ahead of the more recognisable names of Rod Stewart, Lord Weinstock, Posh and Becks, Robert Sangster and Sean Connery. Yes, Tony Brown is indeed a seriously wealthy man.

A close scrutiny of the list will reveal other familiar names. In 168th position with an estimated wealth of £190 million is Andrew Brownsword. Peter and Stan Thomas are valued at £160 million while Nigel Wray, Tom Walkinshaw and Keith Barwell also appear in the lists top six hundred. Like Tony Brown these individuals have all become involved with rugby clubs, Bath, Cardiff, Saracens, Gloucester and Northampton respectively receiving the benefit of their wealth and business expertise. The six men all appear in the Sunday Times Rich List because they are successful businessmen, successful in six different fields, but they are united in their passion for rugby, a passion which is costing them untold sums as they each seek to bring the success they are familiar with in their business lives to their chosen clubs.

Clubs that have attracted the interest of such wealthy individuals are very much in the minority and can be regarded as extremely fortunate to have done so in an era where club rugby is failing to pay its way. We have seen that when the game turned professional there was an immediate interest from entrepreneurs who possibly saw financial gain to be had somewhere down this new road, and how several quickly realised this would not be the case and withdrew their involvement causing casualties among the clubs, some of which failed to recover. Most of the men mentioned above entered the arena after the dust created by the IRB had settled and have subsequently stayed the course. Why do they do it? Why do these men with extremely successful businesses plough money into a venture where there is no realistic chance of recovering the investment never mind seeing a profit? The early departure of those who were involved from day one suggests that their involvement was financially motivated and their hasty withdrawal leads one to believe that they were looking for a return that the club game would never be able satisfy. So what of those who have stayed the course, those men who are prepared to spend millions on their respective clubs in the certain knowledge that they will never see their money again.

If rugby union wanted a sneak preview of what lay ahead of it in the aftermath of Paris '95 it only needed to look at the way Association Football had been developing over the past twenty years. A Premiership had been created at the behest of the major clubs and, although promotion and relegation remained part of the structure, it had become the domain of the big clubs. And the big clubs continued getting bigger while those in the lower divisions fell further behind and could only dream of what might be. While regularly playing to capacity crowds and fully capitalising on the marketing potential, clubs of the stature of Manchester United, Liverpool and Arsenal had created a nationwide base of supporters who would rarely, if ever, see their heroes play in the flesh. This is unique in British sport and has resulted in television companies queuing up to secure the rights to broadcast Premiership football. Rugby union can never hope to aspire to such a following at club level but if the same ingredients are put together with similar emphasis placed on each of them, there would appear to be no reason why a tailored down version of this hugely successful formula could not be achieved.

The entrepreneurs who became involved with Bath, Cardiff,

Gloucester, Northampton and Wasps knew that these clubs were steeped in rugby history and that each had a following that would not disappear if results were poor. There was no apparent reason why a tailored down version of the football Premiership could not see these clubs thrive in the new era of professional rugby. Before this could be put in place however, two major factors would need addressing: how to increase the support base and, once this was achieved, would the club grounds be able to cope with the extra numbers. In Bath and Wasps both extremes of these issues were highlighted.

Bath play rugby at the Recreation Ground which is located in the centre of the city and is rigidly controlled by the local council. It has a capacity of just over 8,000 and there is nothing the club can do to improve on this figure. By the mid-1990s Bath had been the dominant club in English rugby for over a decade. The revenue lost to the club during this period, due to the small capacity of its home ground would, undoubtedly, have been substantial. An extra two thousand seats sold for each home game over the ten-year period and Bath could have welcomed the arrival of the professional game with a much stronger financial base, particularly at the prices visitors to the Rec have to pay.

Contrast the now named London Wasps, who until recently played their home matches at Loftus Road, the home of Queens Park Rangers FC. The ground has a capacity of 19,000, all seated, but attendances rarely threatened half this figure.

With ground capacities of 10,800 and 11,000 respectively, Gloucester and Northampton appear to enjoy something near the optimum capacity when considering the game's popularity going into the twenty-first century. During the early years of professional rugby these four clubs have each enjoyed sufficient success to be able to project a realistic figure for attendances in the medium term. Stadiums with capacities of 12-15,000 will be able to cater for the needs of any rugby club in the foreseeable future and any club that believes otherwise and, more importantly, invests heavily in that belief, is heading for trouble. Welford Road, Leicester holds 16,250 and there are usually seats available behind the posts while Cardiff Arms Park can cater for

14,000 but when were the 'sold out' signs last seen there?

Rodney Parade holds around 11,700 spectators and there have only been a handful of occasions in recent years when it has been full to capacity. For rugby clubs to become viable in the new era they will have to fill their grounds at every given opportunity and even then there will be no guarantee that the sums will add up come the end of the season. Benefactors are marvellous for the clubs lucky enough to be on the receiving end of their generosity but they can only be seriously expected to give their financial support in the short term and it will then be down to the clubs to stand alone and the first step to take in preparing for the day they would be left to their own devices is to ensure that the crowds come in sufficient numbers.

Tony Brown threw his hat in with Newport RFC in 1999, four years after the arrival of professionalism and two years after joining the club as a vice-president. Two years spent watching the club languishing at the bottom of the league and struggling to keep its name at the top end of the game in Wales. Two years spent watching the history, support and facilities that the club had acquired over its 120-plus-year existence gradually fading into oblivion. Two years during which he decided that he could possibly be able to help; possibly be able to do something that would help the club restore itself to its previous stature in the game. Two years at the end of which he decided to underwrite Newport RFC for three seasons and see what happened. While this was a decision that would ultimately save the club from ending up in the lower divisions with nothing more than a proud and distant history to look back on, it was a decision taken in the hope that after three years Newport would be enjoying the level of success that would enable it to be financially viable. The crowds would have returned, the team would be a winning one and Brown's support would only be required vocally.

Why Tony Brown wanted to become involved with Newport is a story that starts some thirty years ago and 150 miles away in the Home Counties. The town of Bisley is located in the stockbroker belt of London, between Ascot and Woking, and it is here that the revival of Newport RFC can be said to have begun.

Although originally founded in 1931 as a car repair firm, a change of direction in 1960 saw the formation of Bisley Office Equipment. The manufacture of steel office equipment helped the business flourish over the next decade and by 1970 annual turnover had increased to a then impressive £300,000. When Tony Brown's father decided the time was right to sell the business and retire his son put into place what he regards as 'the first management buyout seen in the UK'.

Tony Brown was always destined to end up running the family business. His formal education had seen him attend boarding school at St Edmunds, Ware and it was here that he was introduced to the game of rugby football. He played hooker for the school's first XV, but by the time National Service saw him in the Army and an overseas posting to Malaya, his extra inches in height took him into the second row. On his return to the UK and civilian life Brown joined the family business and continued his rugby career at Guildford and Godalming where he played out the rest of his days on the wing. In the 1960s moving a player from hooker to the second row and finally out to the wing may have been misconstrued to mean that the farther away from the ball he was the better, a suggestion Tony Brown would certainly contest. At the end of his playing days Brown had little further involvement with the game until his business activities saw him on the receiving end of invitations to enjoy corporate hospitality on the big occasions at Twickenham.

After the 'management buyout' in 1970 Bisley Office Equipment quickly established itself as one of the leaders in the field and by the end of the 1980s expansion was necessary if the growth was to continue. More factory space and more staff were needed which presented a problem that had to be given serious consideration. While a Home Counties location had obvious advantages - accessibility together with good distribution links for both home and overseas markets - the big disadvantage reared its head when plans to expand on the existing site were considered. Being in a green belt area these were not acceptable and any expansion would have to take place somewhere other than Bisley. When considering where to set up a second factory, accessibility and distribution potential were top of the list of requirements. An M4 corridor location would be ideal and after discussions with the Welsh Development Agency, Newport got the thumbs up.

The new premises opened in 1989 and the company has continued to go from strength to strength. From a turnover of £300,000 in 1970 the figure stood at £75 million in 2001. The company employs approximately 1,000 people and over half of these are based in Newport which now accounts for 60% of the annual turnover. Exports account for 30% of turnover and, again, over half of this figure originates in Newport. With two Queen's Awards for Export, Bisley Office Equipment is now recognised as the leader in its field, a fact which Tony Brown attributes in no small way to the factory in Newport. With all this success Brown still places most importance on the fact that 'there have never been any redundancies at Bisley and I would never sacrifice any jobs for profit'. It is statements like this that help open up and explain the thinking and priorities of the man who would be the prime mover and shaker in the future of Newport RFC.

Okay, you've expanded your business in a new location, turnover's up, profits are up and everything's looking good. Do you sit back and enjoy all the benefits that this success brings or do you look to put something back into the community that has helped you achieve it? Many people would go with the first option and think no more about it, but in Tony Brown we have one of the few who would feel that he wants to give something back, show his gratitude to the community that helped his business flourish. Enter David Watkins.

Now David Watkins is one of the all time greats of Newport rugby but it is doubtful that he ever scored a try, dropped a goal or made a break that was anywhere near as important as the day he invited the businessman from England who made office furniture in the town to come and watch a match at Rodney Parade. And that's how it all started, how Tony Brown came to spend a small fortune on a club that will never be able to repay him. To his eternal credit, Tony Brown decided that he would like to put something back into Newport and he chose to do this via the town's ailing rugby club. Large sums of money would be involved but this was not going to be just a case of writing out large cheques, that in itself would not be enough. It was also the business brain that came with the money, that would ensure the all-important off-the-field factors would be addressed in addition to enticing top players in a massive recruitment campaign. Together with his money and business acumen Tony Brown would bring one other vital ingredient to the table at Rodney Parade - himself. This may seem obvious but it was an ingredient that would play a huge part when it came to the pursuit of some of the game's leading players, and in some instances it would be the deciding factor when it came to getting that all-important signature on the dotted line.

When Tony Brown took his place on the top table at the extraordinary general meeting held in the summer of 1998 to decide the future of Newport RFC he kept a low profile. The motion to form a limited liability company, Newport Athletic Club Limited, was comfortably passed and the net asset value of the club was distributed among the existing membership, each member receiving 936 Ordinary Shares. Directors of the newly formed limited company, Tony Brown among them, received the same allocation, but with an authorised share capital of £5 million there was plenty of scope for further investment after the original issue of 994,968 shares had been allocated.

Tony Brown became the club's first Chief Executive and was joined on the Board of Directors by Bob Atkins, Peter Banner, Tom Burge, Will Godfrey, Terry Greenhaf, Martin Hazell, Christopher J. Hill, Allan Lewis and David Watkins. Banner and Hill would be gone by the end of the 1998-99 season, the latter being replaced as Company Secretary and Financial Director by Roger Eady, while the role of Commercial Director would be reviewed.

However, one thing was clear, there would be no room within the new structure for many of the previous seasons committee men. Gone were the various rugby committees and honorary positions that had been readily filled by ex players and long serving club members. Newport RFC had, albeit belatedly, grabbed the nettle of professional rugby and now there was a new focus within the club. Change, like old age, doesn't come alone and there would be toes trodden on, noses put out of place - casualties - but it definitely was a case of 'shit or bust' and although it had taken three years to happen, the club was now in the real world of professional rugby.

The title Chief Executive suggests a high profile position, a position that requires, in addition to business experience, a knowledge of all things pertaining to the running of a company. Add to this the need for man management skills, social skills and the ability to sell the product and it is clear that the Chief Executives of this world do not grow on trees. While many of these specialist areas would be delegated to other individuals the need to understand what each involves remains. Come the first home match of the new season and one would expect to find Tony Brown in the boardroom entertaining the visiting team's top brass or in the hospitality areas welcoming the corporate guests who would be so important in the future of Newport RFC. But come match day and the Chief Executive of Newport RFC is not to be found in either of the above. No, Tony Brown is to be found walking around the entrance gates selling programmes. As the season unfolded this is how Newport's CEO introduced himself to the paying public and they loved him for it. If nothing else Tony Brown is certainly a man of the people. He would listen to any comments that were aimed in his direction and take on board any doubts and criticisms the old members had. There were plenty in the early days and they had to be acknowledged. Gone was the club of old, the Saturday afternoon and evening meeting place where the same people had done the same things season after season. This was all going to change and for a lot of people the change was going to be hard if not impossible to accept. It was really a simple case of either watching Newport fail week after week in front of small crowds of disinterested spectators while enjoying the habits of a lifetime or hope that the new regime would reverse the trend, attract the public and change the club of old forever. No contest really but many of the stalwarts were upset by the changes to their routines and, while wanting success on the field, were reluctant to accept that this would alter the way things were off it; they wanted to have the cake and to be able to eat it and this was not going to happen.

Tony Brown had sensed this feeling and did all that was reasonably possible to make the transition from a club to a business as painless as possible. One of the first concerns to rear its head was Rodney Parade itself. Owned by the club there was a feeling that the principal shareholders in years to come would be able to sell it without any input from the minority shareholders, i.e. the original members. To dispel these fears Brown agreed that no sale of the ground would take place unless approved by 75% of the shareholders, regardless of their shareholding. Each shareholder would have an equal vote thereby eliminating a majority shareholder influencing the outcome of a ballot. It was inevitable that majority shareholders would come to the fore and in 2000 a new share issue was allocated that saw a further 2,275,000 shares being taken up by the directors in lieu of loans and Tony Brown became the company's major shareholder with 1,330,936, thereby creating an extremely strong position for one individual to have. However, what becomes more and more apparent as one peels off the layers of this most complex of individuals are the genuine reasons for his involvement with the rugby club. As we have seen Brown is seriously wealthy and a controlling interest in a piece of land with a book value of some £1.5 million was never on his agenda. In the early days of incorporation there was talk of a prospectus being issued that would give the public the opportunity to purchase shares in the company. The new CEO referred to this in his programme notes for the opening match of the season and apologised for the delay in its production. However, to this day no prospectus has been produced. There is nothing sinister to be read into this, the Board quite simply feel that there would not be any takers wishing to invest in a company that is making the losses seen at Newport RFC Ltd. But as Brown says 'if there is anybody interested in purchasing shares they will be accommodated'. With the club seemingly somewhere between a rock and a hard place in that first year of incorporation the Board of Directors were pretty much on their own. Although having observed a level of prudence, the Annual Report for 1997-98 declared an operating loss of £299,433. The following Report, which covered fifteen months to enable the Company to adjust to a new accounting period, saw this figure double to £598,514. These losses had been financed by Directors' loans which would in due course be capitalised by way of the second share issue. There were now two options to consider: Newport RFC could live within its means or it could go out and buy a team and, hopefully, a future. It was as simple as that.

This was the decision that had to be made at the end of the 1998-99 season. Money was the only factor that was having a serious impact on the game and without it clubs were going to at best tread water. Treading water was not what Tony Brown had in mind when he made his decision to get involved at Newport and he wasn't going to accept it as the only option now. The capitalisation of the Directors' loans had restored the club to a level of financial stability. What was really only an accounting exercise that meant for loans read shares, the effect this had on strengthening the balance sheet was important. However, the club now needed more financial assistance, it needed somebody to underwrite its expenditure on players and this was not going to be small change. It needed Tony Brown to put his hand in his pocket and to keep doing so for the foreseeable future. This was a big ask and Brown knew it, but he also knew that it was the only way forward. He agreed to underwrite Newport RFC for the next three seasons, unreservedly, a commitment that would see him part with some £4 million of his own money, money he will never see again. 'I don't crave a yacht or any of the other trappings that are normally associated with wealth. I have made a commitment to this club and I will stand by that. My reward comes from seeing the crowds turn out on match day, the families and the pleasure on the faces when the team have won. I'm also particularly proud of what is being achieved through the Gateway Project and the other community work that is being driven by the club.'

Twelve months on, what was now Newport Rugby Football Club Ltd, the change of name had been approved on 12 June 2000, reported a loss for the financial year of £1,473,660. Turnover may have increased by £526,421 to £1,333,987 but this couldn't prevent an increase in the operating loss for the year of £875,146. And the reason for this apparent imbalance? Wages. Players' wages to be precise.

The summer of 1999 had seen the club go on a shopping spree that resulted in the recruitment of several high profile players. David Llewellyn, Peter Rogers and Shane Howarth were attracted to the club by the positive feedback that was coming from Rodney Parade as were Simon Raiwalui, Andy Marinos, Franco Smith, Jason Jones-Hughes and Gary Teichmann. Certainly there were strings being pulled and there was also the small matter of the money on offer but the fact remained that money or no money, twelve months earlier players of this calibre would not have risked their playing careers by joining Newport. There was more to it than that and the CEO had a big part to play in their arrival at the club.

Tony Brown would usually meet the overseas players when they arrived at Heathrow Airport and drive them together with their agents to Newport. When Andy Marinos arrived from Cape Town he was accompanied by Craig Livingston who represented many of the South African players. Brown recalls Livingston taking call after call on his mobile phone during the journey down the M4. On arriving at Rodney Parade, while Marinos went into the offices to complete the paperwork, Brown and Livingston walked around the ground with the phone still working overtime. 'It was then that I first heard that Gary Teichmann was looking for a club in the UK after his dismissal from the Springbok squad. That was the reason the phone hadn't stopped ringing and I became intrigued to know what amount of money a player of Teichmann's pedigree was looking for. When Livingston told me I had no hesitation in offering to pay it and the ball began rolling. Shortly after Teichmann flew over to take a look at Newport and what the club was offering. As before, I met the player and his agent at the airport and drove them to Wales. But this time one thing was different. On the previous occasions the player had sat in the back of the car and the agent had joined me in the front. Not Gary, he was in the front and Craig Livingston in the back. That told me something about the man that I was hoping would sign for Newport, he was used to leading and not following, he was in charge here and not the agent, we weren't only going to be talking money, there had to be something else on offer.'

That Tony Brown got his man is well documented but Teichmann would always say that his early impressions of his new paymaster were the deciding factor in his signing for the club. Let's face it, the money on offer was big, a reported £250,000 over two years, but it was a sum that many other clubs would have been prepared to pay. No, this was an instance when there was more than just money involved. Many overseas players have turned to the UK to boost their pension funds in the twilight of their careers. But few have offered more than just a name to the clubs that have written the cheques and while this practice continues home grown talent will struggle to come to the surface. That Gary Teichmann brought more than just his name to Newport is accepted by all involved in the game. He still had a point to prove and Tony Brown and Newport offered him the opportunity to end his playing career on a high after the disappointments back home in South Africa. In a few short months Newport RFC, with one mans backing had started to put together a squad of players that could, just maybe, turn things around; time would tell.

Whether Tony Brown knew what he was letting himself in for when he made his three year commitment to Newport is debatable. He knew it would be an expensive exercise but that even with the huge sums of money that would change hands over the three years there was no guarantee that success would come Newport's way. And without some measure of success there would be plenty of cynics waiting in the wings to ridicule the club. We live in a material world and envy is currently topping the list of the seven deadly sins as Brown would find out. In 1999 Newport RFC was way off the pace when compared to its rivals. The only solution was the 'quick fix', the short term injection of capital and the introduction of a new crop of players that it was hoped would redress the balance. Then and only then would the club be able to look at medium term and, indeed, long term planning strategies. Outsiders viewed the events at Rodney Parade with untold amounts of sarcasm and uneducated comment. Every defeat was welcomed with raised eyebrows and 'told you so' looks and the weight of responsibility that Tony Brown was carrying would soon begin to tell. Brown is an emotional man and never more so than when he is watching the club he has grown to love. Here is a man who is well used to the pressures that come with running a multi million pound business but make him sit and watch Newport playing in front of ten thousand supporters at Rodney Parade, behind on the scoreboard with time running out and he gets very edgy. The man was 62 years of age when he got on board the Black and Amber train and the last three years of rugby have seemingly advanced him beyond his 65 years.

He is a casual smoker most of the time but this escalates for an eighty minute period most weeks of the rugby season. He drinks whisky and has been known to walk out of a match when things are not looking good to brace himself with a tipple in the clubhouse. We're not talking vices here just ways of relieving the stresses and strains of watching rugby football which are unavoidable when you are so close to the game through such huge involvement with a particular club. Most supporters can watch a match and, win or lose, walk away from it and get on with their lives. Tony Brown is different, he can't even watch a game from the directors' seats in the stand any more, preferring to view with some anonymity from the corner flag at the clubhouse end of the pitch.

Of course, this is all very different at away matches. Then the directors enjoy the hospitality of the home club before and after the match and sit in the appropriate place for the duration of the game. But away from home expectation is very often not as great and the pressures fewer. Then again, there is the odd occasion when the hospitality of the hosts is non-existent, in fact they won't even let you into the ground. On 15 March 2002 Newport visited Eugene Cross Park in Ebbw Vale and there followed a sequence of events that would prove beyond doubt that club rugby in Wales had, with a handful of exceptions, failed to grasp the meaning of professional sport.

Going Over the Rugby

'Why did football bring me so to life? - Whatever it was I gave myself up to the Giants utterly. The recompense I gained was the feeling of being alive.'

Frederick Exley - A Fan's Notes

If a barometer were needed to gauge the highs and lows of Newport RFC during its 125 year history then we need look no further than Newport Bridge. Among bridges, the one built in Newport in 1800 is pretty ordinary. On a global scale it is neither a 'Golden Gate' or a 'Coat hanger', and more locally it pales into insignificance when compared to the Transporter Bridge a mile down river. Or is that up river? No matter. Newport Bridge is purely and simply functional, linking the main shopping centre, rail and bus stations with Maindee, Liswerry, Ringland and other districts found across the River Usk - or, Newport having attained city status, Downtown with the Eastern Suburbs.

Whenever Newport RFC was enjoying periods of sustained success the public would pour over the bridge on their way to Rodney Parade. Programme sellers would stand on the corner of Clarence Place and Artillery Place waiting to be swamped by the oncoming tide of human bodies. Then there were the bad times. The odd fan would wander over the same bridge wondering if the match was on or off as so few people were heading in the direction of the ground. Of course, spectators would approach the ground from all points of the compass but it was the activity on Newport Bridge that measured if the club was on a high or a low.

The Oxford English Dictionary describes a fan as 'a devotee of a particular activity, performer etc', while a supporter, in addition to being an heraldic term or a jockstrap, is listed as 'a person or thing that supports, especially a person supporting a cause, team or sport'. Fans or supporters? Maybe both, but it's decision time, so it's supporters that come from all corners to Rodney Parade and it's supporters who follow the Black and Ambers the length and breadth of the country. But why? Why do thousands of people, male and female, young and old, follow Newport RFC through thick and thin and pay handsomely for the privilege?

In the 2001-02 season Newport had a base of over four thousand season ticket holders. With the advent of the club's incorporation, the members' club and all that it stood for had become a thing of the past. The committees had been replaced by a controlling Board of Directors and the members were now season ticket holders alongside the ever-increasing number of new supporters who took up the option of an up-front payment at a reduced cost that would guarantee them entry to most home matches. Many of the club's long suffering members took exception to this. Why? Because it hurt that's why, it hurt bad. Not many people welcome change in their lives unless they have instigated it themselves so when change is forced on them it becomes difficult to accept. This was certainly the case with a lot of Newport's long-suffering members, the fact that they themselves had voted almost unanimously for it had been conveniently forgotten. None could have honestly believed when they raised their hand in support of the change to the club's constitution that things would ever be the same again.

It wouldn't take long before the members' lounge became out of bounds, the free parking at the club disappear and for several long-time seat holders in the grandstand there would be a relocated position to get used to. In fact, these facilities were still available to anybody wishing to take advantage of them, but at a price, and one that not many were prepared to pay. Then there was the personal contact between members and the office staff that had built up over many years. This all but disappeared, Jean Evans and Colin Taylor were now hidden away and, well, it all became a bit impersonal. Similarly, where the players would always make their way to the members' lounge after the match, there were new demands on their time that prevented this practice continuing. From being a club where every-body near as dammit knew everybody else Newport became, in many people's eyes, a victim of its own success. This was inevitable but, rather than shoot themselves in the foot and walk away, most of the old members accepted the changes - for better or worse.

In addition to the season ticket holders, estimates suggest that a further two thousand supporters regularly attend home matches but prefer to pay match by match. This figure is arrived at by studying the attendances at Rodney Parade for the visits of Edinburgh, Glasgow and Connacht. These three matches are unlikely to have attracted much casual interest and the travelling support can also be assumed to have been negligible. In 2001-02 the average attendance at the three matches was 6,460 and it is not unreasonable to suggest that this can be taken to represent the home support Newport is currently enjoying on a regular basis. The average attendance for the season fell just short of 8,000 with the biggest numbers turning out for the visit of Leinster in the Heineken Cup, when a large travelling support boosted the gate to 10,809, and the Boxing Day fixture with Ebbw Vale when 10,501 people packed the ground.

What do these figures tell us? Very little if Disraeli's 'lies, damned lies and statistics' theory is correct. However, long gone are the days of match attendances always being nicely rounded up, which leaves those now produced to be taken at face value. With the 11,676 capacity at Rodney Parade only coming under threat on two occasions in the season one has to ask the question whether the attendances are sufficient to sustain a club in the era of professional rugby. The answer to that being a resounding no, the future of Newport, and indeed all other clubs, is very uncertain.

It is not unreasonable to suggest that of all the major clubs in the UK only Leicester RFC are a viable business. There are many lesser clubs that can boast healthy balance sheets but they are not in the real world of professional rugby and are deluding themselves if they believe otherwise. Accepting Leicester as the role model leads one to ask why they are in this enviable position. The simple answer is that they are the most successful club the professional game has seen. Back-to-back Heineken Cup victories confirm this, while their achievements on the domestic front have come to be taken for granted. Financially, the club starts each campaign on an equal footing with other clubs in the English Premiership, each receiving an equal amount of income from the RFU, but when the revenue generated by the club itself is considered, then we see the huge difference that gives it a chance to run on solid financial foundations. The bottom line here is the support base that the club is able to draw on. Attendances of 15,000 are the norm at Welford Road with the home supporters making up a large percentage of the figure. Contrast Newport's estimated home support of 6,460 and you begin to see the problems facing the Marketing Department at Rodney Parade. While Leicester could possibly ride out a couple of seasons of under achievement on the back of their support base the same would probably not happen at Newport.

To be in a position to encourage greater numbers to turn out at Rodney Parade on a regular basis the psyche of the animal has to be understood. What do these people want from a game of rugby? Is the club's success topmost in the list of requirements or does it go deeper than that? If it is the simple case of following, being part of a club that is successful then Newport has to live with the almost certainty that fail and the supporters will walk away quicker than they came. The arrival of the day when cries of 'we won' are exchanged for cries of 'they lost' hangs over Newport like the sword of Damocles. But if there is more to it than that, if the supporters are given more in return for their money and their time, then they may be encouraged to continue following the clubs fortunes even when events on the playing field don't live up to expectations, and that is what has to be addressed.

In August 1995 Newport could lay claim to a regular support base of little more than 1,000, a poor figure when compared to the thousands that used to pour over Newport Bridge in the 1950s. Comparisons of this nature are academic however, society and its demands having changed considerably over the past fifty years. All spectator sports can throw up figures showing an overall decline in attendances with only the top clubs managing to retain the same level of interest previously witnessed. Television is seen as the major reason for this decline with the armchair viewers having access to the biggest sporting events worldwide from the comfort of their own home. And not only the major events. Club rugby in Wales is now given extensive live coverage, a development that many blame for the poor attendances plaguing the club game. This is an argument that doesn't always hold water particularly at Newport where the biggest gates seen in recent seasons have been at matches which were being broadcast live on television.

When all the arguments regarding money from the WRU, the input of a benefactor, the effect of live television together with the myriad of other issues surrounding the game are laid to rest, the bottom line regarding a club's survival will be the number of people it gets through the turnstiles on match day. This is the key issue that all clubs are having to address and to blame the surfeit of club rugby shown live on television, or for that matter, any of the other excuses that are regularly raised, is simply to hide from the truth in the hope that it will go away. It won't. And the reason why people don't turn out in great numbers to watch club rugby won't go away, is that very few clubs have been able to identify it. But surely it's television and the unpopular kick-off times? The poor state of the national team, the lack of home-grown superstars, the cost? Well maybe. Each of these reasons has undoubtedly had an impact on declining attendances in the club game but where the clubs have got it wrong is in their belief that these are the only reasons. They aren't. These are general reasons that have had an impact on all clubs across the country and, rather than take them on board as a fait accompli, clubs should be looking closer to home in their search for the truth as it applies to them, their own individual problem.

For example: does it really matter what time matches kick off at Caerphilly? Here is a club that hasn't been able to awaken any public interest to speak of since arriving in the top flight. The clubhouse is comfortable, the team play an entertaining game, there is the best gents facility in Welsh rugby to be admired and yet the support base at Caerphilly can be counted in the hundreds. The easy answer here is that Caerphilly hasn't got a winning team but, realistically, there is more to it than that; much more. If winning or losing were the only criteria by which a club is measured then most would have fallen by the wayside long since. Take Pontypool as another example. A club that swept all before it in the 1980s playing in front of huge crowds that filled the bank at the Park, 'Pooler' now play in front of a couple of thousand at best. Riding high in Division One the club is regularly in the promotion race at the end of the season but the crowd has disappeared. Why don't the people of a town which has such a great rugby tradition bother any more? Perhaps it's because the clubhouse is some half a mile from the ground or possibly it's because of the lack of facilities at the Park, sure you can get a hot dog and a coffee but for any call of nature, pick your tree, and if you happen to be one of the many females in the crowd, well the mind boggles. Watching rugby at Pontypool Park has never been any different but the potential spectator has changed, more specifically the needs of the potential spectator has changed and they want more for their money than most clubs are offering.

So, at Caerphilly there are adequate facilities but the team isn't winning and at Pontypool the reverse is seen, but neither club is benefiting from numbers through the turnstiles. And in the big city, in Cardiff, at the Arms Park, there are different problems to deal with. Here is a club which has excellent facilities, a good playing record and the biggest population in Wales to call on and yet it can't fill a 15,000 capacity stadium. The problems here tend to come from other sports with Cardiff City FC currently posing the biggest threat. If the 'City' can gain promotion to the higher divisions of the Football League, rugby in South Wales will feel the backlash and nowhere will this be more noticeable than in the capital.

Millions of pounds have been spent both on and off the field at Bridgend courtesy of local businessman Leighton Samuel, but still they don't come; no 'Field of Dreams' this. Estimates as high as 20,000 were attributed to the support that accompanied Llanelli to Nottingham for the semi-final of the Heineken Cup, but where are they on match days at Stradey Park? Any player will tell you that the playing surface at St Helens, Swansea, is the best, while any supporter will tell you that the viewing areas are the worst. Neath, Pontypridd and Ebbw Vale are small towns and the infrastructure at each is not conducive to accommodating large crowds, unless 5-6,000 is considered large, figures which are nowhere near enough if a professional game is to be supported.

It is clear that each Premiership club in Wales has problems way beyond those generally attributed to the decline in public interest in the game. These problems vary from club to club and it is for each to identify those relating to it and take the appropriate action. Eighty minutes rugby followed by a pie and a pint is no longer good enough. The public want more and if rugby doesn't provide it then they will find an alternative that will.

To suggest that Newport RFC has succeeded where all other clubs in Wales have failed would be wrong. At the end of the 2001-02 season Newport was certainly leading the way but the other clubs had taken note of the changes at Rodney Parade and were starting to look at how they could implement them at their own grounds. Over three seasons Newport's hard core support base, i.e. the season ticket holders, had been more than quadrupled while there was a growing number of casual supporters that the club hoped to capitalise on in the near future. Attracting more people to Rodney Parade on match days and then making sure that they came again had been the key to the club's rejuvenation but there was no room for complacency and the exercise would have to be repeated every season. Attract the customers, get them to come again and then encourage them to become season ticket holders; introduction and retention.

Who are the people that follow Newport RFC? This is a question that must be considered before the club can expect to understand, and then be able to fully capitalise on its market. Broadly speaking there are two main categories to be considered. Firstly there are those who have supported the club for many years; those with the long service medal, look older than their years and prefer the club tie to the replica jersey. Secondly, there is the new breed of supporter, which will include those who may have followed the club in years gone by, became disillusioned but have now returned and those who hadn't any previous interest but came to have a look, liked what they saw and got into the habit.

To qualify for category one you had to have been to hell and back, many times over. When the bad times set in they tended to resemble something akin to a modern 'Ice Age' and from a good support base in the 60s, 70s, even into the 80s, the hard core fell away to around the thousand mark. This seasonal figure was only adjusted by the passing away of an existing member or the introduction of a new one by its doting parents who would proudly dress their offspring from head to foot in the club's colours and hope the child would not jump ship when it was old enough to think for itself. It invariably would. Working to these parameters it seemed inevitable that in the fullness of time the membership would be chipped away at and the day would arrive when nobody would be watching Newport RFC.

In addition to having the long service medal, qualification for category one is dependent on several other criteria not least among which is the ability to find ones way blindfold to the seat or couple of square feet of terracing from which home matches are always watched. The same unwritten rules apply for before and after match routines. Before its demise the members' lounge was sacred, not only the room but the part of the room that each member had laid claim to as their own.

What these long-standing members of Newport RFC have in common with each other is a resilience, in fact an immunity, to the many failures they have had to live with over the years as supporters of the Black and Ambers. Many of them are able to go back far enough to recall the good times; victories over the All Blacks, Wallabies and Springboks, the exploits of the great players, Ken Jones, Roy Burnett, David Watkins and Brian Price. They have needed these memories to see them through the more recent years when times have not been so memorable. But it is the club that is foremost in their priorities not the results on the field, and the success, or lack of it, would not appear to be the thing that leads them to Rodney Parade through the winter months. There must be something in this because, let's face it, they would have stopped going long since if there isn't. Belonging is something that many people crave. Being able to put their hand up and say 'I'm part of that' gives an identity, a purpose to one's very existence and whether that identity is achieved through an organisation such as the Masons, the Round Table, the Ramblers' Association or Newport RFC is of no consequence. It is the belonging that is the important thing and with it the association with a group of like minded individuals.

This sense of belonging is what has kept the hard core of supporters together at Rodney Parade. Of course they want the club to be successful but that was not the prime motivation in making sure their membership fee was paid on time and looking forward to the start of each new season, even with the almost certain knowledge that it would bring another eight months' disappointment with it. Perhaps they shouldn't have joined a club that would have them as a member, life would have been a lot easier. But they did, and now the club has changed, become successful and in doing so attracted more supporters. The new breed of supporters dominate and things may never be the same again. Gone are the routines that fell nicely into place on match days, now it's an effort to get served immediately after the match never mind having got a drink, being able to choose where to stand to enjoy it. In the club's eyes, where supporters who fall into the first category are seen to be representative of its past those in the second category are seen as the future. What must be realised however, is that for the club to go forward and expand its hard core supporter base, at some stage the new wave of support will have to be converted, they will have to become part of the first category. They will have to be brainwashed, neutered, whatever you wish to call it but at some stage they have to be prepared to go through all that the old brigade have been through and come out the other side smiling. And that raises huge doubts - have they got the bottle for it?

The influx of new supporters that descended on Rodney Parade arrived in a remarkably short space of time. They now represent the nucleus of the club's following and travel in huge numbers to all away fixtures where their presence on the terraces is more often than not greater than that of the home team. Travelling support will also include those to whom the delights of Sardis Road, the Gnoll and the Brewery Field are well known, but the make-up of the support that Newport RFC takes on the road with it is irrelevant, the colour and the noise generated by a bank of Black and Amber supporters chanting 'Who Let The Dogs Out?' being all that matters to the players on the field. The club has sold itself well to this new-found support but only time will tell if it will retain the interest in the event of a decline in fortune on the playing field.

It is to the eternal credit of all those concerned with the marketing of Newport RFC that in a short space of time over 5,000 people were drawn to watch rugby at Rodney Parade and would still be doing so three years down the road. How they did it, and the fact that they are going to have to do it again and again in order to attract the numbers that are needed to make the club commercially viable, is looked into elsewhere, but this increase in support from an area that is traditionally apathetic in its following of sport has to be viewed with some caution while still in its infancy.

The message has been sent out loud and clear. Newport RFC is the family club where there is something on offer for everybody. Parents can take their children, comfortable in the knowledge that they will be safe and not likely to get bored because of the attractions that are on offer at Rodney Parade. Having picked up their evening paper and read the adverts that were always prominent, they came. Then they came again and they told their friends about this new experience that was such a great day out. The place resembled a village fete more than a rugby match and the public were sold on it. With jazz bands playing in the tented village, beer tents, fast food outlets, face painting and bouncy castles for the youngsters, this was a very different rugby experience on offer, and it had attracted a very different type of person.

A sporting analogy can be seen by comparing the sedate experience of county cricket with the noise and colour of the one day game.

Newport RFC had transformed itself from the traditional members' club, it had taken down the barriers that were linked with such tradition and opened its gates to everybody.

Made up of both the old and the new, the groundswell of support that now follows Newport RFC is the club's bread and butter but there is a third group of supporters that must not be forgotten. Small in number they may be but their financial contribution to the club is massive; these are the club's sponsors who pay most for the privilege of being involved on match days. They are a valuable asset to the club and as such are treated differently to everybody else. Sponsors and their invited guests take over the hospitality boxes behind the posts where they are wined and dined before the match. Some have the opportunity to take a prime seat in the stand for the match before returning to the hospitality boxes for further refreshment. Also to be included in this small group are the club's Vice-Presidents and the members of the Brecon Club. They enjoy pre-match drinks and refreshments in the Brecon Lounge which is at their disposal on match days. Nevertheless, with prices ranging from £1,800-£4,000 there weren't many takers. But that's the whole point really. The exclusivity of such clubs would be lost if the comfort factor disappeared. Regardless of many people's opinion on the matter, the Brecon Lounge has never been as profitable, the turnover it generates far exceeding anything seen in years gone by, and in the age of professional rugby that's what matters: turnover and more importantly, profit.

Newport RFC is slowly bringing together a wide cross section of the community it serves. Clubs will always have to cater for their financial backers away from the general match day melee but this is not to be seen in any way as an elitist divide, there was more likelihood of such a divide when Newport was a members' club. Having sold itself on the back of being somewhere to bring the family Newport must use every asset at its disposal to develop the concept. It's no longer about eighty minutes rugby followed by a pie and a pint rather five or six hours of entertainment. Never before have so many arrived at the ground so early or stayed so late after the match thereby proving that there is much more on offer and it is this that represents the future for all spectator sport in the twenty-first century.

If there are any followers of Newport RFC who want what the club is offering and more, who want to feel even more involved and are intent on seeing all matches both at home and away, then there is a further option to consider. Every club has got one, the club within the club. The club that caters for those who want to take their allegiance that bit further, who want to watch rugby with like-minded dedicated supporters, travel in numbers to away matches and enjoy social occasions with a rugby bias. All this is available to those who, for a nominal fee, become members of Newport Rugby Official Supporters Club.

The Supporters Club is run on a proper constitutional basis. It has an elected committee of eight, holds an annual general meeting and is recognised by Newport RFC as an essential part of its development. There is no doubt that the main appeal of the Supporters Club are the organised trips to all away matches. Not long ago Llanelli was the furthest the club would travel but that has all changed with the introduction of European competition. Visits to France, Ireland and Scotland have become part of the fixture list and the Supporters Club offers an option to the many followers looking to accompany the team on its travels. These organised trips were once open to anybody but membership of the Supporters Club is now required. This enables the committee to retain an element of control which is felt necessary when transporting large numbers of people who are effectively representing Newport RFC and as such, expected to show an appropriate level of responsibility.

One of the few negatives to have reared its head as a result of the marked increase in support seen by Newport RFC is the behaviour of some of its followers. Newly appointed CEO Keith Grainger is adamant that behaviour of any kind that threatens the reputation of Newport will be stamped out at source. On two occasions in the 2001-02 season there was the need to draw attention to this in the matchday programme. Rivalry between opposing supporters is a part of the game and long may it continue to be so. Banter on the terraces can be both amusing and harmless but lately the humour has gone out of the rivalry and something more sinister is beginning to rear its head. Foul language is not uncommon and, with Newport trying to promote itself as a family club, is something that has to be firmly handled.

'For those of you who feel that they cannot enjoy watching the Black and Ambers without directly swearing abuse at the referee or without confronting the oppositions followers with intimidating language or actions... we don't want your company, we don't want your money and we don't want your support.' These comments were made by Grainger in his column in the club's programme. Newport are not the only club seeing this inane subculture begin to rear its head, and all clubs need to adopt a similar approach if it is to be quickly stamped out. Newport can control or quickly react to any problems that occur at Rodney Parade but at away matches that responsibility is handed over and it is essential that all clubs are united in their stance towards what, while only amounting to a small number of incidents today, could escalate and become another of the many problems that bedevil rugby. Football has learnt many worthwhile lessons over the years, the benefit of which should not go unnoticed by rugby union's hierarchy, but the problem of hooliganism is one that it is still struggling to control and to pretend that it won't infiltrate into rugby would be a serious error of judgement.

Less than ten years ago the Supporters Club had barely enough members to fill a coach but now the membership is over a thousand strong making it the biggest club of its kind in Wales. That is not surprising in view if all the recent events at Newport but what is surprising is the fact that there are still people who are prepared to give their time to run the club. Sending out fifty newsletters three times a season is no big task but make that a thousand newsletters and it becomes a different proposition. Add to this the organisation of away trips and there is a mountain to climb.

The marked increase in membership and the added pressures that came with it meant that committee members were having to field hundreds of phone calls from people wanting details of the up and coming away matches and the situation soon reached saturation point.

The Supporters Club took 200 people to Limerick for Newport's first Heineken Cup match. By land, sea and air 200 supporters were taken to Ireland to watch Newport play. In addition to the travel arrangements there were hotels to be booked, transfers to arrange and the no small matter of getting everybody at the right place at the right time. What had started out as a hobby was now a huge job and help was needed. What can loosely be called a partnership, there is nothing official about it, was formed between the Supporters Club and Newport RFC, which saw the latter taking responsibility for all telephone enquiries and bookings for away trips. A considerable burden was passed on and the Supporters Club reciprocated by ensuring that members were on hand to help the staff at Newport send out thousands of envelopes at the start each season. As well as containing information regarding season ticket renewal the envelopes also included information regarding the Supporters Club, an exercise at once efficient and cost effective. The momentum of this fine institution is gathering pace season by season but there must be concerns that it too could become a victim of its own success.

Dennis Bennett is Chairman of Newport Rugby Official Supporters Club. Asked to sum up what the attraction was, why people joined the Supporters Club he summed it up quite simply - 'fun'. Nothing more nothing less. Followers of Newport could join the club, travel away without having to do any more than decide how many pairs of socks to pack, and enjoy themselves. He describes the ongoing relationship with Newport RFC as excellent, identifying Keith Grainger as a staunch backer of the Supporters Club. Players are on hand to attend functions and the club's facilities are made available at no cost. All in all there is what Bennett describes as 'a general feeling of trust and mutual support' between the two factions.

In many ways the Supporters Club resembles the rugby club of old. It has a similar number of members, time and effort are given freely by the keenest and the club tie is still seen as de rigueur by many of them. Most of the members probably belong to what has been described as 'the old school' and will be there in the future come rain or shine but the Supporters Club can help establish a bigger hard core support base for Newport with its ongoing enrolment drive ensuring that extra commitment is made.

A little bit of rivalry never did anybody any harm and there is evidence of this coming into play at Newport. Having always held functions at the club for the benefit of its members, the Supporters Club is now experiencing competition from within. People will only attend so many functions in a season and the frequency of those now held by both Newport RFC and its Supporters Club will see one or the other end up with egg on its face. Also, while there is still an annual Supporters Club dance, the players' awards that were once a highlight of these events are now very much a part of the end of season dinner held by Newport RFC at the Celtic Manor Hotel Resort. This event is not one that appeals to everybody, viewed by many as being too formal, but there is no reason why the end of season social calendar shouldn't continue to accommodate both functions.

At the Family Fun Day held at Rodney Parade in July 2002, the Supporters Club was to be found in a section of the tented village. Membership was being sold at £3.50 which included a lapel badge and bookings were being taken for away trips to Connacht, Edinburgh and Toulouse. There was even information regarding a New Year's Eve dinner dance. Boards were covered with photographs of previous events and trips, while the members were doing everything possible to promote the Supporters Club. Proactive it certainly was and long may it continue to be so. There is no accurate information regarding when a Supporters Club was first introduced at Newport but there are photographs taken in 1926 which show presentations being made to the touring New Zealand Maoris on behalf of the club by Gladys Liles, daughter of the then Chairman, Charles Liles. At least seventy-six years old there is every reason to believe that the biggest contribution to Newport RFC from its official Supporters Club is about to be seen.

Back on Track 1999-2000

'Captaincy is 90 per cent luck and 10 per cent skill. But don't try it without that 10 per cent.'

Richie Benaud

Fifty-three supporters had made the trip. Fifty-three supporters had travelled over six thousand miles to watch Newport RFC play two matches. Not that long ago you wouldn't have got many more travelling sixty miles. However, this was a bit different.

Durban, capital of KwaZulu-Natal Province, is on the east coast of South Africa. The Indian Ocean crashes onto mile after mile of golden sand making it one of the country's favourite playgrounds .The climate borders on the sub-tropical, when it rains it rains but the rest of the time it's damn near perfect. The beaches are a haven for swimmers and surfers - and sharks!

Half a mile inland from North Beach stands the imposing structure that is the ABSA Stadium, home to another kind of shark, the Natal Sharks. One of South Africa's leading rugby provinces, Natal had always stumbled at the final hurdle. It took one hundred years before the Currie Cup, the country's top rugby prize, graced the trophy cabinet. That was in 1990 and the next ten years saw success heaped upon success as the famous old trophy was won on three more occasions - in 1992, 1995 and 1996 with 1993 and 1999 seeing Natal contest two further finals but having to settle for second place. The only common denominator to be found was the coach, Ian McIntosh. But look a bit further and, excepting 1990, another name is ever present, Gary Teichmann, and it was because of Teichmann that fifty-three Newport supporters found themselves six thousand miles from home in June 2000.

Twelve months earlier Teichmann had been the Springbok captain. Forty-two caps had been won, including thirty-four as captain, when the team had amassed an impressive run of results including the record equalling seventeen consecutive victories. Now in World Cup year, Springbok coach Nick Mallett controversially dropped the captain, at the same time making it clear that Teichmann was not going to figure in his tournament squad. The argument still rages. Many South Africans believe the World Cup would have been retained had Mallet continued with Teichmann, we shall never know. What Mallett's decision meant, however, was that one of the world's leading players was now going to be open to offers.

Acting on behalf of Teichmann, Craig Livingston, Managing Director of Players Sport Management started making enquiries. By email, fax and the good old-fashioned telephone Teichmann's availability quickly became known in rugby circles worldwide. When the name of Newport RFC was first mentioned Gary Teichmann admits to having not been familiar with it, in fact he had never heard of Newport. That aside the club were showing a lot of interest and perhaps it would be worth while taking the matter further.

Teichmann is quite definite when he talks about his reasons for pursuing, initially talks, and then negotiations with Newport. In Newport Chief Executive, Tony Brown, he knew he had met somebody he could work with and, more importantly, somebody he could trust. This element of trust was high on the list of a man who was contemplating uprooting his family and taking them a long way from home. He wanted to know there was going to be somebody he could rely on if things didn't go according to plan. And with Tony Brown he was sure that such a person had been found.

It had been Tony Brown who had met Teichmann at Heathrow Airport and driven him to Newport on his first visit. Brown made him feel comfortable immediately and the foundations of a friendship that would reach beyond the game of rugby were laid on that two hour journey to Rodney Parade.

That had been in August 1999 and now, less than twelve months later, Newport together with the fifty-three supporters, had arrived in Durban to take part in a testimonial match that would give the Sharks supporters an opportunity to salute one of their favourite sons. Teichmann's move to Newport had been sorted out in double quick time but his arrival at his new club had to wait until after the Currie Cup. Natal had reached a sixth final in ten years and were to play the Golden Lions on 11 September at the ABSA Stadium. Also making his final appearance for the Sharks was full back Andre Joubert but it was not to be the fairy tale ending that the home crowd had hoped for. The Lions ran out comfortable winners 32-9 but the Sharks were well below strength with the seven players included in the Springbok squad for the World Cup ruled out of selection. Take Mark Andrews, Adrian Garvey, Henry Honiball, Ollie le Roux, Pieter Muller, Chris Rossouw and Stefan Terblanche out of a starting line-up and the loss is enormous. Admittedly, the Lions were without three leading players for the very same reason but the Sharks loss was the greater and it told on the day.

No sooner was the match over than Teichmann was packing his bags to leave for Newport and the celebration of his time in Natal would have to be put on hold.

One week Durban and a 52,000 sell out, the next Rodney Parade, the visitors Pontypridd and an expectant 7-8,000 spectators. No gentle introduction to club rugby in Wales and by full time the visiting supporters were leaving nobody in any doubt how they felt about the so-called Newport revival. Cries of 'What a waste of money' and 'Cheque book Charlies' were heard on the terraces and would continue for some time to come. Such banal, uneducated comment would have to be put up with until the results started to speak for themselves. This first game for Gary Teichmann ended in the same manner as his last for Natal - defeat. Leading 15-3 at one stage, the home side eventually went down 33-28. Also making his debut for the club against Pontypridd was ex-Springbok outside half Franco Smith and when prop forward Robbie Kempson came on as a replacement there was a certain justification in the cries of 'Bok and Ambers'. Who would have believed that three of the South African team that had defeated Wales at Wembley Stadium the previous November would now be playing for Newport, and that a fourth would shortly join them. However, Kempson was only on a short-term contract that would last until the completion of the World Cup, clubs having received dispensation to make up any squad deficiencies due to international requirements during the tournament.

Spare a thought for centre Andy Marinos. Two weeks earlier he had been on the threshold of the Welsh squad only to lose out at the last minute to another Newport signing, Jason Jones-Hughes, who had been brought over to Wales amid much controversy, the Australian Rugby Union claiming an appearance for the Australian Barbarians ruled out his eligibility to play for another country. The matter resolved, Jones-Hughes took his place in the Welsh squad and Marinos would have to bide his time and settle for his appearance in an uncapped match against the USA; but his day would come.

Andy Marinos was another player with South African connections. A replacement at Neath, like Teichmann, he also had his first start for the club in the home defeat against Pontypridd. The two players' careers had previously crossed when Marinos spent a couple of seasons with the Sharks in the 1990s but he decided to sign professional papers and went to Australia where he played for the rugby league club, Sydney Bulldogs. On his return to South Africa he continued to play league before eventually returning to the union game, joining the Western Stormers in Cape Town where he is fondly remembered for his leading role in a players' strike which saw the team refusing to play a Super 12 semi final against the Otago Highlanders at Newlands until their financial demands had been met. At the eleventh hour a cheque from a major sponsor was delivered to the team hotel and the match duly went ahead.

Newport's 'Summer of Signings' had started with scrum half David Llewellyn who was quickly joined by other Welsh squad members, prop Peter Rogers and full back Shane Howarth. Rogers and Howarth had arrived at Rodney Parade via Allied Dunbar Premier sides London Irish and Manchester Sale respectively and were joined by Fijian, Simon Raiwalui, also from Sale, Australian, Damien Cummins from London Scottish and Welshmen, Gareth Cull, Justin Thomas and Jason Forster. With Llewellyn, Rogers, Howarth and Raiwalui, together with Rod Snow, all on World Cup duty, ten league matches had been played before coach Allan Lewis had his full squad of players to select from. With many clubs in a similar situation the WRU had decided that league matches played prior to and during the RWC would earn two league points for the winning team, while those played after the completion of the tournament would see this increased to four points.

League positions at the end of the RWC showed Llanelli on top with seven wins and fourteen points, closely followed by Neath, Newport and Pontypridd all on thirteen points, with six wins and one drawn match to their credit. Six penalties by Gareth Cull had got the season off to the perfect start when Cardiff visited Rodney Parade but the high spot among the early matches played was the away win at Stradey Park. A visit to Llanelli is a daunting challenge for any team and Newport had fared worse than most on their travels west. The last victory had been way back in 1978 but all those lean years were forgotten on a Friday night in October. Cull continued his prolific scoring with four penalties and two conversions while Jon Pritchard and Ben Breeze scored the all important tries that saw Newport home 26-20. After scoring 139 points in the first ten matches of the season Gareth Cull was released by Newport, club captain Shane Howarth was now available and took over the reins for his debut, a league match away to Dunvant. Firstly Jason Forster and then Gary Teichmann had led the side in his absence but Howarth would play in all the remaining matches, excepting a friendly with Pontypool, alternating between full back and outside half.

It's a funny old game. One minute you're riding high in the league with a string of good results under the belt, and this with a lot of star players missing. Then, on their return to the fold, things start to go pear-shaped.

No sooner was the RWC over than clubs were turning their heads towards Europe, in Newport's case the European Shield and six group matches against Bedford, Castres and Rovigo. Intersperse these with away matches at Cardiff, Pontypridd and Ebbw Vale and it was clearly going to be a testing few months for the club. The European campaign began with an unexpected defeat at Bedford quickly followed by a home reverse against Castres. The back-to-back matches with Rovigo provided the expected wins but an away defeat to the French club meant the home game with Bedford was of no significance even though Newport gained ample revenge with a comfortable victory.

In among these matches was the visit to Cardiff. Full of optimism and expectancy thousands of supporters descended on the Arms Park only to come away bitterly disappointed having seen their side go down 26-22. Missed opportunities resulted in a disastrous night that highlighted how fickle supporters can be. Shane Howarth had an instantly forgettable game and the finger of blame was firmly pointed in his direction. It happens to the best and on this occasion it was Howarth who the supporters felt had cost Newport a rare victory at the Arms Park. Maybe, but this was nothing compared to the controversy that would shortly steal the headlines. For the moment, this was just a bad day at the office that had contributed to another defeat at the hands of the old enemy. There was much of the 'we could have won' mentality that follows many a defeat but as NFL coach Vince Lombardi was famous for saying 'if you could have won you should have won'.

Newport couldn't have won at Pontypridd, not in a month of Sundays. The weather was against them, the crowd were against them and, sure enough, the final scoreline was against them. Pontypridd strolled to a 25-7 win and the home crowd took up where they had left off earlier in the season. Once again Newport players were subjected to cries of 'what a waste of money' as Pontypridd slowly dismantled the star studded visitors. Pretty it certainly wasn't and most travelling supporters couldn't wait to distance themselves from the self-styled 'House of Pain'. Little could they have known that their day would come and that it would be sooner rather than later.

A month after the visit to Sardis Road Newport entertained Pontypool in a friendly at Rodney Parade. The match was well attended and supporters saw Emyr Lewis, son of coach Allan, make his debut at full back and a young Andrew Powell come on as a replacement for Simon Raiwalui in the second row. But what made the match particularly interesting was some of the banter heard on the terraces. 'Get in there Teichmann', 'look at him, he doesn't like doing the graft does he?' and 'what's he doing over there?'. By early February such touchline comment was old hat, but this time it was different; this time it was coming from the Newport supporters!

Rugby followers in Wales were not used to seeing a number eight forward roaming the field, often away from the action. They were used to seeing the ball picked up at the base of the scrum by the eighth man who would then make some hard yards and set up the second phase. Scott Quinnell for Wales and Llanelli, Emyr Lewis at Cardiff, Mark Jones at Ebbw Vale, Dale McIntosh at Pontypridd - the list goes on. What the rugby public weren't used to seeing, not since Mervyn Davies in the seventies, was a number eight forward who played a lot of his game in the open parts of the field, corner flagging in defence, linking with the three quarters and comfortable with ball in hand. Gary Teichmann was all these things and more, he just didn't waste time and energy in areas of the game where he wasn't needed - in other words he had vision. Teichmann was used to a faster game, played on hard surfaces by players who would claim greater fitness levels than the majority of their Northern Hemisphere counterparts.

Football offers a good analogy. Take Ryan Giggs out of the Manchester United team he plays with week in week out and put him in the Welsh team alongside players from the lower divisions. He starts putting the ball about, long searching passes that would see Beckham, Scholes or Veron on the end of them at Old Trafford but playing for Wales such passes would not find their mark. Giggs would have to adjust accordingly and make the necessary allowances for the players around him. A world class player such as Ryan Giggs has no problem with this and the players respond by upping the level of their game. In short both the individuals and the team benefit from his presence.

In time this would happen at Newport. In time players and coaches alike would make the necessary minor adjustments to their respective approach to the game that would see the team go further along the road to greater days. However, before this could happen there was one matter that would have to be addressed: the captaincy. When Shane Howarth signed for Newport, Allan Lewis had no hesitation in offering him the captaincy, a decision that was well received throughout the club. The arrival of Peter Rogers would result in a shuffle in the front row, Rod Snow moving to tight head where he was expected to be first choice and thereby replace Sven Cronk, who had led Newport in the previous season. With Teichmann not yet in the frame, the choice of Howarth to lead the club would ensure that a high profile player with a wealth of experience and undoubted class, would have no problem in getting the respect of his players which would be essential if old and new alike were to begin to play as a unit.

Captaincy doesn't come alone. It brings a lot of baggage with it and not many players have the necessary talent to cope with the added responsibilities while, at the same time, not seeing their game affected. Shane Howarth was no different to many others before him and, by the turn of the year, he found that the pressure of international rugby, together with the demands being put on him at club level, were starting to tell. When he returned from World Cup duty it was to a fairly settled side and to take over the reins in such circumstances and at the same time make your club debut could not have been easy. Add to this the change in fortune on the field of play and things had started to reach breaking point when the time came to visit Eugene Cross Park, Ebbw Vale.

Newport had experienced some forgettable days during the season to date but this match would easily top the list of poor performances come the end of the season. It wasn't so much the defeat that rankled, rather the manner of it. Try scoring opportunities went begging with experienced players Marinos and Teichmann the main culprits. Then, in the second period, the forwards found themselves on the back foot and there was only one outcome, a 29-17 defeat for the visitors and the trip back down the valley to reassess the situation and decide how to approach the remaining seven league matches and the next round of the Welsh Cup which would see Cardiff at Rodney Parade.

Every cloud has a silver lining and the defeat at Ebbw Vale was no different. When Shane Howarth decided to step down from his role as club captain he showed a lot of character. He realised that the club needed to improve significantly if it was to secure a top four finish and secure a place in the Heineken Cup in the following season. He needed to be at his best for the remaining matches, added to which there was the Six Nations, and he could only achieve this if he was left to get on with his own game and not have the extra pressure to contend with. Newport were fortunate to have at their disposal a man who had all the leadership qualities the role demanded and who was in a position to be totally focused on the job in hand - Gary Teichmann. The change was implemented, Newport had a new captain, and he would be in charge for the visit of Cardiff.

Unfortunately, this wasn't the end of Shane Howarth's problems Within weeks of stepping down from the captaincy at Rodney Parade, Howarth was involved in a scandal that rocked Welsh rugby to its very foundations. 'Grannygate' or 'Kiwigate,' the media had a field day when the eligibility of certain players to represent Wales was brought into question and Shane Howarth was at the centre of it. The IRB regulations require that to represent a country at international level a player should either be born in the country, have a parent or grand-parent who was born in the country or be qualified on a residential basis having lived in the country for an uninterrupted period of three years. This would appear simple enough but the problems start when the Unions don't make the necessary enquiries and obtain documentary evidence to substantiate a player's selection.

Welsh coach Graham Henry had cast his net far and wide in the search for players who were eligible to play for Wales. Adverts appeared in rugby magazines in New Zealand asking players who could claim Welsh ancestry to contact the WRU, similarly, rugby league players were sounded out. This was fine subject to the criteria being observed - but it wasn't. This was the case with regard to Howarth, fellow Welsh player Brett Sinkinson and Scot, Dave Hilton. The search for documentary evidence which would prove Howarth's grandfather had been born in Wales drew a blank while in Sinkinson's case the documentation was found but it showed his grandfather to have been born in Oldham, Lancashire; not what the WRU were hoping for. Hilton, after winning 41 caps for Scotland on the basis that a grandfather had been born in Edinburgh, was deemed ineligible when it materialised that this ancestor had entered the world in Bristol.

The IRB, in finding Howarth ineligible to play for Wales, accepted that he had acted in good faith in the belief that he qualified through his grandfather. However, a regulation introduced on 1 January 2000 now prevented Howarth appearing for Wales again until after three years' residency as he had previously played for New Zealand. This was later overruled, Howarth's circumstances being unusual to say the least, and the player could again be available for Welsh selection in June 2002 - by which time he would be almost 34 years of age.

The cup match against Cardiff saw Newport's season put well and truly back on track. Howarth kicked five penalties and converted Snow's try to see the club clinch a 22-13 victory and a place in the quarter-final. However, the draw was not favourable, Newport would have to travel to Llanelli and repeat the performance that earlier in the season had brought about a rare victory at Stradey Park. History would not repeat itself and the Scarlets ran out comfortable winners 36-17. That left the league and a top four finish that would see the club in the Heineken Cup in the following season.

A home win over Swansea played between the two cup matches left Newport with six games to play. Arwel Thomas missed an injury time penalty that would have won the game for Swansea but the home side edged it 23-21. In the remaining matches Newport started to show what they were capable of. It had been an up and down season and there was a sense of under achievement at Rodney Parade. Nobody could have forecast that the club would be looking to finish runners up in the league on that forgettable day in Ebbw Vale. But that was exactly what it had in its sights going into the remaining matches.

The players revelled in the good weather that April and May brought along, none more so than those from the Southern Hemisphere. The six remaining matches saw the team score an impressive 335 points which included 47 tries - averaging 57 points and almost 8 tries per match. It was breathtaking rugby with the best of the performances coming at the Brewery Field, Bridgend. Each of the seven tries scored was straight out of the top drawer and all the hours spent on the training ground were rewarded in style. Even the thousands of supporters who had made the journey were in forgiving mood at the final whistle; Ebbw Vale was a bad dream, history, forget it. It was in this match that a significant change in the line-up behind the scrum paved the way for the remainder of the season, a change that would become permanent in the next season. It was against Bridgend that Shane Howarth stepped into the number 10 jersey, a position he would make his own.

Newport secured second spot in the table, the club's best finish to date, and could now look forward to the next season with some anticipation. It would be a while before the draw for the Heineken Cup would take place, but the interest among the supporters suggested that when it came to the away games, they would be there in numbers. Before then, however, there was a trip to South Africa and an encounter with the Sharks.

In the shadow of the east stand at the ABSA Stadium lie two playing fields. Kings Park 3 is home to College Rovers, Gary Teichmann's club in KwaZulu-Natal and it was here that Newport played the first of their two matches in Durban. Four thousand spectators turned out, standing three or four deep along the touch lines and in goal areas. Newport won a close game 21-13 and could be forgiven for having slipped into end of season party mode. There was a real buzz about the ground and every indication that the match against the Sharks in seven days time was creating a lot of interest and would be well attended.

Coach Allan Lewis and his assistant, Ian Smith, a Scot, were making the most of this time away with the players. The team had started to realise its potential at the end of the season and the opportunity to work with the players in a relatively pressure-free environment presented a rare chance to experiment and consider previously untried options. Lewis had always preached an 'off the cuff' approach to the game, believing that natural flair should always be given its head. He had worked with Graham Henry and the Welsh squad as National Selector and took on board Henry's philosophy that club and country should be playing the same style of game. There were many who felt that Newport didn't have the players behind the scrum to play such adventurous rugby but it appeared that Lewis was starting to get it right come the end of the 1999-2000 season.

If there had been any doubting the high esteem in which Teichmann was held in Natal rugby circles it would be laid to rest on Saturday 3 June. After a week of golf, deep sea fishing and trips on safari, the players were ready for the big day. The weather was glorious, the temperature reaching the high seventies come kick-off, added to which the locals had turned out in numbers. Over 36,000 poured into the stadium for an afternoon that saw the clock well and truly wound back.

Newport were always going to find it difficult, the pace of the game cruelly exposing the deficiencies that were behind the scrum, a lack of genuine pace being uppermost among them. Twenty minutes into the game the Sharks were 21-3 ahead, two tries by Rodger Smith on the wing with a third scored by Stefan Terblanche in the centre. To their great credit Newport held on and produced some fine rugby which led to tries by Popham and Forster resulting in a 28-15 half-time score. When Teichmann scored early in the second period, closing the lead to eight points, things looked decidedly better but it was short lived. With ten minutes remaining, and to the delight of the crowd, the Sharks rang the changes bringing on old favourites Andre Joubert, Henry Honniball, James Small, Kevin Putt, Dick Muir and Jeremy Thompson. The match ended 52-25 to the home team but Newport could take a lot of credit out of their performance scoring four tries, all by forwards, and contributing in a big way to the party atmosphere.

Newport had taken a twenty-five man playing squad to South Africa. Franco Smith stayed behind when the team returned home, while Damian Cummins carried on to Australia. Steve Moore, Mark Workman, Justin Thomas and Lee Fortey would not renew contracts but two members of the tour party had signed with the club, one new face and one old. Peter Buxton was an English Under 21 product who many had earmarked for major international honours and, after two seasons at Pontypridd, Ian Gough was once again a Newport player.

Setting up Shop

'You can create excitement, you can do wonderful promotion and get all kinds of press... but if you don't deliver the goods, people will eventually catch on.'

Donald Trump

Marketing is a science. There are university courses designed to cater for it, degrees to be gained, letters after one's name. We all come under the influence of marketing every day of our lives. We are made aware of the latest products on offer, the latest superstar to be launched, the best place to invest our money... every possible need is catered for. We live in a world where many decisions are being made for us. We may not be aware of this but the marketing machine is in full swing and an unsuspecting public is the target.

Over the course of the last twenty years marketing has reached into a new aspect of our lives. Love it or hate it, sport is an important part of modern day life. Everybody is touched by it, whether as a participant, as a spectator or by simply picking up a daily newspaper and reading about it. Even if the back pages are avoided sport is regularly to be found on the front page; there's no escape. Is there anyone who hasn't heard of Muhammad Ali? That's the power of sport, or rather, the power of sports marketing. Many people ridicule the claim that wrestling is a bona fide sport. That may well be so, but the WWF in the United States has developed into one of the biggest phenomena of recent years. While it boasts only a handful of participants it is watched by millions and has acquired a global following. The spin-offs generated have produced huge revenue and there is no sign of a reversal in interest. Quite the opposite in fact. Why? Because it has been marketed successfully. Without good marketing the interest in two outrageous characters going through a sequence of pre-determined moves would have long since been consigned to the scrap heap.

With many options now available to the public all sports have to work hard to get a market share and can no longer rely on people turning up - the sport has to go out and get them. This is why the marketing people have to be taken on board. People who understand the difference between demographic profiling and psychographic profiling, geoclusters and outer rims, terminology previously unfamiliar to most sporting organisations.

There are two distinctly separate aspects involved in the marketing of any particular sport. Firstly there is the marketing of the sport itself, how one sport is sold against another: rugby against football, golf against tennis. Secondly there is the way in which the individual constituents that make up the sport, in the case of rugby union, the clubs, market themselves.

The marketing of rugby union falls largely within the remit of the IRB. The governing body controls the very ethos of the game as was seen when the decision to become a professional sport was taken. The laws of the game are controlled by the IRB with any variations being rubber stamped at its Dublin-based headquarters and it bears ultimate responsibility for the image of the game as it is portrayed to the general public. Any misrepresentation, damaging publicity or miscreant players are dealt with at this highest of levels.

Individual member unions take control of their own international interests together with the domestic leagues and cup tournaments that their member clubs participate in. Then it falls to the clubs to capitalise on their involvement and reap any benefits they can from their own unique position in the bigger picture. Which brings us to Newport RFC and the most successful marketing campaign the game of rugby in Wales has seen. Beyond Wales it would be difficult to find many stories to match the one that has evolved, and is still evolving, at Rodney Parade, a fact born out by the number of clubs that are looking at Newport and following its lead.

There were many pitfalls that had to be avoided by rugby clubs entering the new era of professional sport. Many believed, and still do, that winning is paramount, whilst failing to identify the difference between a winning team and a successful club. In recent years

Treorchy and Dunvant have had winning teams but failed to take this forward and develop into successful clubs in the top tier of the game. Short-term planning is essential as, equally so, are both medium- and long-term strategies, and all three have to be taken on board for a club to have any chance of realising its potential. Then there is the importance of identifying the needs of the supporter, the consumer, the customer. This has been largely taken for granted over the years, eighty minutes of rugby and a couple of pints, but with more sectors of the marketplace seeking a slice of the cake this is no longer enough. There has to be more on offer and while Newport were slow in recognising the need for professional marketing staff the situation has now been addressed and the benefits are there to be seen.

Accepting that the game as a concept is marketed by the IRB it would appear a not unrealistic assumption that, once the domestic structure was in place, clubs would have control over all the other factors that would impact on their future. This, however, is far from the reality of the situation and the biggest obstacle preventing the clubs having total control over their own affairs is one which is, at the same time, essential to their very future - television. Television in whatever guise, terrestrial or satellite, is rugby union's most important working partner and having been very instrumental in the sport's professional awakening it was always going to have an impact on the every day running of it. Jack Nicklaus is quoted as saying that 'Television controls the game of golf. It's a matter of the tail wagging the dog.' That was in 1984 and now, almost twenty years on, rugby union is finding itself bowing to the same paymaster. The television networks pay handsomely for the rights to cover sport and cannot be denied their input into its presentation through the medium, but rugby union as the latest addition to the world of professional sport is finding it difficult to come to terms with the demands put on it by this dominant partner.

Largest among these demands, and the biggest bone of contention with supporters, is the networks' control over the timing of live matches. When a match kicks off and even on which day it takes place, has caused enormous problems for the clubs who are largely losing their ongoing battle to get attendances to a level that would give them a glimmer of hope of financial stability. Welsh club rugby is now played on Friday nights and Saturday evenings, with matches starting at 7.05 pm and 5.30 pm respectively and very few games enjoying the traditional 2.30 pm kick off on Saturday. If a club is enjoying a successful run the problem is compounded with the television programme planners able to pick and choose which matches will be screened live as the season unfolds. The scheduling is totally unsympathetic to the needs of the regular supporter and the clubs have no apparent input into the selection process. This leads to the strong argument that important revenue is being lost to the clubs by the reduced attendances that are experienced when a match is live on television and starting at an inconvenient time. But is it? Is there a loss in revenue at every club each time the cameras turn up?

In 2000 a five-year contract was signed by the WRU and the BBC/S4C granting sole broadcasting rights of the Welsh Scottish Premier Division matches. The BBC would show a selected match on Friday night and S4C would continue its early Saturday evening coverage of matches. At the start and end of the season, matches would be played mid-week and these would also be available to the broadcasters to transmit as they felt appropriate. It is accepted that supporters are not happy with the scheduling but what about the clubs?

Over five years the television companies will pay the WRU £22.5 million, virtually all of which will be paid directly to the Premier clubs, the Welsh Premier clubs that is, Edinburgh and Glasgow being excluded from the contract. Out of £4.5 million received each season £750,000 is put to one side and the remainder is distributed equally between the nine Welsh clubs each receiving approximately £400,000. The £750,000 is then used as payment to clubs when their home matches are broadcast live. While this is a standard payment for each match shown, some clubs will benefit more than others depending on the number of times they play host to the cameras. In 2001-02 the amount received by the clubs per match was approximately £17,000, this after some 40 plus matches had been shown live.

Are the clubs happy with the arrangement? You bet your life they are, in fact some of them were questioning why their home matches couldn't feature live on television more often. It needs a lot of people on the terraces to generate £17,000, somewhere between 1,500 and 2,000, and most clubs are happier in the knowledge that the money is in the bank rather than relying on the numbers turning up.

Newport had the best of both worlds in 2001-02. Seven home league matches were broadcast live and with an average attendance of over 7,500 at these games, the club was getting two bites of the cherry. What these figures do not take into consideration however, is the damage such irregular match days and kick-off times do to a club's customer base development programme; the way each club is trying to get its supporters into a routine which guarantees their attendance at every home match.

During the 2001-02 season only three of Newport's home matches kicked off at 2.30 pm on a Saturday - these were played on 25 August, 1 September and 11 May. For over eight months there was no first team rugby on offer at Rodney Parade on a Saturday afternoon. While this is a ludicrous situation for any club, and Newport were not on their own, it is the way that the game is heading and the marketing departments are going to have to take the fact on board and respond accordingly.

Newport have had to react quickly to the factors that are beyond their control. Out of a total of fourteen home fixtures during the 2001-02 season, ten were transmitted live on television. Nine of the seventeen away matches were broadcast live in Wales with a further six getting coverage by the local networks in France, Ireland and Scotland, and nowhere were the attendances unacceptable. Quite the opposite in fact, with the visit of Newport usually producing the biggest crowd of the season wherever they played.

What was happening at Rodney Parade was a complete reversal to the trends being experienced by virtually every other club in Wales. Newport had started to negotiate the recognised pitfalls; it had implemented short-, medium- and long-term strategies and it had put in place a professional marketing team that clearly identified the customers' needs. And, even if more by accident than design, through its shortcomings on the playing field the club began to put into perspective how important winning would be to its long-term success. The day will come when the supporters will demand more success on the playing field but in the meantime a period of consolidation is currently being enjoyed at Rodney Parade. Not many clubs dominate for long periods in any sport. There are a few exceptions to this but success tends to come on an irregular basis and is all the sweeter for it. This is why the argument that winning is paramount has its critics. The more the total match-day experience is enjoyed the less the emphasis on winning becomes, and this is the key to long-term success. There are many clubs in the lower reaches of their particular sport that amply illustrate this, a period of short-term success almost inevitably followed by a decline that more often than not became irreversible. This, because the clubs didn't make the time to put the necessary infrastructure in place, the time to take stock and plan for tomorrow, preferring to enjoy the ride and let tomorrow look after itself. The real winners are those that are always challenging for honours, while at the same time keeping their supporters satisfied by offering more than the occasional silverware.

To fully understand how Newport RFC sold itself to a public which had previously shown little or no interest in its existence we need to look at two very different marketing strategies. One was put in place to attract the customers to the concept of watching rugby union at Rodney Parade and the other to ensure that once converted the customers would be retained. Both strategies are ongoing and very much interdependent on one another. There is little point in attracting a host of new customers to a concept if they don't enjoy it. Customer retention is achieved by satisfying a need which can then, by word of mouth, lead to further growth, but get it wrong and the reverse effect can just as easily be realised.

At the outset of professional rugby Newport had less than a thousand members. Four years later nothing had been done to impact on this figure. Both on the field and off it the club was failing to make any impression that would see an increase in interest, but then came the summer of 1999 which saw the big names arriving at the club giving the marketing department something to work with. Newport didn't actually have a marketing department at the time, preferring to call it the commercial department, and although there is a difference in the two functions it was from here that the club would try and promote itself to the community it hoped would eventually come to support it.

In its last years as a members' club, committee men Brian Cresswell and Martyn Kirtland had been responsible for sponsorship then, after the formation of the limited company in 1998, ex-rugby league player Peter Banner was appointed as the club's first Commercial Director. Banner was joined in the commercial department by first team player Shaun Connor and Alan Williams, previously the Commercial Manager at Swansea City FC. And if you wanted to buy a Lottery ticket these were the people to see. Lottery tickets, Sunday lunches, Ladies' Nights with exotic dancers, all the club's Scottish members could enjoy their Burns Night celebrations at the club; yes, it was all starting to happen at Rodney Parade!

Early in the 1998-99 season the club had opened the Roy Burnett Suite. Named after one of Newport's great players of the 50s, the suite offered excellent facilities for corporate entertaining on match days with its corner flag position allowing guests to view proceedings without having to relocate to the grandstand. The facilities were certainly in place at the club but the necessary interest was not forthcoming. Much of the effort put in had been aimed at the existing support base rather than the huge, untapped market that was sitting on the club's doorstep. Mediocre performances on the field aside, Peter Banner and his team had not grasped the potential the town and its environs had to offer; if they had, they certainly failed to capitalise on it, and it came as no surprise that the commercial department was there in name only long before the end of the season.

Newport has a population of 130,000, give or take, and it was little different in 1999. Add to this a catchment area taking in the south-east corner of Wales and the figure is nearer 500,000. Half a million people out of which 0.2% could be called regular supporters of Newport RFC. What did the other 99.8% do with themselves on a Saturday afternoon - this before television took over - where did they go? None of the other senior clubs in close proximity to Newport were enjoying great success, a fact reflected in their dismal attendances. At Pontypool, the great days of the 'Front Row', Cobner and 'Bish', were long gone while at Newbridge and Cross Keys things were no better. All three clubs were in Division One of the Welsh League and struggling to get out of it; in an upward direction anyway. In what had always been recognised as a strong rugby area it is doubtful if more than 7-8,000 people in total were watching the game on a regular basis. Neither was there any competition from another sport. Without a major club in the area, football, the biggest of spectator sports could not be seen as a serious competitor vying for the public's attention. Newport County had lost its place in the Football League and now competed in the less prestigious Doc Martens League while Cwmbran Town played in the League of Wales. The crowds would certainly not be big at these clubs which left the public with the alternative of either watching televised sport, getting involved in a participant sport or taking no interest in sport at all. It would appear from the figures that sport in and around Newport was getting a huge thumbs down from the public which was probably no bad thing when it came to seriously starting to market Newport RFC.

From an army background, Simon Lee had been running a health club in London prior to taking on the position of Commercial Director at Newport. His job was certainly made easier by Tony Brown's commitment but the development of the club as a focal point in a town starved of sporting success would depend on a lot more than simply having some high profile names on the books. Lee was joined by Mark Rollings, a local man and regular supporter of the club, and they began by looking for a new image for the club, something different to the public perception of what rugby in Newport stood for.

For the start of the new season Newport RFC adopted a 'branding' that would give it a new identity in the market place. A black and amber rugby ball would feature prominently in the club's new logo

104

and would be used on match programmes, advertisements, stationery and a range of leisure wear would soon be available at the club shop. Club ties were still popular but it was clear that a new audience would want to be identified with Newport RFC in a different way. T-shirts with the new logo prominently displayed were used to test the market and it would not be long before replica jerseys and polo shirts were put on sale to satisfy demand. With the RWC being hosted by Wales there was no better time to promote Newport than that 1999-2000 season. The high profile that the game would receive from the World Cup was unlikely to be repeated in the near future. This, together with the faith shown in Newport RFC by its millionaire backer meant that the moment had arrived - now all the club had to do was seize it!

That 1999-2000 season wasn't many months old before Tony Brown grasped the enormity of the off-field task that was now facing the club. The players and coaching staff were in place but elsewhere it was a different matter. Simon Lee and Mark Rollings were joined in the commercial department by Phil Davies who would soon be appointed Executive Director. His input into the commercial activities of the club reflected his previous experience at Treorchy, Llanelli and Cardiff and how close Newport came to being called the 'Giants' is a question best left unanswered. Phil Davies is a big man in every sense of the word and he had big ideas for the club but he was way down the road in his thinking and appeared to have overlooked the fact that Newport RFC had to learn to walk before it could run. Perhaps Davies wasn't exactly what was needed at that point in time and Tony Brown had some more thinking to do. The following season Phil Davies would become the club's first Community Development Director, eventually renamed Communications Director, a position that would see the him excel in the organisation and running of a project that would take the club in a totally new direction. That was not going to solve the immediate problem however and some other input was going to have to be found which would point the club in the direction Brown had in mind.

As Christmas approached Tony Brown was keen to have some

input from outside the club. He wanted another opinion on the way things were developing at Rodney Parade, some input totally free of any bias. Rob Cole of Westgate Sports Agency had built up many contacts throughout the game in both Wales and England and he suggested Brown should contact Keith Grainger who had just parted company with Northampton. Grainger had been Commercial Manager at Newcastle and Leicester before joining Northampton as Sales Director. The inner politics of club rugby had finally caught up with him and he was pondering a future as far from rugby as possible. Consequently, when he took Brown's call he was far from receptive, in fact he didn't want to know. Having reached a stalemate Tony Brown suggested Grainger enjoy his Christmas, rethink the situation, and that they should speak again in the new year.

When he is in Newport, Tony Brown is to be found at the Priory Hotel in Caerleon and it was here that the two men first met in January 2000. The first thing Brown wanted to know was what advice Grainger had with regard to his financial involvement with Newport RFC. 'Get out now' was the simple answer and it was not what Brown wanted to hear. He had made a commitment, he was certainly going to honour it and here was this in-your-face Geordie telling him to do a U-turn. Although they started off poles apart in their thinking, after a while it became clear that there was a lot of common ground between them and Grainger agreed to come to Newport and have a look at the way the club was operating.

Keith Grainger's first experience of match day at Rodney Parade was Newport's cup win against Cardiff. He couldn't help but be impressed by events on the field and it was obvious that there was a lot of potential that could be developed off it. Between them Tony Brown and Keith Grainger came to an agreement that would see the latter spend three days a week at Newport, basically as an observer, with a brief to make appropriate comments and recommendations as he saw fit. This was probably not a sensible arrangement, nobody likes to have an outsider looking over their shoulders in the work place and the administrative staff at Newport were no different. First impressions stick and there were some formed by both the staff and

Grainger that time would fail to repair.

Chris Rea and 'Auf Wiedersehn Pets' Oz were probably the closest many people in Newport had ever got to the Geordie persona and without hearing Keith Grainger sing it would be a brave man that likened him to the travelling brickie. Suffice to say most Geordies are blunt individuals and some people can easily take this the wrong way, so when Keith Grainger accepted Tony Brown's subsequent offer to become Acting Chief Executive at Newport there were some raised eyebrows. A different animal to all that had gone before, Keith Grainger was a man who knew what was required and quickly set about introducing a more organised approach to the job, laying the foundations that would eventually see Newport become the role model that other clubs would look to imitate. Brown was keen to, if not distance himself from the sharp end at Rodney Parade, take more of a back seat role and by installing Grainger in this new position he could see an opportunity to pass a lot of the day-to-day decision making to a new face.

With his background in commercial development and marketing at three English Premiership clubs it was inevitable that this would be one of the first areas that Keith Grainger would address on his arrival. When talking about commercial and marketing opportunities Newport's new Acting Chief Executive continually refers to the C word... Cash! First impressions had told him that Newport RFC was being sold cheap and he intended to correct this imbalance sooner rather than later. Sponsors had their name associated with a club that was attracting a lot of media attention and they weren't paying anything like the going rate. Neither were supporters paying what would be considered appropriate for the level of rugby and the quality of player that they were now watching. Before too long both sponsors and supporters alike were going to have to dig a bit deeper if they wanted to be involved. And they did, they may not have liked it, but they did.

Every square metre of Rodney Parade was now looked at with a view as to how much cash it could generate. How much it could contribute to the ever-increasing running costs of the business that the club had become. The function rooms, the car park, pitchside advertising, programme advertising all would undergo change in the drive to generate more income. Sections of the ground would be named after the club's sponsors, players could be sponsored. Match sponsorship, previously £1,000, now cost from £4,000 for the lower profile league matches to £7,500 for the Heineken Cup fixtures which would include use of the prestigious Burnett Suite and twenty-four hospitality boxes would be available for hire at £12,000 for the season or between £1,500-£2,000 per match. Nothing was overlooked and the new pricing structuring surprisingly proved to be less of a barrier, in fact it became a case of the more expensive the product, the greater the demand.

Simon Lee and Mark Rollings departed, Lee to become Sales and Marketing Director at the Millennium Stadium, and it was now the turn of Janet Harris and Jonathan Cook to take on the task of promoting Newport RFC. Ensuring all matches are sponsored, the hospitality boxes sold and the Vice-Presidents' and Brecon Lounge memberships taken up, is a big responsibility. Over the course of a season these four facilities alone are capable of generating £600,000. Add on programme and pitchside advertising and the importance of a well-run commercial department is not difficult to see. The team sponsors are Bisley Office Equipment and while one could be forgiven for thinking that this is a perk for Tony Brown, far from it. His company pays the going rate adding another significant sum to the total.

Newport RFC has a corporate customer base of 400 companies. They utilise every promotional opportunity offered by the club, from matchday programme advertising through to the sponsoring of matches, and with very few exceptions they are companies local to the community served by Newport. This is the sensible way to market the club and while some more nationally recognised names may wish to become involved in the future it is those names that are more locally known that are currently getting the benefits from their involvement with Newport.

The real growth area in sports sponsorship is seen in the hospitality market and it was no coincidence that after a season with twelve suites for hire there are now twenty-four available at Rodney Parade

These are temporary fixtures that are rented for the duration of each season thereby making their cost-effectiveness easy to measure. Sponsors can entertain their guests within the confines of a well-appointed facility that offers privacy and comfort while still enjoying the total matchday experience. Players will visit the boxes after the match and this ongoing cementing of relationships with the club's business partners is proving to be beneficial to all parties. In addition to their marketing potential the hospitality boxes, by being positioned behind the posts, have helped to create a much tighter feel to the ground. Modern in design, they have helped to uplift the overall appearance of Rodney Parade and with the Family Stand behind the opposite posts the ground now creates a very intimidating atmosphere for visiting teams to contend with.

Club sponsors and corporate clients are essential to the everyday survival of a rugby club. Small in numbers they may be on match days, but their contribution per head is high, each generating as much as twenty times the revenue of other spectators. But by virtue of their numbers it is the other spectators that must be recognised as the club's bread and butter.

Not that long ago, if Newport had a home match, unless someone actively followed the club there was every likelihood that they would be none the wiser. Certainly this would be true if they didn't take the local newspaper, the South Wales Argus, and it was this glaring lack of communication that needed to be looked at. While it is impossible to underestimate the immediate impact and interest the arrival of players such as Shane Howarth and Gary Teichmann had on the club, this could easily have been allowed to disappear after a handful of matches and that wasn't going to be the answer. However, the big signings did give the marketing department something to work with and they began to set about the task in earnest.

Every book published on marketing has identified the importance of awakening in the potential customer a need for the product. If Delia Smith tells her viewers that they need a particular brand of saucepan to boil an egg, millions will go out and buy one, the fact that every household kitchen probably has one or more saucepans that will adequately do the job being irrelevant. This is the first stage in the selling process and it is the most important. The marketing people had to get the message across that something was happening at Rodney Parade and the public had to be a part of it; indeed, they needed to be a part of it.

Advertising works. Make no mistake about it, push something in front of the public often enough and the message starts to get across. Newport RFC began a major advertising campaign that continues to this day on the premise that the second most important stage in the selling process is the last, i.e. ensuring that the customer isn't allowed to forget. Ever wondered why household names such as Kelloggs Corn Flakes, Heinz Baked Beans and Cadburys Chocolate spend millions of pounds annually on promotional campaigns? To make sure the customer doesn't forget, and the thinking isn't any different at Rodney Parade.

Block advertising in the local paper, glossy leaflets inside each copy of the paper, banners stretched across the width of the main shopping thoroughfare, radio advertising, mail shots; on it went until there wasn't anybody within a ten-mile radius who didn't know what was happening at Newport RFC. Now there are two names in sport that everybody within that ten-mile radius of Newport have heard of - Muhammad Ali and Newport RFC.

Having made the immediate market fully aware of its existence, the club now had to address the second phase of its strategy which would be aimed at ensuring those that had responded positively to the initial campaign, got into the habit.

Bees Round a Honey Pot

**'One week he's in polka dots, the next week he's in stripes.
'Cos he's a dedicated follower of fashion.'**

Ray Davies

Two events took place at Rodney Parade on Sunday 30 July 2000. The first Family Fun Day saw Newport RFC open its gates to the public, and a new club merchandise shop was launched. The Fun Day was an innovation which gave people the opportunity to enjoy the club and its facilities away from the pressures of match day. It allowed them to view the hospitality areas, the changing rooms, in fact it was access all areas, and there was plenty of entertainment on offer for young and old alike. The players were there to put the youngsters through their paces; they scrummaged, worked line-out drills and kicked goals with their heroes while their parents did what parents do best when their children are being amused by someone else. There was music, face painting, a bouncy castle and touch rugby. People could have their photograph taken holding the Heineken Cup, they could meet the players, meet Tony Brown, in fact they could do all the things that were becoming part of the matchday experience - except watch a match.

It was the first day supporters could collect their season tickets and, of course, new supporters could join the club. As a public relations exercise the Fun Day was a resounding success. Over two thousand people turned up to enjoy the family experience that Newport were working so hard to promote. It would be down to the marketing department to ensure that these people and many others like them would return when it mattered - on match day.

Accepting that phase one of the marketing strategy put in place by Newport was aimed at introducing the club to both the corporate and private sectors of the market, phase two was there to ensure that the new wave of interest was not allowed to disappear. Converting the casual spectators to season ticket holders, catering for their matchday needs and giving them the opportunity to identify with the club would play a big part in securing a healthy future. Ticket sales, bar receipts and merchandising - the three main factors in second phase marketing.

To watch a game of rugby at Rodney Parade members of the paying public have always had two options at their disposal: buy a season ticket or pay at the gate. While this system had certainly stood the test of time it was inevitable that it would have to be updated, in fact it would have to be totally overhauled, to meet the requirements of a professional club. What was wrong with it? Basically, it was a system that was open to abuse and at the same time, it was a system from which the club learned absolutely nothing about the people who were turning up on the day to watch Newport play.

The club had always kept a record of season ticket holders and at the end of each season these would be mailed with all the necessary information required to enable them to purchase their season ticket for the next campaign. This was fine, but there was little else done to promote the purchase of season tickets, in fact not that long ago there was a requirement that new applicants had to have a proposer and seconder, both existing members, before they could be considered for club membership. These policies were in place for a reason but they would now have to be changed and brought in line with the club's future demands.

One of the observations made by Keith Grainger after watching a couple of matches at Rodney Parade was the lack of control at the entrances. He noted that shortly after the kick off the gates on Corporation Road were flung open allowing as many as a hundred people to walk in free of charge, after missing only a few minutes' play. Under the system then in place the club had little or no control over these 'gatecrashers' while elsewhere in the ground there were similar problems with people moving from the enclosure to the grandstand and season tickets being taken out of the ground by one person and passed on to others, thereby getting two or more in on the same ticket. What all this amounted to was a significant loss of revenue over the course of a season.

Expensive to introduce it may be, but a sophisticated ticketing system was going to have to be put into place, not only one that would help tighten matchday security, but one that could be used as a marketing tool. The club wanted to know who was coming to the matches. It wanted a customer profile, the mix of men, women and children, and it wanted addresses. Where did they come from? How often did they come?

This all meant the end of the road for the small season ticket that would fit nicely into a credit card holder and the cloakroom ticket stub issued at the turnstiles would also become a thing of the past. Season ticket holders would now be issued with a book of numbered vouchers and on match day the appropriate number would be posted at the entrances and duly detached from the book; simple. For non-season ticket holders and visiting supporters, tickets would have to be bought in advance and there would be ample opportunity to do so in the days and weeks leading up to each match. This facility would obviously be available on match days but, after a rocky start, 60-80% of tickets sold are now bought in advance of match day. The rocky start was experienced on a wet night in February 2000 when people were having to be sent from the ground's entrances back to the ticket office to purchase the tickets that would allow them to view the match. The queue was long, tempers became frayed but the public quickly caught on and the system now in place works well.

The marketing advantages produced by such a system are quite significant. Many tickets are ordered over the phone and customers' information is stored on the database which can be triggered to produce a list of people who used the system and, more importantly, how many times. In the close season, not only will existing season ticket holders be sent the club's promotional material, but a second mailing campaign will follow targeting those people on the database who attended two or more matches at Rodney Parade - 7,000 in the 2001-02 season. Add this to the 4,270 season ticket holders already on the books and the number targeted is substantial.

The control and marketing benefits such a ticketing system brings to the club more than justify its existence but perhaps the most important benefit it introduces is not immediately apparent. As we have seen, attendances at Rodney Parade have significantly increased in recent years which has resulted in the ground being full to its capacity of 11,676 on three occasions and catering for crowds in excess of 8,000 on many more. Known as 'critical crowd density', CCD is a problem that not many people would ever have envisaged applying to Newport RFC. At its simplest, CCD relates to the safety issues that must be observed at all sporting venues and in particular, the tendency for spectators to congregate at the best vantage points, such as the half-way line. Where the choice used to be grandstand, enclosure and field there are now sub-divisions within each category and these are particularly important in the standing areas of the ground which are now divided into paddocks, each with a capacity level that must not be exceeded. Each has a separate entrance and, despite its name, those in the Walkabout Paddock can do no such thing.

'You pay your money and you take your choice.' There are six different spectator options on offer at Rodney Parade, four seating and two terracing. Adult season ticket prices for the 2002-03 season range from the top priced Platinum seats at £250 to a place on the uncovered terrace for £100 while Junior tickets are available ranging from £220-£25 together with various concessions. Individual matches are priced between £20-£10 for adults and as low as £5 for juniors with particularly good value on offer from the multiple choice family tickets. Not a particularly expensive pastime then but neither is watching rugby cheap. For regular supporters the season ticket offers significant savings and from the club's point of view creates a much welcome boost to cash flow in the early part of the season. Newport's 4,270 season ticket holders probably generated £400,000 revenue by the start of the season and the club will wish to see this number grow in the future. Similarly, pre-selling tickets helps eliminate the risk of losing supporters if, come match day, the heavens open and the game is live on television.

Initially viewed as yet another case of bureaucracy gone mad and more red tape, the ticketing facilities at Newport are now well accepted and there are few problems for Ticketing Manager, Jackie Page, and her staff to contend with. The public has been made aware of the system and how it works and now, having got their tickets, it's usually a case of 'Where's the bar?'

Pouring Guinness is an art. In Dublin the locals will tell you that it takes eight minutes to pour the perfect pint. Customers don't have to wait eight minutes because every pub has a dozen or more pumps and under each one is a glass containing varying levels of the black stuff. Barmen continually add an inch or so until the glass is full and ready for drinking. They know what they are doing these barmen and many pubs won't let them near the Guinness until a suitable apprenticeship has been served. Eight minutes. That means that to pour 5,500 perfect pints of Guinness will take 44,000 minutes, or 733 hours and 20 minutes, or 30 days 13 hours and 20 minutes - one month!

Between 5 pm on Friday 12 January and 11 pm on Saturday 13 January 2001, Newport RFC sold 5,500 pints of Guinness. During the same period total bar sales topped £30,000 - yes, the Irish had come to town. The men of Munster to be exact, and they had a ball. And just think about it; this consumption was largely after seeing their team win. Imagine what it would have been had they lost! On the Friday night the club had held a Ceilidh, an Irish Night with fiddles, tin whistles and bodhran, funny dancing and serious drinking. Then on the Saturday, and despite a 5.35 pm kick-off with the match being shown live on S4C, a genuine full house, and the best part of those 5,500 pints of Guinness consumed. It probably took a minute to pour each pint but nobody was complaining if there wasn't a shamrock artistically placed on the head that would still be there when the glass was empty; the true test of a pint well poured.

The following week the club's website was full of emails received from the visitors from across the water. Most referred to the 'best rugby experience' adding more fuel to the argument that the Heineken Cup is starting to replace the Six Nations as the fans' preference when planning their weekends away during the season.

Unfortunately, you don't get many weekends like this, and while things are always buzzing at the ground on match days, the reality of the situation is that the excellent facilities Rodney Parade has to offer are rarely used during the remainder of the year. Unlike Cardiff RFC with its city centre location, Newport has never been able to build up a lunch-time trade, the fact of the matter being that it is the wrong side of the river. Evenings should be different with comfortable lounges and ample parking and there must be scope to develop this; Newport, the city centre that is, offers very little in the way of night-time entertainment, unless you are of a certain age, i.e. under twenty-five, so an as yet untapped marketing opportunity is waiting to be looked at. Until then, it's match days and as many bar staff as possible, pouring as much beer as possible as quickly as possible.

While the clubhouse offers more comfort, with drinks served in glasses and the full range of beverages, the place to be seen is the Tented Village. With the best part of an acre of land between the club house and the stadium at its disposal, the club decided to put a number of interlinked marquees on the hard standing that was previously a base for four tennis courts. The Tented Village was introduced during the 1999-2000 season and more than paid its way. Initially it was rented at a cost of £12,000 but such was its popularity that the club invested £50,000 and bought a much improved version. Rain or shine, the Tented Village is equally popular on match days and, in addition to the many activities that are geared towards keeping the kids happy, it has three bar areas that ensure the inevitable pre- and post-match demand is satisfied. Beer and lager are available, served in plastic containers admittedly, but the customers are not kept waiting which is the priority at peak periods.

And there are more bars. If supporters want sustenance during the game there are two situated within the ground which do surprisingly good business. The availability of alcohol at sporting venues is an issue that causes a great divide among spectators. Football often outlaws it for obvious reasons but many other sports have allowed it and it is unlikely that the sale of alcohol during matches is going to stop. The WRU allows spectators to take drinks to their seats at the Millennium Stadium, if they are bought at one of the many on-site bars, and appears oblivious to the numerous complaints that are aired through the press relating stories of spilt beer, ruined clothing etc. There is only a social responsibility lacking at this point in time, but a responsibility that will certainly have to be recognised when the inevitable violence-related problems rear their head. Most clubs have followed the lead of the WRU with regard to the availability of drink during matches, probably the only thing both have been in agreement on in the professional era, and at Rodney Parade there doesn't appear to be a problem. The ratio of stewards to spectators is high and any sign of trouble can be quickly addressed and, at a self styled family club, the shutters would come down for good on the bars within the ground if behaviour directly related to the facility became unacceptable.

It goes without saying that the contribution realised from bar sales at Rodney Parade has considerably increased over the past three seasons. Now standing at £300,000, the turnover has trebled and there is no sign yet of demand being satiated. The sales generated at the Munster game can be repeated if overall attendance levels increase and this is where the two separate aspects of marketing begin to rely on each other.

Bees around a honey pot. That's what Rodney Parade resembles on match days. Supporters have got their ticket, they've had a drink and now they want to watch their team and they want to be identified with it. What better way than putting the jersey on?

Demand for club-related merchandise had escalated with the change in public attitude towards casual clothing. The market leaders, Nike, Adidas, and Reebok, fought for the contracts that would see their products worn by the world's top clubs and sporting personalities. The publicity received by being involved with the best was of enormous value when it came to selling the product in the retail market. From trainers to polo shirts to replica jerseys, and before we knew it we had all become walking adverts. It didn't take clubs long to realise there was a marketing opportunity here and with that awareness came the club shop. At Old Trafford it's the Megastore and customers have shopping baskets and trolleys at their disposal. But this is big business and it would not be unreasonable to suggest that Manchester United make more money from their retail operation than rugby's four home unions and their affiliated clubs make between them.

Club shop has not always been an appropriate name for it but like most, Newport has always had an outlet where club sweaters, ties, car stickers and lapel badges could be bought. The club office, a Portakabin and by 1998-99, a ground floor room at the end of the clubhouse, were all used to sell the club's wares. The club's kit sponsors in 1998-99 were Rossco and a range of leisure wear was introduced to go on sale with the replica jerseys. The season was a nightmare for the club and the home and away jerseys were as bad, the worst the team has ever played in. It came as no surprise when almost fifteen hundred items were left unsold at the end of the season, but what to do with them? Commercial Manager, Mark Rollings, recruited Alison Smith to help sort out the stock and three years later she is still there, not sorting the stock but managing the new club shop. The surplus stock was finally sold - a 'buy one get ten free' offer proving irresistible - but what happened in the next three seasons more than made up for any losses suffered.

Alison Smith had a room, some trestle tables, a cash box and a manual credit card machine. She had to beg, steal and borrow to make the selling space presentable. Local fashion shops supplied old tailors' dummies and a few yards of black cloth worked wonders in transforming the trestle tables. With a new line in T-shirts displaying the club logo and a new jersey sponsor supplying something a bit more pleasant on the eye, how could she fail? Really, Alison Smith couldn't fail, she was on a sure fire winner; after all, the club shop had only generated £4,000 turnover in the previous season!

If there had been any doubts about the potential profitability of a well-run club shop then they were laid to rest at the end of that 1999-2000 season. With turnover increased to an impressive £50,000 everyone concerned could pat themselves on the back and look forward to more of the same in a few months time. Admittedly, this figure.

included the offloading of the previous season's unwanted stock at give-away prices but it proved there was a market for in-house products. However successful the marked increase was seen to be Newport's newly appointed Acting Chief Executive thought differently. Keith Grainger knew from experience the revenue potential that was available from a thriving club shop and as he saw it, Newport hadn't even begun to scratch the surface.

The summer months were spent ripping the shop apart. While the builders were in, the telephone lines were busy with new suppliers being offered the chance to come on board. Cotton Traders were given a three-year contract to supply the first team's kit together with the replica jerseys, both home and away. A separate deal was negotiated with New Zealand sportswear manufacturer, Canterbury, who would supply the Under 21s' jerseys together with a full range of branded leisure wear and winter clothing. And for people looking for something other than clothing there were many alternatives on offer: clocks, glassware, mugs, books, pens, mouse mats and much else besides.

The shop was totally refurbished, the stock in place, two full-time staff ready to operate two new tills and two new electric credit card machines; now all that was left to be done was to open the doors, let the punters in and take the money. The shop took £2,000 on that first Family Fun Day and by the end of the season the total turnover had reached an impressive £350,000, a seven-fold increase on the previous season. When Bath were the visitors to Rodney Parade for a Heineken Cup match it took over £10,000. Two part-time staff are now employed on match days and there is a security presence on the door. The shop is open six days a week and at Christmas a barrow is set up in the Kingsway Shopping Centre which needs restocking daily.

Top selling items in the 2000-01 season were the replica jerseys. There was a surge of interest when the club got to the Principality Cup final and over fifteen hundred in total were sold during the season at £40 a time. A limited edition jersey commemorating Gary Teichmann's two years at the club was also put on sale. Even at £55 all two hundred were snapped up which resulted in a total of over

£70,000 being taken on the sale of replica jerseys alone.

The only change in the jersey's design for the 2001-02 season was the sponsor's name on the front. Bisley replaced Robert Price and sales were not expected to match the previous season's figures. Neither was there a cup final to generate interest, but remarkably, the demand for replica jerseys continued and not only did sales match the previous year but overall total turnover once again topped £350,000. The shop now offers a personalising service so supporters can have Snow, Howarth or Raiwalui put on the back of their jersey. It is impossible to go shopping in Newport without seeing the club's jersey being proudly worn by men, women and children alike. Forget fcuk, Quiksilver and Tommy Hilfiger - in Newport, Cotton Traders, Canterbury and Bisley are the names to be seen in.

Ticket sales, bar receipts and merchandising. The three principal areas of second phase marketing are each proving to be success stories in their own right and, within the success story that is Newport RFC, in the coming years they are probably going to be the most important sources of revenue of those that are within the club's control. They are what the majority of the supporters that arrive at Rodney Parade relate to, and they represent what 'going over the rugby' is all about.

It's Getting Better - 2000-01

'The time to repair the roof is when the sun is shining.'
John Fitzgerald Kennedy

The 2000-01 season was going to be the most important in the history of Newport RFC. Success in at least one of the three competitions the club would be involved in was of the utmost importance if the faith shown by Tony Brown, his board of directors and the thousands of supporters who were now following the club was to be rewarded.

In its long history Newport had seen many seasons where the results and performances were of the highest quality, seasons that unfolded match by match, evolved as the weeks went by and they rightly stand in the record books, never to be forgotten. Without a doubt, the players and administrators in the past had set about each new season with an intent. An intent to win matches and produce quality rugby football, but the pressures that the professional era had brought with it would have been totally alien to them. In 2000-01 the players had to win something, they had to maintain the new-found interest that had been seen in the previous season, the club had to move forward.

The close season had seen several players depart. Principal among them had been Franco Smith, Damian Cummins, Justin Thomas and scrum half Steve Moore. David Llewellyn had picked up a long-term injury at the end of the previous campaign while early in the season Peter Rogers was allowed to move to Cardiff who took over the remaining term of his contract. To replace them Newport signed second row Ian Gough, wing forward Peter Buxton, hooker James Richards and South African prop Adrian Garvey, together with scrum half Darren Edwards, wing Matt Mostyn and full back Matt Pini. Garvey needed no introduction, he was the fourth member of the South African team that defeated Wales at Wembley in 1998 to join the club, while Mostyn had played in all Ireland's RWC matches in 1999. Garvey's inclusion meant that Rod Snow could now revert to his favoured loose head position, allowing the front row to develop into one of the team's strengths as the season unfolded.

It was clear that Shane Howarth was going to continue where he had left off in the previous season, at outside half, and finding a full back with experience and pace was paramount to the club's aspirations. Matt Pini was a dual international having appeared for both Australia and Italy, and looked an ideal player to bring into the squad. He certainly had the pace that was previously lacking behind the scrum. This was a more balanced looking squad, the forwards looked particularly strong while the back division would benefit from the added pace in the back three. Now it was time to deliver - would they be good enough?

Where Frank Sinatra had failed, the Baha Men succeeded. Looking for a song that would create some crowd participation and be identified with Newport, the marketing department had experimented with Old Blue Eyes' rendering of New York, New York. When the chorus arrived the speakers would be silenced leaving the crowd to substitute New Port, New Port. Well, surprisingly, this didn't come off so an alternative had to be found. From September through November 2000 'Who Let the Dogs Out?' had spent a total of twelve weeks in the UK music charts, peaking at number two in the week of 14th October. Marketing manager, Jonathan Cook, has to take the dubious credit for introducing this infectious chant into the matchday proceedings and the crowd love it. Thankfully, to date the Baha Men have proved to be one-hit wonders, but if royalty payments are made for crowd renderings of that one-off hit record, they must be very rich Baha Men indeed. Why the Newport supporters took 'Who Let the Dogs Out?' on board as their signature tune is a mystery. When the team takes the field, scores a try, gains any form of ascendancy, needs a bit of touchline assistance from the fans or just for the sheer hell of it, 'Who Let the Dogs Out?' is heard echoing around the four corners of the ground. The dogs look as if they are here to stay - they certainly helped in the search for a title for this book!

The fixture list for the season was the most exciting for many years. Twenty-two matches in the Welsh-Scottish League, an initial six matches in the Heineken Cup and whatever the Principality Cup produced after the club entered in the sixth round. However, the season lacked structure, of the twenty-nine matches Newport were guaranteed, seventeen would be played before the end of the year. Incredibly, seven league games would be completed before the end of September. The following month would be taken over by the Heineken Cup with four matches scheduled to be played while in November there were no matches due to the now ever-present autumn internationals but there would be room to squeeze in a further six league games in December!

The season got off to a bad start with the visit to Llanelli. Leading 11-9 into injury time, Simon Raiwalui was penalised for obstructing Stephen Jones as he attempted to follow up a kick ahead. Jones converted the penalty and a lot of hard work went unrewarded. Newport had done enough to win the match but one basic error cost them dearly. Three home matches followed, Neath, Swansea and Ebbw Vale were all beaten in a frantic eight days, the latter 56-24 which showed the improvement from the previous February's defeat at Eugene Cross Park.

Three wins out of four. Next up Cardiff at the Arms Park - three wins out of five. What is it about the Blue and Blacks that Newport cannot seem to contend with? In recent seasons there has never been much between the sides at the final whistle but Cardiff have invariably won the game. This time the score was 29-16 and come the return fixture at Rodney Parade on Boxing Day it would be more of the same. What made it all the more difficult to understand was compounded a week later at Pontypridd when Newport were unrecognisable from the team at the Arms Park in putting another jinx to rest with an emphatic 44-22 victory. The Newport backs ran in five tries, Howarth converted them all and added three penalties. The most vociferous home supporters in Wales were silenced - it wasn't such a waste of money after all, was it? The seven league matches played had produced five wins and two defeats, but now it was time to put the spotlight on Europe and the Heineken Cup.

When the draw had taken place in the summer Newport had been placed in Group 4 with Bath, Munster and Castres. The first phase would see the club visit Munster, play Bath at Rodney Parade and then the back-to-back matches with Castres. To be in with any chance of progress two wins were essential but three would probably be the requirement if hopes of advancement in the competition were to be realised. The Heineken Cup was a new level of competition for Newport RFC. The European Shield had introduced the club to the demands of travelling to play English and French clubs on their own territory, but now they would be facing the best teams in Europe and there would be no time for the much relied on 'learning curve'.

Not that Thomond Park, Limerick was ever going to be the place to start learning. Munster had not lost a European game there in five years and only five months earlier had contested the previous final losing to Northampton 9-8 at a packed Twickenham. Talisman, Keith Wood, had returned to Harlequins but the side was still able to field thirteen internationals, among them Peter Clohessy, John Hayes, Mick Galway and David Wallace in the forwards and Peter Stringer and Ronan O'Gara at half back. Munster were an experienced, streetwise outfit and in front of their own crowd in a packed stadium they certainly started the match as favourites. Not that Newport didn't have support in the crowd. Far from it. Estimates vary but it would not be exaggerating to suggest that the best part of five or six hundred Black and Amber followers had crossed the Irish Sea for the rugby and the undoubted craic that would both precede and follow the game.

Newport got it wrong. Coach Allan Lewis was right when he said that the first two tries came from forward power. They did, but the field positions that the moves started from were a result of extreme naivety on the visitors' part. What this game needed from Newport was a steady first quarter, a period of calm, simple, basic rugby. When Matt Pini made a comfortable mark the ball should have been kicked into touch and the game played in the opponents' half. Instead, he preferred to run the ball and a penalty was conceded which led to a try being scored from the resultant line-out. Within minutes the Munster pack forged another try by captain Mick Galway and Newport were 15-0 down in as many minutes.

To their eternal credit the team regrouped and took the game to the home side. Two Shane Howarth penalties reduced the deficit to nine points and the visitors were more than holding their own as the interval approached. In first half stoppage time they were awarded a penalty just outside their twenty-two metre line with the only obvious option being a kick into touch and then head off to the changing rooms. Gary Teichmann didn't do much wrong in his two seasons at Newport but of the few errors he made, electing to run this penalty tops the list. A turnover, kick and chase, Munster get the benefit of the doubt and at half time Newport are left trailing 20-6 with a mountain to climb.

And climb they did. Within minutes of the restart, with the Newport forwards in irrepressible form, the ball was spread wide to Ben Breeze who touched down in the corner. Howarth's touchline conversion made the score 20-13 and it was game on. But then Teichmann was once again the villain of the piece when he handled the ball on the ground at a ruck, in front of both the referee and the posts. Ronan O'Gara rarely misses these and he shortly added another to take the game away from Newport. A second try by Breeze was little consolation and the match ended with a 26-18 score line in favour of the home side.

The visit to Thomond Park had ended in defeat, but there were lessons to be learned and if these could be taken on board quickly all was not lost. That the Newport players took time to adjust to the pace of the game was clearly apparent. They also learnt that at this level the game must be played in the opponents' half and that risks should be kept to a minimum if not ruled out completely. The last three Heineken Cup champions were Bath, Ulster and Northampton. Champions maybe, but none of them were the best side in the tournament when they lifted the trophy. All three just played simple, basic rugby and their success was built around risk elimination, solid defence and consistent goal kicking. Newport had to adjust to this percentage rugby and quickly - in six days' time Bath would be visiting Rodney Parade.

Whoever said that live television was killing club rugby in Wales obviously hadn't visited Newport. For this match it was the turn of the BBC and the Scrum V team. The programme started with one of those cinema noir pieces, all shadows, angles and mood music. The camera was focused on a sign which read - 'Do Not Disturb - Sleeping Giant'. What did this mean? Newport RFC or Eddie Butler? Next up Eddie and Jonathan Davies wide awake and raring to go. So the sleeping giant must be Newport - not tonight!

There's always a moment in a game of rugby when the players, coaches and supporters know which side is going to win. More often than not this is when the referee blows the whistle for full time. However, some games have defining moments, moments which clearly decide the outcome. For example, even if it was in the first couple of minutes, the Barbarians were never going to lose after that try. Neil was never going to miss that kick at Wembley and Wales wouldn't beat England in Cardiff in February 2001 - and that was before the teams even took the field!

Such a moment occurred for Newport against Bath. In front of a capacity crowd, Shane Howarth lined up a conversion way out on the touchline, went through his usual routine and missed by a country mile. Bring on Dan Lyle, captain of the USA, captain of Bath. Lyle charged the conversion attempt early, got a ticking off from the referee and Howarth took the conversion again. Same routine but a better kick, this time it hit an upright, in fact it hit both uprights before it dropped over the cross bar. That was one of those moments. Newport were now leading 12-3, the two tries scored by Matthew J Watkins and Matt Mostyn, and despite Bath being allowed to pull back some of the deficit a third try by Andy Marinos saw Newport 22-10 in the lead at the interval.

While not quite reaching the heights of the first the second half ended with Bath piling on the pressure. Newport were penalised for continually killing the ball which led to referee David Tyndall warning

Teichmann that the next offender would receive a yellow card and ten minutes off the field. One minute later and the next Newport offender was shown the yellow card - Teichmann. The captain spent the last few minutes of the match anxiously watching from behind the goal line; nobody had told him that it had been won way back in the first half with Howarth's conversion. Final score 28-17.

If the start of the revival in the fortunes of Newport RFC had to be pinpointed, then this Heineken Cup match against Bath would surely be it. Not only was the club successful on the field, it also experienced unprecedented success off it. Two weeks earlier the match programme for the Bridgend game advised that over 7,000 tickets had already been sold for the visit of Bath and that a corporate marquee would cater for 200 guests on the night. Dinner, wine, a free pre-match bar, a covered seat and a match programme was on offer at £950 + VAT per table of ten. Not only did this sell out but there was a reserve list. The match may have been played on Friday, 13 October, but there were only good omens on offer at Rodney Parade.

Like Newport, Castres had taken part in the European Shield competition in the previous season losing to Pau in an all French final. Indeed, the two clubs had contested the same group, with Castres winning both matches. A year on it was essential that Newport win the home leg while for Castres who were struggling after losing their first two group matches, nothing short of two victories over Newport would be good enough. The first encounter was at Rodney Parade and the most familiar names in the visitors' line up were captain Jeremy Davidson and Gregor Townsend, both British Lions. Newport edged home 21-20 after being awarded a dubious last minute penalty by Italian referee Giovanni Morandin. The French club had shown enough flair and skill to suggest that things could be different in the return match and sure enough, Newport suffered a 43-21 defeat, but the group was still wide open and there would be everything to play for in January.

With no domestic rugby in November, the clubs in Wales had a serious interruption to cash flow that they could only hope would be redressed by the glut of matches scheduled for December. Newport played a total of seven matches in the month and with them went any aspirations the club may have had of improving on the previous season's runners-up spot. Three of the games were lost including the home match against Cardiff. Played in front of a full house on Boxing Day this was another game that saw Newport flattering to deceive. Beaten 23-16, one could be forgiven for thinking the team were developing something of an inferior complex when faced by their greatest rivals. In fact, when it came to the big matches, those that really mattered, the record didn't bear close inspection.

If Tony Brown, Allan Lewis and Gary Teichmann had sat down pre-season to discuss the fixture list they would more than likely have viewed the six Heineken Cup matches together with the home and away matches against Cardiff, Llanelli and Swansea in the domestic league, as the biggest of the season and games that would have to be won if the club was going to make an impression in either tournament. At the end of the season the record showed that two European group matches had been won plus two of the six league matches that might have been targeted. A thirty-three per cent success rate never won anybody anything as Newport were starting to find out to their cost. Using the same criteria for the previous season would show Newport had won seven of the matches, four in the league, which saw them finish in second place, and three in the Shield which still hadn't been enough to take the club into the latter stages. At the end of 2000-01 the league structure in Wales had been in place for eleven seasons. The number of clubs contesting the top division has varied but comparisons are possible on a percentage basis. The lowest percentage of matches won by any of the champions is 72% with an average of 81%. Newport's best achievement to date was 68% in 1999-2000 which would fall to 64% in 2000-01 and improve to 70% in the following season, but still not high enough to suggest the club was capable of winning the championship.

Having lost five league matches of the fourteen played Newport were unlikely to be challenging for the title at the end of the season but a top four finish was essential if the club was to qualify for the Heineken Cup in 2001-02. The current season's two remaining group

Newport benefactor Tony Brown looks on from one of the hospitality boxes as the players prepare for the start of another season.

Club Chairman David Watkins fields the question at an Annual General Meeting as Chief Executive Keith Grainger and Tony Brown wait for their turn with the microphone.

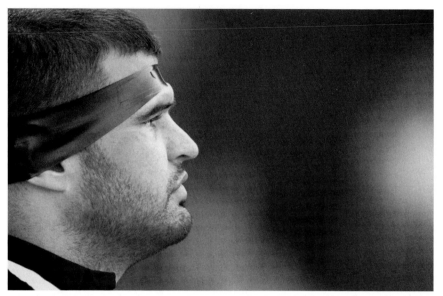

The face of Newport rugby since 6 January 1996. Rod Snow has been at the club for virtually all of the seven-year period of professional rugby and made his first team debut against Pontypridd. Now with a new two-year contract, there will be many more opportunities to stake a claim for a place on the wing!

But there again maybe he should stick to what he does best. Adrian Garvey, James Richards and Snow size up the opposition.

Shane Howarth, the consummate professional rugby player weighs up the options. Whether at full back or outside half, Howarth's basic skills are of the highest standard but many of the Rodney Parade faithful tended to forget this when he missed crucial place kicks. What they didn't realise was that the player felt the hurt more than anybody.

One of the blackest days for the club game in Wales. Tony Brown is refused entry to the match at Eugene Cross Park, Ebbw Vale as a protest by the home club against his involvement in the 'Gang of Six'. Already a ridiculous situation, things were made worse when not allowing Brown to watch the match was likened to 'Churchill not allowing Hitler to come to dinner'.

Things were no better at international level where the public's patience was being pushed to the limit. Whether this leaflet is spelt correctly or not, the message comes across loud and clear.

The Heineken Cup match at Bath was postponed twice as a result of a section of the pitch being frozen. Captain Gary Teichmann and Team Manager Jim McCreedy discuss the options with Bath coach Jon Callard.

The home tie with Leinster in the following year's tournament got under way but proceedings were brought to a premature halt when the lights went out in one corner of the ground. Simon Raiwalui and match referee Chris White talk things over but the match was stopped for ten minutes which was long enough for Newport to go off the boil and, on its resumption, lose a match that they really should have won.

At last! After a wait of twenty-four years, the Principality sponsored WRU Challenge Cup returned to Rodney Parade. Gary Teichmann holds the trophy flanked by Matt Pini and Jason Forster.

At the final whistle, Coach Alan Lewis congratulated all the players individually.

When the team returned to the club they were greeted by some thousand or more supporters who had patiently waited for their arrival. The picture sees Teichmann and Tony Brown show the silverware to the delighted crowd.

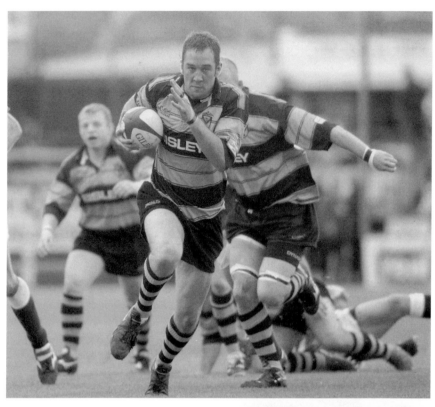

A squad of players is a constantly evolving entity and it is inevitable that there will be new faces replacing old favourites season by season. When Joe Powell, above, left to join Swansea at the end of the 2001-02 season it was on the back of being voted the Supporters Club Player of the Year and many felt he had still plenty to offer Newport. Peter Buxton, right, also ended his two years at the club in May 2002 but the move to Gloucester was prompted by aspirations towards gaining international honours with England having already been capped at 'A' level while a Newport player.

Mark Workman, seen here winning a line out ball against Cardiff, joined Newport in 1994 but as the strength of the squad improved so there became less opportunity of regular first team rugby and Workman left to join Caerphilly where he is still producing quality performances.

Jason Forster shared the captaincy with Gary Teichmann at the start of the 1999-2000 season before Shane Howarth took up his duties at the end of the World Cup.

The highs and lows of being a coach. Allan Lewis enjoys the aftermath of the clubs cup success while Ian MacIntosh can only look on in frustration as his season in charge starts to fall apart at St. Helens, Swansea.

The highs and lows of a player. Ian Gough secures a good line out ball straight off the top but, below, can only watch with the rest of the Newport bench as the team implode at Swansea.

Hi - I'm Simon Raiwalui. The current captain takes time out to let off some steam. By popular demand, Raiwalui will lead the club for a second term in the 2002-03 season with his eyes firmly set on going one-step further than the runners up spot achieved in the previous campaign.

It didn't take long for Ofisa Tonu'u to make his mark at Rodney Parade. 'Joost the Ticket' was soon forgotten, the consensus being that Tonu'u was a far better option.

If much is expected from Tonu'u then spare a thought for Andrew Powell. It all happened a bit quick for this rare and raw talent, seen here playing at number eight behind Peter Buxton at six, and that is now the critical decision to be made. Will it be eight or six for the young man? The smart money is on six!

Whoever said you should never go back was wrong. Mike Voyle is playing the best rugby of his life in his second spell with the club, and some of his performances have left people wondering why he hasn't caught the eye of the Welsh coach and been given the opportunity to add to his twenty-two caps.

Andy Marinos is the most recent Newport player to have represented Wales. After a false start - he was replaced in the World Cup squad at the last minute - he now has seven caps to his credit.

The two Matts. Matt Mostyn, above, is an Irish international seen here breaking through against some of his fellow countrymen when Leinster were the visitors to Rodney Parade while Matt Pini, below, is a dual international having represented both Australia and Italy.

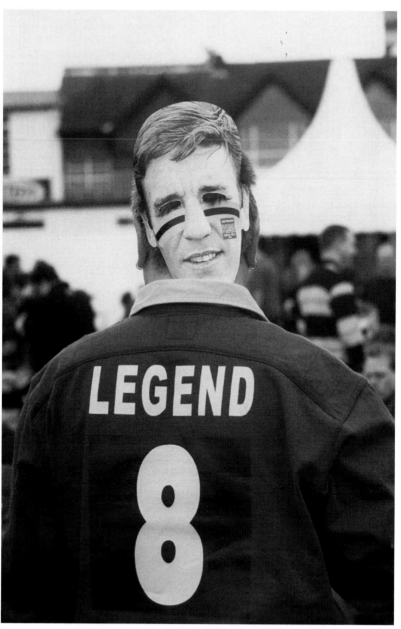

Gone but not forgotten.

matches were played in January, both ending in defeats. It seemed Rodney Parade had become a corner of the Emerald Isle when the men from Munster arrived. The game had a touch of déjà vu about it, but this time it was Newport who led 15-0. Mostyn and Pini were the early try scorers but eventually the strength and experience of the visitors, particularly in the forwards, told and they deserved their 39-24 victory. There was nothing at stake for Newport in the last game at Bath although if the home team could score eleven tries they would progress to the quarter final stage. Amid great controversy the match was called off by the referee less than an hour before the scheduled kick-off. One corner of the pitch was frozen solid, the hosts having felt it unnecessary to cover it despite the weather forecast. Two thousand Newport supporters had arrived at the Recreation Ground and they were not in a happy frame of mind when the announcement was made. Hopes that the game could get under way on the Sunday disappeared when a thaw failed to materialise and it was Tuesday when the last match in the tournament's group stages finally kicked off. Gone was the ice rink and in its place was a swimming pool. Monsoon conditions had descended on Bath and the match would surely have been postponed again if the next stage of the competition had been further than four days away. To both teams' credit some excellent rugby was played in atrocious conditions but, though winning 38-10, Bath only scored six tries and their tournament was over.

Out of Europe and struggling in the league Newport were starting to focus on the Principality Cup. The WRU Challenge Trophy had been introduced into the rugby calendar in 1972 and Newport had only been successful in 1977. In 2001 the Premier Division entered the competition in the sixth round. Newport defeated UWIC 47-17 in a home tie but not before the students had entertained the crowd with some adventurous running that saw them in the lead at the interval. Aberavon were the visitors in the next round and Newport won convincingly 33-13. The gods were certainly looking favourably on the Black and Ambers who were paired with Dunvant in the quarter-final. Away this time but Newport were never in any danger of being on the end of an upset and scored eight tries winning emphatically

62-14. Ebbw Vale, Neath and Swansea were the other clubs involved in the draw for the semi-finals and while no opponents can be taken lightly at this stage of the competition, if Newport could have chosen who they would play they would certainly have gone for Ebbw Vale, and that's exactly who they were paired with.

Back-to-back semi-finals at the Millennium Stadium are not a good idea. The four clubs will struggle to sell twenty thousand tickets between them and not everybody will watch both games. Even allowing for neutral interest there are unlikely to be more than fifteen thousand spectators at either game and the atmosphere created by so few in such an arena is poor. The days of neutral grounds packed to the rafters with the crowd all but on the pitch made for much better occasions and preserved the thrill of playing on the biggest stage only for the deserving finalists.

Ebbw Vale and Newport were first up, the match kicking off at 2.30 pm and Newport were soon wondering if maybe Neath or Swansea would have been preferable after all. Semi-finals are no place for the fainthearted and the tag of pre-match favourites doesn't do anything to help calm the nerves. The Newport players were carrying an enormous amount of expectation on their shoulders added to which, they dearly wanted to send their charismatic captain home to South Africa with some silverware having found its way into the club's trophy cabinet. Ebbw Vale nearly denied them. A Matt Pini try, converted by Howarth, separated the sides at the final whistle, the remaining points coming from penalty goals, four apiece to Howarth and Jason Strange. Coach Mike Ruddock confounded supporters in both camps with his substitutions in the latter part of the match. With Ebbw Vale piling on the pressure and Newport looking more and more stretched he replaced the hooker and the half backs. It wasn't so much the substitutions, rather the timing of them and press reports would later suggest that this had been determined before the game. Strange! Newport's game plan seemed to have gone out of the window. In a complete reversal of what had been seen at Thomond Park, Newport now decided to play a tight game keeping the ball in front of the forwards but this was one match where they would certainly have benefited from a much more open approach. However, Newport were happy to reach their first final for fifteen years ending 19-12 winners and their opponents would be Neath who later accounted for Swansea in by far the better of the two semis.

Newport finished the league campaign with some mixed performances. Three more games were lost: Swansea at St Helens (the banker in any season) and home and away to the Glasgow Caledonians. Five victories were sufficient to ensure a place in the following season's Heineken Cup but the club ended the campaign in a disappointing fourth place. But there was still the Principality Cup - and Newport were going to have to win it. There is a fine line between success and failure and Newport's season was about to be measured on eighty minutes' rugby, the highs and lows in the other competitions were now confined to the record books, as would be the cup final if Newport lost. Everybody remembers who won the cup but not many will tell you who they beat.

With the FA Cup Final being played in Cardiff until somebody decides what to do with Wembley, the Principality Cup Final had to play second fiddle and take place on a Sunday. Liverpool had overcome Arsenal in front of a full house and now Neath and Newport would meet in front of 37,000 spectators meaning the Millennium Stadium was either half full or half empty. This was some indication in the decline in popularity of the game in Wales. In its early days the cup final attracted little interest beyond that generated by the two finalists. Then there had been a gradual increase in demand for tickets which saw the finals of the late 1980s and the 1990s played in front of capacity crowds of 54,000. It must be of some concern to the organisers that with almost 20,000 more tickets available the demand has returned to levels last seen some fifteen years ago.

'Neath Play Sexy Rugby' - so thought the girls and they told every-body by way of glittery lettering on the front of black T-shirts. Well, Newport could handle that, it was good rugby that was likely to cause a problem. The Newport supporters had their own message to convey - 'On The Eighth Day God Created Teich'. It may not have been as good to look at but it made as good a point. This was Teichmann's last game for the club and when he and Neath captain Gareth Llewellyn led their teams onto the pitch the 37,000 stood and the noise more than made up for the empty seats.

There are only two things that matter in cup finals - winning and losing. A spectacle is not on the agenda, if it happens fine, but the final of any competition in any sport is there to be won and any participant would prefer to win a poor match then lose a memorable one. And all supporters would, without a doubt, prefer success to failure. As for the neutrals in the crowd, well, they don't count, simple as that. So when Neath whinged on about 'tries' that weren't given and penalties that were, and when the media reported on a poor match that offered very little in the way of quality rugby - did they care back at Rodney Parade? Did they hell!

When half time arrived with the teams tied at 3-3 any thoughts of a classic encounter had long disappeared. Referee Clayton Thomas was kept busy as both teams gave away penalties with the inevitable warning regarding killing the ball on the ground not long in coming. The first kickable penalty came after Ian Gough had been adjudged to have put in a high tackle on Patrick Horgan but in truth it was just a clumsy effort that did little harm. Shane Williams took this first opportunity and Neath were in front. There followed a period of intense Neath pressure and twice decisions went against them when they thought tries had been scored. Firstly Shane Williams was denied after he had followed up a kick ahead, beaten to the touch-down by Shane Howarth, and minutes later right wing Kevin James was deemed to have been forced into touch by Peter Buxton before he had grounded the ball. Newport were on the ropes at this stage and television replays suggested Neath were hard done by on at least one, if not both occasions.

Howarth had been a marked man from the start. While a kick that saw him leave for attention to a cut lip was accidental, a late tackle by Gareth Morris resulted in referee Thomas getting the yellow card out and Howarth converted the subsequent penalty from in front of the posts. Nothing between the sides at the interval with what looked like being a tense forty minutes to come.

Newport started the second period looking the more likely and when they had the put-in at a line-out eight metres from the Neath line they made no mistake. Gough took the ball cleanly, the drive was on and Adrian Garvey forced his way over. Howarth converted, 10-3, and the Black and Amber army could breath a little easier. Gough had been prominent throughout the match and it was unfortunate when he had to be replaced midway through the second half after dislocating his shoulder but club stalwart Gareth Taylor was born for occasions like this and his moment was enjoyed by players and supporters alike.

The game may have fallen short in the skill department but it was not lacking when it came to effort. Both sides were in with a chance of glory all the way to the final whistle and the tension continued to rise when Neath scored a well worked try that brought them back to within two points. Denied in the first half, Kevin James made amends in the 69th minute and once more it was game on. Substitutions in the last ten minutes added to the incontinuity of both teams and when Shane Williams found himself taking over at outside half the game took on a new look. Here was a player who could swing a match in a moment with his electrifying turn of speed and deceptive running. Howarth had increased Newport's lead with a drop goal and so it was caution to the wind for Neath and Williams led the way. One run from inside the Neath twenty-two metre line turned several Newport players inside out. Williams looked to be clear only for Teichmann to hamper his progress for a vital second while Rod Snow got in position to launch an all encompassing tackle on the Neath player.

Newport held on. The five minutes of stoppage time may have seemed an eternity but when Taylor kicked the ball into touch and the whistle went for the last time the emotions took over.

Both sets of players were exhausted. A classic it certainly wasn't but for Newport RFC it was a victory that would stand alongside anything achieved in its long history. It was a victory that represented one man's total belief in the club, the unwavering faith of thousands of supporters and a squad of players who were determined that such commitment would not go unrewarded. When Gary Teichmann received the Principality Cup from Sir Tasker Watkins the slate was wiped clean.

Even for the best supported club in Wales, the scene that greeted the team when it returned to Rodney Parade must have come as a shock. The clubhouse and the open ground in front of it were packed with supporters who had returned and patiently waited for the arrival of the team and the opportunity to play their part in the celebrations. The party would go on a while yet - it had been a very good day.

Teichmann Revisited - a 12,000 Mile Diversion

'I believe that all of us ought to retire relatively young.'

Fidel Castro

Gary Teichmann's last appearance for Newport had been in the Principality Cup Final on 13 May 2001. It was his 51st appearance for the club and, although not quite marking the end of his playing career - he would play two games for the Barbarians - the victory ensured it would finish on an appropriate note.

A close look at Teichmann's playing career reveals that, in addition to his time at Rodney Parade, he played 144 games for Natal and 52 for the Springboks, winning 42 test caps in the process. He is his country's most capped number eight forward, holds the record for the number of consecutive caps won with 39 and he captained South Africa 36 times, another record. During his time as captain seventeen consecutive test matches were won equalling the world record set by New Zealand in the 1960s. At Provincial level Teichmann led Natal to back to back Currie Cup victories in 1995 and 1996 but in his final game for the Province, the 1999 Currie Cup Final, he had been on the losing side. With such a record it would have perhaps been a travesty of justice if his career had ended with another defeat in a cup final, but that didn't happen and his playing record has rarely, if ever, been equalled.

With such emotional scenes as those which greeted Newport's triumph fresh in the memory, it was not the right time to quiz Teichmann about his thoughts on the club and his time spent in Wales. Better to wait a few months and meet him on his own patch. Time would have helped put everything into perspective and he would be able to talk more objectively about Newport, Tony Brown and his two seasons of Welsh club rugby.

The Crowne Plaza Hotel dominates the skyline of Durban's North Beach. Each of its 446 rooms is ocean facing and with two swimming pools and three first class restaurants it is a popular choice with visiting touring teams. The All Blacks and the British Lions use it as do the Australian cricketers. It was here that Newport RFC stayed in May 2000 and it was here that King Goodwill Zwelithini was staying in February 2002.

King Goodwill Zwelithini is the ninth in a line of succession that goes back many years and he was in town to give his backing to the newly formed KwaZulu-Natal Taxi Council which had been established to sort out the taxi wars that were tearing the industry apart in the city. There had been an influx of new companies who were trying to take control and the existing operators were having none of it. This had resulted in the outbreak of gang wars which were getting out of control. A look around the Continental Restaurant at breakfast would suggest nothing would get out of control when the king was around.

King Goodwill Zwelithini is an immaculately turned out man. Difficult to age, but probably in his mid-fifties, he looks fit, intelligent and, well, regal. No fuss was made when he entered the restaurant and he seemed relaxed giving a reporter an interview while enjoying his fruit juice, omelette and coffee. An ordinary working breakfast if you ignored the four large individuals who had taken up strategic vantage points in the four corners of the room. Big men by any standards, they would ensure that things didn't get out of control.

Ronnie runs the Continental Restaurant and he is only too happy to talk about the people who have visited, people like King Goodwill Zwelithini and the many other dignitaries before him, but Ronnie's first love is sport and sportsmen and during his thirty years at the hotel he has met them all. All, that is, except the Springboks who always stay at the Umhlanga Rocks some ten kilometres north of Durban. When the teams arrive they are placed in Ronnie's care. He looks after their every requirement and counts the likes of Shane Warne and Steve Waugh among his friends. He remembers the 1974 British Lions, a team that swept all before them, and more recently the 1997 side that sealed the Test series in Durban. The Australian and New Zealand teams stay at the hotel for Tri-Nations matches, even those played in Johannesburg, and there have been many others over the years, Grasshoppers Zurich being the latest name to be added to the long list. The RWC saw the hotel cater for many of the game's leading players and it will be the same in 2003 when the cricket equivalent takes place. Ronnie has kept a scrapbook during all this time and it contains the autographs of all the sportsmen and sports-women that he has looked after when they have stayed at the Crowne Plaza and it must be worth a fortune even allowing for the South African names that are missing.

This probably goes some way to explaining why the tall, fit, athletic looking man that entered the hotel's reception area didn't go unnoticed. Staff working behind the reception desk stopped what they were doing and followed his progress through the lobby. The doormen and porters did likewise and the arriving and departing hotel guests seemed to recognise him. This was Natal's favourite son. This was Gary Teichmann and he was at the hotel to have lunch and to talk about rugby, Newport rugby, some nine months on from that last game at the Millennium Stadium.

It is still one of the major talking points in South African rugby circles and likely to remain so. Should coach Nick Mallett have dropped Springbok captain Gary Teichmann for the 1999 RWC? In his autobiography 'For the Record' Teichmann describes in great detail the events leading up to his sacking. The matches lost, the injuries and the leaning towards Bobby Skinstad were all factors that contributed to the decision to drop him. Teichmann's reign came to an end shortly after the Springboks had lost to Wales for the first time. His final appearance in a Springbok jersey came two weeks later, a Tri-Nations game in Dunedin which saw the All Blacks record a 28-0 victory, the biggest defeat ever suffered by South Africa and the only occasion on which the Springboks failed to score with Teichmann in the side.

In his book Teichmann had the perfect opportunity to be critical of Mallett, to take him to task and throw the Boks' failure to win the

1999 World Cup in his face, few would have criticised him if he had taken this action, many would have applauded him. Instead, he chose to lay down the facts as they happened and let readers form their own opinion. His only recorded criticism of Mallett being the way in which he handled the affair. He's still reluctant to talk about it referring to it as 'my thing with Mallett'. To this day the two haven't spoken since Nick Mallett informed Gary Teichmann of his decision to replace him in the squad for the RWC.

Whether Gary Teichmann would have led South Africa to a second consecutive World Cup victory is academic now but from a Newport point of view his sacking was very timely indeed. His first meeting with Tony Brown and that journey up the M4 all but convinced him that he would make the move if his family were happy. They were, and Teichmann arrived in Wales amid the build-up to the biggest tournament in the game's calendar. How did this feel, knowing that the side he was leading a few months earlier was likely to be based down the road in Cardiff if they reached the latter stages of the competition?

'Well, it was probably better than it would have been if I was still in South Africa. If that had been the case everybody would have wanted to discuss the issues and the sacking and I would have found that much harder. As it turned out I had a new focus with Newport, there were some big games to be played and it was a case of getting on with the job in hand. I remember winning at Llanelli on the eve of the quarter-finals and this was a big result. The club hadn't won there for many years and I could see what it meant to the regular guys. That was a big night for me. I was starting to feel a part of the team.'

Having decided to take lunch in the hotel's outstanding Indian restaurant the table was now covered with dishes of lamb curry - 'not too spicy' - rice, poppadoms and all the other trappings associated with the eastern cuisine. More lagers were on the way.

'If anything hurt in those early months with Newport it was the abuse the players were getting from the opposition supporters. You learn to expect criticism but at the club grounds in Wales the crowd seems to be on top of you and you are more aware of what is being said. We had a disappointing run in the European Shield and by the New Year things were not looking to good. The away defeats at Pontypridd and Ebbw Vale were probably the turning point for me. When the crowd at Pontypridd started chanting 'what a waste of money' we were playing so badly I began to wonder if they may be right.

'Shane was having a tough time of it with all his international commitments and when he decided to step down from the captaincy it was for all the right reasons and I was honoured to be asked to take over. That first game against Cardiff in the cup put us back on track and we were a different side for the remainder of the season only losing at Llanelli in the next round but winning all the league games.'

A few weeks before this meeting in the Crowne Plaza, Gary Teichmann had taken part in a sporting event about as far removed from a rugby ball as it is possible to get. The Dusi Canoe Marathon is a three-day event which sees competitors paddle their canoes down the Umsundusi and Umgeni rivers to the end of the course which is where the Umgeni flows into the Indian Ocean just north of Durban. Teichmann competed in a two-man canoe and completed the course in 11 hours and 53 minutes rating this achievement alongside many of his those he is remembered for on the rugby field.

Gary Teichmann is a natural athlete. He is a more than competent golfer and spends time on the squash court. You have to ask the question - could he have played on another season? There had undoubtedly been the opportunity to do so if he had wanted to take it, Tony Brown would have had no hesitation in resigning him.

'We had a marvellous time at Newport. My wife, Nicky, and my eldest daughter, Danielle, were very happy and our second daughter, Dominique, was born there. We were very sad when the time came to leave but to stay I would have had to play another season, and the body was telling me to call it a day. You have to listen to your body and I know it was the right decision. Newport gave me a fresh challenge after the disappointments I'd experienced in South Africa and I will always be grateful for that. I hope I gave something in return for the faith shown in me by people like Tony Brown, David Watkins and Martyn Hazell. I hope to return in a few months to meet up with old friends and maybe catch a game. But no, I have no regrets about calling it a day.'

Having read about Teichmann's proposed visit in the local press, it was inevitable that there would be speculation that he was going to return to the club and take on a coaching role.

'I'm helping an old friend with a bit of coaching at my old club College Rovers but beyond that I have no immediate plans in that direction. My business is very demanding on my time and I have to prioritise this in the next few years.' Teichmann Civil Engineering is a successful company with contracts throughout South Africa which means a lot of travelling and time spent away from home. Any further involvement in rugby is going to have to be put on hold for the fore-seeable future.

And what about Joost? Trying to get anything controversial out of Teichmann makes pulling hens' teeth look a doddle. It just isn't in his make up to say anything that might upset somebody and when that somebody is a former playing associate of some standing in the game, forget it. But there was a look that maybe just said something. Maybe just the slightest suggestion that perhaps Newport were better off without the scrum half. Who knows?

Teichmann's second season at Newport would prove to be his last in the game. Going into it he knew this was likely to be the case and so it was doubly important that the club did well. Newport were a club starved of honours for far too long and Teichmann dearly wanted to end his career on a high.

The coffee came and it was cold. Back it went and now was the time to talk about Munster. What on earth made Teichmann run the penalty in injury time of the first half at Thomond Park. 'You don't win games at places like Munster by adopting a conservative approach. You have to take the game to them and it really doesn't matter what stage in the game it is. Sometimes things come off and win matches and other times... well that was what happened in Munster. But I still believe we had to show them we weren't there to make up the numbers. I'd do the same again.'

And Bath? 'We learnt a lot in Ireland. The Heineken Cup is a big step up and we weren't going to find it easy to adjust. But we were ready for Bath and Rodney Parade was fantastic that night - one of the highlights of my time at the club. There were several that season, we played great rugby at Pontypridd and Bridgend and of course there was the cup.'

If you want to embarrass Gary Teichmann, really want to stop him in his tracks, put him on the defensive, just ask him what God did on the eighth day. 'I've taken more stick over that than anything else in my rugby career. The lads wouldn't let it go and I think it will stay with me forever. It makes a change from talking about the sacking anyway.' Teichmann's modesty is one of his most redeeming features and it was interesting to read that when asked at a public function 'When had he become a good captain?' he replied 'When I was sacked'.

There is no doubt that Newport RFC and Gary Teichmann were good for each other. Which party got most out of the deal is debatable. Newport obviously saw a change in the club's fortunes during his time there but equally Teichmann needed something to take him away from the game in South Africa and Newport offered him both the challenge and the security that he was looking for.

The supporters would be one of his lasting impressions. 'They were incredible. There weren't the numbers that I had been used to but the noise could be deafening on the field.' Teichmann and the rest of the team had made a point of visiting the hotel where the fifty-three supporters who had travelled to South Africa for his testimonial match were staying. And this would be repeated back at Newport, Teichmann was always accessible to the fans.

Curry, lager and coffee duly despatched it was time to leave. Gary Teichmann paid the bill 'You're in my country now' and it was back through the hotel's reception area and more raised eyes. The weather wasn't good, heavy rain forecast, and he recommended a trip to an out-of-town shopping mall he visits with Nicky and the children. You can safely bet he still turns a few heads there.

Gary and Nicky Teichmann came to Newport and saw the League match against Cardiff late in the season. He kept a particularly low profile and after all the hype built up in the press regarding his visit many were left wondering if he had come. There was no half-time introduction to the crowd from the pitch, he didn't sit in the main stand and after the match he kept his head down in the room reserved for players and their families. His day was over, now it was for some-body else to win over the crowd. Teichmann's place in the team had been taken by Andrew Powell, a name he wasn't familiar with, but he had heard good things about the youngster. Impressed? 'Yes, he looks the part' - and that from one who knows.

Whether Newport will continue to look overseas for crowd-pulling players only time will tell. They are not the only club to have done so but it is widely acknowledged that in Gary Teichmann they came up with a gem. His input off the field was obviously not as widely broadcast but his school visits, attendance at business functions and general professionalism away from the playing side of things helped Newport progress in the off the field development it is so keen to develop. Yes, 'Teich' is a good man, and so he should be - it took a day to make him!

'Do You Want To Be in My Gang?'

'I'll thcream, and thcream, and thcream till I'm thick.'
Violet Elizabeth Bott

William Brown had a gang. There was William, Ginger, Henry and Douglas and they were collectively known as the Outlaws. William's dog Jumble was an honorary member but there was no room in the gang for Violet Elizabeth, after all, she was a girl! The gang would meet in an old barn in a field near William's home where they would make liquorice water and cook potatoes on a fire while plotting what great deeds they would perform in the school holidays. These would usually involve money-making rackets such as putting on plays or a circus which would invariably boast some long extinct animal, Jumble in disguise, and the local children would queue up ready to part with their pocket money to see the beast. That was the theory anyway.

In May 2001 Welsh rugby acquired its own gang made up of five Premier Division clubs with a sixth set to join in October. Officially called Rugby Partnership Wales it would not be long before the members, Bridgend, Cardiff, Llanelli, Newport, Pontypridd and Swansea would be given the unimaginative sobriquet 'The Gang of Six' by the media who took an instant dislike to all they stood for. Like the Outlaws, representatives of the clubs would meet to enjoy food and drink and discuss how they were going to get more money to help them run their everyday businesses.

Before trying to decide the rights and wrongs of such a collective it is important that the background to their formation is understood. This isn't easy - rugby politics in Wales make all other forms of the species look simple - but let's try.

Anybody who viewed international rugby from a distance during the past thirty years or more would be correct in assuming that the game was thriving at this highest of levels. Full houses at all the major stadiums for the Five Nations tournament were the order of the day, a demand that would be repeated when the major sides from the Southern Hemisphere visited. Tickets were desperately sought after by fans who felt short-changed by the distribution of these valued bits of paper and it was no exaggeration when the unions suggested that the grounds could be sold twice over for the big matches. So the obvious thing to do was create bigger stadiums. France built the Stade de France, admittedly for the 1998 FIFA World Cup, but it is now the home of the Fédération Française de Rugby, while Twickenham and Murrayfield received major facelifts. In Cardiff, the National Stadium was dismantled to make way for the Millennium Stadium which would be built in time to allow Wales to host the 1999 RWC, and in Dublin the Irish Rugby Football Union did nothing. They sensibly sat back and watched developments unfold across the water, which has probably resulted in their being the wealthiest of the four home unions.

With English rugby on a high at the end of the twentieth and the start of the twenty-first century, tickets for matches at Twickenham are harder than ever to come by with a similar scarcity being seen in Paris. Contrast this with Murrayfield where tickets for recent matches have been sold through various city centre outlets with visiting supporters only having to pick up the phone and call the SRU to buy as many as they want. The restructuring of the domestic game together with the pricing of tickets are perceived to be the reasons for this lack of demand north of the border but in Wales, where there is a similar lack of interest beginning to work its way to the surface, the reasons are not quite so easily explained. True, if England are the visitors tickets are like gold dust, but any other team and supporters have recently had the opportunity to buy tickets direct from the WRU in the days leading up to the match.

Following the building of a new 72,000 seater stadium, the next stage in the dismantling of the game at international level in Wales was the number of matches that began to appear in the fixture list. Familiarity breeds contempt and this has become apparent with the poor attendances some games billed as 'Internationals' began to see. With 20,000 more seats available and eight or nine matches to pick from each season, it became clear that supply would soon outweigh demand. The paying public would no longer be prepared to fork out money for the second-rate fare that was on offer, it would become a case of quality not quantity that was wanted. The novelty of the new stadium has long since worn off and the RWC is a distant memory leaving the no small matter of paying for it which explains the surfeit of mediocrity that is now being served up. With the burden of massive capital and interest repayments the WRU is under enormous pressure to make ends meet which is starting to throw up some strange anomalies. While the players are likely to see a dramatic change in their financial situation with a reduction in the monies received for pulling on the Welsh jersey, the coach, after losing six out of seven matches in charge - a victory over Italy the only plus - is paid a handsome six figure salary! Obsessed with looking to the Southern Hemisphere for its off-the-field expertise the WRU has recruited further highly paid individuals with scant regard for any home grown talent. Sponsorship for such a high profile organisation is poor and until the performances on the field dramatically improve the additional revenue that comes with success will have to be put on hold. One swallow doesn't make a summer and Wales will have to come up with more than the occasional worthwhile victory that has been the sum total of its success in recent seasons. Memorable days they may have been, but the victories seen in Paris and particularly at Wembley have not been repeated in Cardiff and until such time as they are Welsh rugby will struggle. The Millennium Stadium will always be near to capacity for the traditional fixtures but it is the extra ones, the games that are played to generate the additional income needed, that witness the disinterest of the general public. The Barbarians, Samoa, the USA and even Italy in the Six Nations, these are the matches that are truly testing the patience of the Welsh public.

What has all this got to do with the Gang of Six? Well, plenty is the simple answer because it is to the WRU that the six clubs would turn for additional revenue to help them run their businesses and the bottom line is that the WRU hasn't got the money they seek. While the Union continues to be burdened with the loan on the Stadium any additional funding being placed in the direction of the clubs is simply not on the agenda. Hence the Gang of Six. Their suggestion is that if there is no more money for the pot then they should have all the money that is in the pot. Near as dammit anyway. This is a selfish argument in the extreme but, at the same time, it is an argument not without some credence. If the international game in Wales is starting to struggle financially then what about the game at club level? This has been on a downward curve since August 1995 and if it hadn't been for the generosity of a few individuals then it would have long since imploded.

In a nutshell then, the game in Wales is being forced onto the public in large quantities at international level and the public are gradually waking up to the fact that they are not always getting value for money. This leads to the decreasing attendances which in turn leaves a shortfall in the anticipated, indeed necessary, revenue of the governing body. Nor are the television companies showing a competitive interest in covering the matches which will mean a further possible shortfall of revenue in the Union's books. Add to this the fact that the league has failed to attract a sponsor for the past few seasons and a bleak picture is starting to develop. Sadly, while the national team shows no sign of any significant improvement, this situation can only be expected to deteriorate, certainly in the short term, and probably for much longer. Therein lie the problems that plague Welsh Rugby in their most simplistic form. Many more exist but these lead to a situation where it becomes difficult to see the wood from the trees, in itself a further problem which is best avoided.

Welsh Rugby is in a mess. A situation that worsens quicker than these words find their way onto the page. This situation has arisen as a result of the Union's inexplicable refusal to address the factors fundamental to it. Three years after the game went open the WRU decided that a plan should be introduced that would review all aspects of rugby in Wales and, over a ten-year period, the changes necessary to reflect a professional game would be gradually implemented. It took a further two years before a Working Party was given a brief 'To conduct a comprehensive review of the structure of and the ways in which Welsh rugby is governed and to propose appropriate recommendations for change'. After five years of inaction could the WRU be about to wake up to the fact that Welsh rugby had become a joke; become a laughing stock wherever the game was played?

Under the Chairmanship of Sir Tasker Watkins, President of the WRU, the Working Party was made up of individuals with a wealth of experience and knowledge pertaining to Welsh rugby. WRU staff and General Committee members were included, although some would withdraw before the report was completed, WRU Chairman, Glanmor Griffiths, and national representatives, David Pickering and Howard Watkins, among them. Independent representation was seen with the inclusion of Gerald Davies, Gwyn Jones and Ken Jones, ex-players held in the highest esteem, and clubs and interested parties were advised that any input they wished to contribute would be welcome.

The Report was finally published in January 2002, but not before much of its content had been leaked to the media and thereby widely reported. Among twenty-seven main recommendations the following were of particular interest to the Clubs:

- Premier to be the only professional Division.

- Number of Premier Clubs should be reduced, certainly to eight. Further reduction problematical.

- Criteria proposed to help determine the number of Premier Clubs.

- Premier Division alone to receive WRU financial support for the payment of players.

- The present organisation and governance structure to be replaced.

It came as no surprise when the Report was apparently rejected in its entirety by the WRU whose principals had already clearly distanced themselves from it. When one of the members of the Working Party suggested of the Report that 'It may as well have been written on the back of a fag packet!' the general public were left in no doubt that Welsh rugby was nowhere nearer to finding a way forward; they could only expect more of the same, both on and off the field.

While the WRU Working Party was preparing its report, Rugby Partnership Wales had put together a document outlining how its members saw the future of Welsh rugby. Having, by its very existence, already alienated the majority of Welsh clubs, RPW now pressed the self-destruct button. It produced 'A Vision Statement' which was distributed throughout Wales and made readily available to the public at large. In it the clubs gave a brief background to why RPW had been formed, outlined their observations on the running of the game by the WRU and listed their proposals for how the game should be restructured. It all made for very interesting reading and much of the content was based on solid thinking but RPW made one mistake in their presentation, one big mistake that probably saw any future they might have had destroyed before it even started. The first of five points listed as 'The Vision' read - 'A reduction of the Premier Division to six clubs'- and by implication it was interpreted to mean the six member clubs of RPW. They never stood a chance and time would see their proposals firmly rejected.

What is very clear when comparing the WRU Working Party Report with the Vision Statement issued by RPW are the many issues on which both are in agreement. A reduced Premier League with relegation and promotion to be determined by play-offs between the bottom-placed club and the First Division Champions. Clubs in the Premier Division having to comply with laid-down criteria which would include ground facilities, youth academies, Under 21 squads, and clubs run on sound financial principles. Also, both reports wanted to see an Executive Board put in place to oversee the running of the game. Here, however, there was a difference of opinion. While the WRU Working Party wanted a Board to run the game in Wales, on behalf of Wales, RPW wanted to form a Joint Company with the WRU which would oversee the running of the professional game. Both reports were of the opinion that Wales could only sustain a professional game at the top level and that elsewhere it should return to being an amateur pursuit.

Let's take a time-out here. Two opinions on the state of health of the game in Wales had been published. One, a report commissioned by the WRU and the other a Strategic Plan which gave air to the voices of six of the country's senior clubs. Many important issues plaguing the game had been considered and the findings of both were consistent when considering a large number of the most contentious issues. These were not the opinions of people who were totally distanced from the game, the reports had not been compiled as part of some school project neither had there been any input from the Simpsons. No, these were the work of educated individuals who not only knew the game of rugby inside out but who were, in the main, individuals who were successful in other walks of life. Men of stature, decision makers, their opinions had to be listened to. Not only that but they were opinions that needed to be acted on - positively.

In the week leading up to an Extraordinary General Meeting of the WRU which would be held in Cardiff on Sunday, 7 April 2002, for the sole purpose of deciding on a reduction in the number of clubs in the Premier Division, Glanmor Griffiths wrote in the Western Mail 'The general committee of the Union passionately believes that a move to six clubs will suit the amount of playing talent we have in Wales, fit our proposed playing structure and go a long way to satisfying the financial needs of the Union and its professional clubs'. The clubs outside RPW thought differently and when the proposal was put to the vote it was unanimously rejected.

With the 'Gang of Six' now firmly put in their place and the report of the Working Party pushed to one side, where would Welsh rugby turn next? Whether or not the General Committee of the WRU really wanted a reduced Premier Division put in place is irrelevant, its member clubs didn't and that was the deciding factor on 7 April. There is no doubt that RPW badly represented themselves from the outset but realistically the substance of their argument, backed up by the Union's own Working Party Report is the only way forward for Welsh rugby. How long it will take before this is finally accepted is another matter but in the meantime the future of the game in Wales looks decidedly fragile.

Three weeks before the meeting in Cardiff the feelings of clubs not involved with RPW were running high. There had been little opportunity for their opinions to be aired in the media where reportage of the developments resembled little more than a slanging match. There had to be another way to air their feelings; there was and it wasn't pretty.

The high profile that had come the way of Tony Brown through his involvement with Newport RFC was about to bring about repercussions that would be both unpleasant and unwarranted. The fact that he was a member of the Board of Directors and that he had stood down from the position of Chief Executive twelve months earlier counted for nothing when the club's association with RPW was viewed from the outside. It was a case of 'for Newport read Tony Brown', an interpretation of the situation that would come to a head at Eugene Cross Park.

The directors of Ebbw Vale viewed the formation of RPW as a threat to their club's future, a feeling certainly shared by all other clubs in the Premier and First Divisions who were not included in the partnership, and they decided to make their feelings clear on the night of 15 March, the night Newport came to visit. The result saw some of the most embarrassing incidents seen at a rugby ground together with the stupidest comment - and all this from professional men!

Tony Brown knew there was a likelihood that he would be refused entry when he arrived at Eugene Cross Park. Earlier in the afternoon a fax had been received at Rodney Parade advising that Brown and Chief Executive, Keith Grainger, would not be welcome at the ground and that they would be refused entry. Grainger was not going to the game but having travelled 150 miles from his home in Surrey Brown decided to travel to Ebbw Vale. Newport team manager, Jim McCreedy, had alerted the WRU of the potential problem and it was hoped that by the time Newport arrived at the ground the situation would be defused. Unfortunately this wasn't the case and together with a welcoming party of stewards, who had been instructed to refuse entry to Brown, there were TV cameramen conveniently on hand to record any confrontation.

Although forewarned, there still appeared to be a look of disbelief on Tony Brown's face when he was politely told that he could not go into the ground. He accepted the rebuff but expressed his disappointment that he would not be able to watch the game live. Petty was the word he chose to describe the action of the host club and petty it certainly was. When Ebbw Vale Director, Paul Russell, likened refusing Brown entry to 'Churchill not allowing Hitler to come to dinner,' club rugby in Wales plummeted to new depths. Newport Chairman, David Watkins, cannot be let off the hook either. His immediate reaction was to call the game off giving scant regard to the huge Newport contingent who were by now standing on the terraces in the pouring rain having paid Ebbw Vale thousands of pounds as they came through the turnstiles.

Fortunately the Newport players were not made aware of developments outside the ground until after the match. Both sets of players deserved credit for the quality of rugby produced on such a foul night but the whole atmosphere at the ground was affected by the situation, fans having heard about the events in the lead-up to the kick-off. Throw in the stupidity of the Tannoy announcer with his inane comments together with the incessant playing of the Strawbs dirge about being part of the Union and you have to wonder why on earth the public choose to spend their leisure time this way.

The Newport directors ended up watching the match on TV in a nearby pub. Mission accomplished, the players were told of events off the field and decided to leave the ground immediately insisting that Brown and co join them for a meal on the way back to Newport bringing to an end an evening that club rugby would do well not to repeat in the future.

After all the unpleasantness a nice postscript is provided by Llyr Lane, Newport's Under 21 scrum half who was on loan to Ebbw Vale and had played against his club. He showed where his loyalty lay having no hesitation in joining the Newport players and directors en route down the valley away from the enmity that had surfaced at one of Newport's greatest friends.

If Tony Brown had walked away from Welsh rugby after this disgraceful night nobody would have blamed him. Note, we are not talking Newport rugby here but Welsh rugby. People have already forgotten how Brown and the other club benefactors have pumped millions into the game in Wales in an effort to take it forward and regain some standing on the world stage. Certainly, Newport RFC has enjoyed the benefits of Brown's financial clout, but for all that, huge losses are still being seen. Where Welsh rugby has benefited is in players being encouraged to stay in Wales to play their club rugby. The real threat that would have seen star players either staying in England or making the move there was staved off by Tony Brown and others like him at a time when the WRU was seemingly helpless to control the movement of players. Why are the biggest gates at Ebbw Vale seen when Cardiff and Newport are the visitors? Would over two thousand Newport supporters have been at Eugene Cross in March if Tony Brown had kept his cheque book closed? No, they certainly wouldn't and this scenario has been happening wherever Newport have played in the last three seasons, a fact that should not be forgotten by clubs that have grievances with RPW. If anybody had ever bothered to ask him they would have learnt that Tony Brown, while agreeing that club rugby in Wales cannot carry on in its present state and that he is in favour of a reduction in the number of clubs in the Premier Division, they would also have found out that he does not agree that the member clubs of RPW have the right to choose which clubs qualify, a conclusion arrived at by many based on inference rather than fact. He would later be critical of the fact that no representative of RPW put their case forward at the subsequent meeting of the WRU at which their proposal was unanimously defeated. No matter, for the time being at least Tony Brown is honouring his commitment to Newport, a commitment that is the envy of most clubs in Wales, and beyond.

He's a rich man is Tony Brown. No, he's a very, indeed seriously rich man. He's also a gentleman, a man of his word, quiet, unassuming and on a very good day he can be quite amusing. Tony Brown is many things but one thing he certainly isn't is stupid and many people throughout the game in Wales would do well to remember that - the last thing you do in any walk of life is kill the goose that lays the golden egg.

Almost There - 2001-2002

'Yes we've had bad times at Anfield; one year we came second.'
Bob Paisley

In a perfect world these pages would draw to a close with Newport being crowned Welsh Scottish Premier League Champions - in a perfect world. Unfortunately we do not live in anything like a perfect world and the records will show that Newport RFC failed in its mission to be crowned the best club in Wales. Why it failed is a matter of some conjecture. Was it really a seventy-ninth minute penalty goal in a match between two other clubs that became the deciding factor or does the truth of the matter lie elsewhere? In its most simplistic form, and to avoid any soul searching, it cannot be denied that if the penalty had been missed Newport would almost certainly have been crowned champions - the element of doubt is only raised because of the additional pressure the team would have had to bear in the final match of the season which may have proved too much. Realistically, however, Newport's ultimate success in the 2001-02 season should not have been in the hands of a player lining up a penalty kick in Cardiff, but why it was is quite a story.

Although the previous campaign had ended with victory in the Principality Cup, the new season would begin with the club prioritising the Heineken Cup and the Welsh Scottish League. Gary Teichmann had left as expected - no amount of persuading would see him change his mind, and there was a huge hole to be filled. Newport not only had to find a player who would replace him at number eight, it also had to appoint a new captain. It was also keen to find a player who would have the charisma and standing on the world stage to maintain the high profile Teichmann had given the club in the local community.

It came as no surprise when Fijian, Simon Raiwalui, was chosen to succeed Teichmann as club captain for the new season, a popular choice with both players and supporters alike, all acknowledging that Raiwalui was a good man to have on your side. The 6ft 6in, nineteen-stone second row forward, had joined Newport at the start of the 1999-2000 season though his début had been delayed due to his participation in the World Cup. From day one his presence in the team had been restricted only by injury and this, together with his international experience made him perfect captaincy material. Teichmann's number eight position was not so easily filled. The obvious candidates at the start of the season appeared to be Alix Popham and the versatile Joe Powell but it would be another Powell, Andrew, who would eventually make the position his own.

The search for another player who commanded a similar standing on the world stage as that held by Gary Teichmann once again led the club to South Africa. This time the target was scrum half Joost van der Westhuizen. Like Teichmann, van der Westhuizen was South African, a Springbok and, indeed, a Springbok captain. Excepting the fact that they represented different provinces, van der Westhuizen played for the Northern Bulls, the two players' rugby careers were not dissimilar, but there any similarity between them ended and if those at Newport ever thought otherwise they were in for a rude awakening. That van der Westhuizen signed a legally binding contract with Newport RFC is fact. That he never played for the club is also fact. Why the one didn't lead to the other is not quite so clear.

The South African Rugby Football Union has a selection policy which it rigidly adheres to, this being that any player not playing his rugby within South Africa will be excluded from selection for the national side. When van der Westhuizen signed for Newport in June 2001 he may well have felt that his international career was all but over and consequently he would not fall victim of SARFU's selection policy. His contract with SARFU was not due to expire until 31 December and the initial understanding of his deal with Newport seemed to allow him to return to South Africa if needed by his province for Currie Cup matches which, in turn, meant the door on further international rugby wouldn't be closed for good.

At this point in the proceedings the Northern Bulls' executive seemed to be happy, Newport were certainly happy and there hadn't been anything to suggest that SARFU saw a problem. Two months later, however, a rather different picture was beginning to appear. Now SARFU were stating that Newport had not followed the correct procedure and that the club had written a letter of apology to that effect. Newport had seemingly only held negotiations with the Northern Bulls through the player's agent and the contract van der Westhuizen had with his Union had been overlooked. There was talk of a further transfer fee being paid to SARFU; Newport had already paid one to the Bulls, and what had seemed a done deal back in June was now looking anything but. SARFU would later confirm that Newport had observed all the IRB requirements but if the player was required by the South African coach before 31 December, then he would be held to his contract. Van der Westhuizen played well in the following Tri-Nations matches, a fact that was instrumental in engineering a change of heart but, what is critical, was whether this change of heart was by SARFU or the player. Perhaps van der Westhuizen wasn't ready to step down from international rugby - not yet anyway.

What followed in the months after the contract was signed was an appalling indictment of the professional game. Newport set out on a marketing campaign that was heavily geared to van der Westhuizen. Promotional material and brochures all led with the slogan 'Joost the Ticket!' while the signing was obviously being built up by the media and press.

After completion of the necessary paperwork, payment of a transfer fee to the Northern Bulls and a press announcement from SARFU confirming the transfer, the management at Rodney Parade had good reason to believe they had got their man. Then the goalposts started to move. The final act in the affair took place in Cape Town on 30 August. At a meeting at SARFU headquarters Joost van der Westhuizen was seen to be given an ultimatum - play for South Africa or Newport - and in making his decision he told the rugby world a lot about himself. Purported to have been written by van der Westhuizen, an article in Newport's match programme for the opening league game of the season, read 'It's disappointing to have missed the early part of the Newport season, because I'm excited about playing in Wales, but as you're reading this, I'm only a week away from arriving in your rugby mad country'.

Newport still had a legally binding contract. It would not have any power over international matches but could, if enforced, prevent van der Westhuizen playing club or provincial rugby. In laying the matter to rest, Tony Brown said 'Joost has a contract with Newport which in a court of law would be enforceable. Nevertheless, it would not, in the club's view, be sensible to bring a player to Newport who would be unhappy there'. This was a level-headed comment and the matter came to, if not a satisfactory conclusion, a logical one. It did however, leave one wondering the true value of player contracts if they can be held in such obvious contempt. Maybe Newport should have sat on van der Westhuizen's for a while, watched developments from a distance, maybe called a few bluffs. Clubs and players must treat each other with the utmost respect and seeing the legal papers that work in both parties' interests so blatantly flaunted is not good for the game. Finally, aware that their campaign to sell season tickets had been heavily marketed around Joost van der Westhuizen, Newport offered to refund any supporter who had purchased a season ticket on the back of it. Only one person took up the offer!

With all the furore surrounding van der Westhuizen one could be forgiven in thinking that all was quiet on the recruitment front at Newport - not so. Swansea prop Chris Anthony had signed a two-year contract adding strength in depth to an experienced front row. With six more than competent players vying for selection this would not be an area that would cause any problems - other than who to leave out! Outside half Jason Strange and second row Mike Voyle were the other major signings. Strange had to come via the scenic route. Ebbw Vale not being prepared to release him to another Premier Division club he signed for Pontypool and quickly moved on to Rodney Parade. For Mike Voyle it was a case of déjà vu. Previously at Newport, his career had taken him to Llanelli and then on to Cardiff where he decided to call it a day and move with his family to New Zealand. Imagine his surprise when he received an SOS from his old club.

Off the field it was much the same with only one new face for the public to get to know. Ian MacIntosh joined the coaching team and during the course of the season television viewers would have ample opportunity to witness this South African's wildly expressed emotions.

So equipped then, did Newport RFC set out on the new season. A season that, like all before it, would be controversial, divisive and destructive, but that was what Welsh rugby was best at so there was no reason to believe that 2001-02 would be any different.

What was different was the introduction of a Celtic League. This comprised the nine Welsh and two Scottish teams in the Welsh Scottish League and the four Irish provinces, Connacht, Leinster, Munster and Ulster. The teams were divided into two pools of eight and seven, the teams playing each other once. The top four in each pool would then progress to a knock-out stage. Just in case this was seen as being too easy to follow, if two teams that were in the Welsh Scottish League met in the pool stages then the fixture would double up and count towards that league's final standings. The only thing Irish about this little conundrum was the fact that the Irish representatives were not involved in it!

The draw for the Heineken Cup had grouped Newport with Leinster, Newcastle and Toulouse. This was a tough group, probably the toughest the draw had thrown up, and it looked an odds-on certainty that only the group winners would be guaranteed to progress to the quarter-final stages of the tournament. As in previous seasons the group stages of this most prestigious of tournaments would be strongly criticised. The six groups of four format is a ludicrous system to have in place when the thing is crying out for four groups of six. The Heineken Cup is the best thing to have happened to club and provincial rugby in the Northern Hemisphere since the game became professional. The public want as much of it as they can get and enlarged groups would provide four more matches leading to more quality rugby and more revenue for the participating teams. And there would be no more best runners-up places, the top two in each group gaining automatic progress to the knock-out stages. There's no such thing as an entente cordiale when it comes to the game of rugby union in

Europe. The Heineken Cup is a gem of a competition so why aren't the administrators getting the best out of it? They should be locked in a room with bread and water and not let out until it's sorted.

Until such time as this unlikely change of heart takes place clubs like Newport, well all clubs involved really, must turn up at the draw each year and keep everything crossed in the hope that they end up with an Italian club in their group. This provides a distinct advantage when the best runners-up places are decided, providing two opportunities to score tries, lots of tries, which help determine the sought after seventh and eighth quarter-final places.

To have any real hope of progressing beyond the group stages of the Heineken Cup clubs have to get at least one victory away from home. This had been Newport's downfall in the previous season and so it was with great determination and a horde of supporters that the club travelled to the north-east to open their campaign against the current English cup holders, Newcastle Falcons. Such was the interest in this match that the clubhouse at Rodney Parade was packed to the rafters and with several television screens showing every move, the atmosphere was electric. Newcastle's main threat was always going to be represented by the boot of Jonny Wilkinson and he didn't let them down. Seven times Newport infringed within kicking distance and seven times Wilkinson punished them. But it was not enough for the home side. Newport showed that they had learnt from the previous season's experiences on the road in Europe and their response was quite magnificent. Jon Pritchard, Matt Mostyn and Peter Buxton scored tries and Shane Howarth converted two and added five penalty kicks to complete a 34-21 victory.

While the team that took the field at Kingston Park had a very familiar look about it, even Mike Voyle looking like he'd never been away, at eight and nine there were two new faces who were both starting to make an impact in the black and amber jersey. After the disappointment brought about by the van der Westhuizen affair, Newport had to look for an alternative and with most players already under contract with a club or having signed new contracts during the close season, options were limited. The previous season had seen two players sharing the scrum half duties and with Darren Edwards leaving the club during the summer the sequence of events resulted in Dale Burn as the club's only experienced player in the pivotal position. He wasn't found wanting in the early matches and supporters were beginning to wonder if further recruitment was indeed necessary. However, even with a promising Under 21 player at the club, it was still felt that another experienced player was essential to Newport's ambitions.

Ofisa Tonu'u had fallen out with London Irish and his future at the club appeared to be over. Newport acted quickly and within a very short time, they had his signature on the dotted line. Keith Grainger met Tonu'u at a hotel at Heathrow Airport when the team were en route for a Celtic League fixture at Munster, and the deal was completed with the player's agent at a hotel in Cork later in the day. The announcement had season ticket holders diving for their old copies of Rothmans' Rugby Yearbook and among its pages were some very interesting facts. Ofisa Tonu'u was an All Black no less. He'd represented New Zealand on eight occasions and, in addition, he'd played for Manu Samoa six times. Add to this spells with Super 12 outfits Wellington Hurricanes and Auckland Blues and it became clear that this was no novice that the club had signed. What about this problem with the not so Irish, London Irish? (not so London, London Irish come to that). This appeared to be more a clash of personalities than anything else and so the deal was done. Newport's second All Black had signed a one-year contract and it only took him a couple of matches to convince all concerned that he was the answer to the problem. Never mind 'Joost the Ticket!' now it was 'Joost who?'

When any club suffers the loss of a world class player who has decided to call it a day the problem of finding a suitable replacement is not easily solved, the player would have dominated in his position, thereby making it difficult to develop a ready-made replacement. This was the situation that faced Newport after the departure of Gary Teichmann. The feeling in the back room was that the likely successor would be youth product Alix Popham who had bided his time through the previous season, grabbing the few opportunities that came his way at number eight and putting in several appearances at wing forward. And, sure enough, the start of the new season saw the heir apparent take over in the middle of the back row. Popham was barely into his stride, having just played the opening two fixtures, when injury struck. Little would he, or anybody else, think that his season at Newport was all but over. Popham only started one more game but as is always the case, one man's misfortune was another's good luck.

Andrew Powell was another player who had come through the junior sides at the club. Coach Allan Lewis decided it would be in the player's interest if he were to get some regular rugby in a lower division rather than spend his time keeping the replacements bench warm. Powell originated from Brecon and had been a pupil at Llandovery College. It seemed a sensible solution to put him on a dual registration with Llandovery, a First Division club, where he could continue playing on a regular basis.

Popham's injury brought Powell back to Rodney Parade sooner than expected and saw him flung in at the deep end, at number eight in the third match of the season with Edinburgh the visitors. During the season Andrew Powell made the position his own and his performances would see him fast-tracked into the Wales A squad and eventual representative honours at that level. Powell had been particularly prominent in the win at Newcastle and he was an automatic selection the following week which saw Newport play host to Toulouse in their second Heineken Cup group match.

Toulouse. This was another step up for the Black and Ambers. The French club had won the inaugural tournament in 1996, beating Cardiff 21-18 in the final, a match that went to extra time. Now they were at Rodney Parade with a team full of experienced and up and coming French stars that would fully test the home side's character. Captain Fabien Pelous, Frank Tournaire, David Aucagne, Nicholas Jeanjean and the exotically named Xavier Garbajosa were in the visitors' line-up together with ex All Black Isitole Maka at number eight, a selection that would not have gone unnoticed by his opposite number.

The match attracted a crowd of over 9,000 and they were not

disappointed. French flair was on view in abundance and a French side that has travelled well, and is in the right frame of mind is the most dangerous animal on a rugby field be it at club or international level. There is a theory that in their own domestic championship French clubs are not expected to win away from home. This may well be the case but in European competition such idiosyncrasies have to be put to one side and Toulouse certainly weren't at Rodney Parade just to make up the numbers. Although trailing 8-7 at the interval events took a dramatic turnaround and the score stood at 20-11 to the visitors with the clock ticking down quicker than any side trailing on the scoreboard likes to see. But Newport were not going to be denied in front of their own supporters and Shane Howarth completed the scoring with a penalty and a try which he duly converted to record the clubs second success in the competition by the slenderest of margins, 21-20.

Next up were Leinster, the Irish province would be played on consecutive weekends, first in Dublin and then Newport. Unfortunately these matches were three weeks away thereby breaking any continuity that teams were putting together. European Cup rugby is a big step up from the regular week-in week-out league matches that clubs are used to in Wales and the participating clubs have to adjust to the more intense competition that the tournament brings with it. To have it taken away for a few weeks just when things are hotting up would not seem to be a sensible option but that is exactly what happened, and after the next two matches had been played there would be an even longer break - two months - before the final pair of matches in the group stage of the tournament would take place.

Donnybrook, home of Leinster rugby was, like Thomond Park in Limerick, a fortress. A stronghold that visiting sides were rarely able to penetrate and seldom would a visiting team come away from with any success. Newport would not prove the exception to the rule, losing by 21-6. Two Shane Howarth penalties were their only reward for eighty minutes of intense cup rugby. Leinster, meanwhile, would maintain their one hundred per cent record in the tournament scoring two valuable tries in the process. They were a side that had a lot of nous, they were streetwise and knew how to win a game of rugby. This would never be better illustrated than in the return fixture at Rodney Parade seven days later.

Another big crowd, another night of intense drama and another night of massive disappointment. A crowd of 10,809 turned out to watch the fourth match in Newport's European campaign. What would be the biggest gate of the season willed their side on in a match that had to be won if Newport were to stand any real chance of going through to the last eight in the tournament. And as the game reached the last quarter the home side were firmly in the driving seat. They may have only been enjoying the comfort of a one point lead but Leinster were on the back foot and the game was Newport's for the taking. And then the lights went out. Rodney Parade wasn't plunged into darkness, far from it, but a fuse had blown and one of the flood-light stanchions in a corner of the ground was affected by the reduced lighting. Yes, there was a reduction in the light coverage in one area of the ground, but matches are played in far worse light and after some fifteen minutes' deliberation, this one was allowed to continue.

The failure was put down to overloading. The hospitality boxes were fed power from the mains and with all the boxes occupied the system was eventually found wanting, unable to cope with the extra demand put on it. At first it appeared that the teams were happy to carry on but Leinster coach, Australian Matt Williams, had other ideas. He was quickly out of his seat in the stand and appeared pitch side, from where, after discussions with the match officials, he instructed his team to leave the field. He wasn't happy with the light and insisted the match be stopped. In reality he wasn't happy with the way things were going on the field, the pressure his side was under and the looming prospect of defeat. That may seem rather cynical but the fact remains that after the break in proceedings the match was allowed to continue even though the lighting hadn't been repaired. A few minutes after the restart the lights were fully operational again, but whereas Leinster had come back onto the field Newport had stayed in the changing room, or that's the way it looked, the home side just didn't get back into the game after the enforced break and the match was lost 26-21.

This result in particular saw the first signs that there was 'trouble at mill' looming on the horizon. The South Wales Argus published letters from supporters who were obviously not happy with the way the team was performing. 'Leinster showed more stomach for a tight game than Newport's star studded mercenaries.... It's time to remove the black and amber tinted monocle and realise that Newport are a barely average team who bottle it on the important occasions.' And, 'After the latest defeat at Rodney Parade things must change dramatically. Our leadership and team are just not good enough.... There are glaring deficiencies which only the Newport management seem not to see.... Allan Lewis must be removed.... Shane Howarth must be either moved back to full back or replaced.... Matt Pini, although a good player, doesn't add an extra edge to the back line.... Jason Jones-Hughes. We should cut our losses and release him.' Oh dear, was the bubble really about to burst?

There was always a possibility that results would go in Newport's favour when the tournament resumed in the new year but this was clutching at straws. Newport would have to win in Toulouse, Leinster would have to slip up twice and, even allowing for these improbabilities, Newport would almost certainly be left having to score a hatful of tries when Newcastle visited Rodney Parade for the last of the group matches. It wasn't likely to happen and it didn't. A creditable performance in France failed to prevent a 36-23 defeat and, though Newcastle were comfortably beaten 53-17, the club's European adventure was over for another season. The final record shows three matches won and three lost, an improvement on the previous effort, but was the current squad ever going to take the club further in its search for glory in European competition? While the Heineken Cup was undoubtedly the biggest prize to be had there were still domestic competitions that demanded attention. After all, qualification for Europe was decided by league placings and there was no room for complacency.

The inaugural Celtic League had been completed before the end of the year. This was seen by the three unions involved as a stepping stone to a competition that would eventually be run along the same lines as the Super 12s in the Southern Hemisphere. Newport were in Pool B and, by winning three of their six matches, had progressed to the quarter-final stages where they would meet - Leinster - the match to be played in Dublin. In a matter of five weeks the two teams had met on three occasions, and Leinster duly completed a hat-trick of victories. The new tournament created a surprising amount of interest, particularly in the latter stages, and the fact that the four semi-finalists were provincial sides, Connacht, Leinster, Munster and Glasgow, certainly gave weight to the argument that this was the way forward for Welsh rugby.

There was a growing feeling among many observers of the club game in Wales that winning the Heineken Cup was beyond the reach of any Welsh club. Cardiff had appeared in the first final and Llanelli had recently looked the club most likely to mount a serious challenge but elsewhere performances had been disappointing. There was no denying the fact that the Irish provinces had fared well in the tournament but the Scottish regional sides had met with less success than the Welsh clubs. This, and the fact that provincial rugby had long been established in Ireland, was conveniently overlooked by those wishing to see a similar format introduced in Wales: four regional sides representing the country in European competition.

Welsh rugby is based on a club ethos. It always has been and it always will be. Any form of regional rugby introduced in the hope of capturing the biggest prize in Europe would completely undermine all the efforts made by the individuals who have kept club rugby in Wales afloat for the past seven years. This is the dream Leighton Samuel has for Bridgend, Peter Thomas has for Cardiff and Tony Brown has for Newport and with Llanelli, Neath, Pontypridd and Swansea all holding similar aspirations the prospect of regional clubs being introduced would appear to be extremely remote.

Another cup, this time the domestic Principality Cup, saw Newport enter in the seventh round drawn away to First Division club

Bonymaen. The first tie in the round had taken place at Pontypool Park on Friday night and all the good that Pontypool had done for rugby in the lower division was rapidly undone on Saturday afternoon by a side that had no intention of playing the game. Pontypool had beaten Swansea in a match that suggested the gap between the two divisions was not that great. At a time when elitism was threatening the very core of league rugby in Wales, this was a timely reminder to all concerned that perhaps there was an alternative. But Bonymaen were out of their depth, knew it, and did everything they could to camouflage the fact. They defended their approach to the game and their opinion had to be respected, but what could not be respected was an incident that overshadowed the rugby.

Newport scrum half Ofisa Tonu'u was the victim of racial abuse from a Bonymaen player during the course of the first half of the match. It was as simple as that. Racial abuse is a totally unacceptable face of society today, but it is something that is proving difficult to drive away. Most people are not confronted by this offensive behaviour in the course of their everyday lives and therefore cannot begin to understand the hurt that it inflicts on those who are. Reports suggest that Tonu'u was distraught in the changing room during the half-time interval, understandably so, and after the match the matter was brought to the attention of the Bonymaen officials and left in their hands to be sorted 'in house'. Both Tonu'u and Newport received written apologies from the player who had been identified by his club and given a two match ban, but matters didn't rest there. Tonu'u was not satisfied with the way the issue had been handled and the South Wales Argus mounted a campaign to ensure that the culprit received more suitable punishment and in doing so named the player, who had until then been given the comfort of anonymity. Some felt that the matter should be laid to rest, the Argus having beaten the drum over a period of days on both front and back pages, and after being referred to the WRU, it eventually was. There isn't any lesson to be learnt from this because racial abuse will inevitably continue to feature in a game as multi-cultured as rugby union. It's just sad that the two have to meet, that thirty players aren't able to show each other the respect that such a physical contest demands without some idiot opening his big mouth. The South Wales Argus named him, these pages will not - he isn't worth it.

'And Cardiff will play - Newport'. Away to Cardiff, a draw to whet the appetite but not a draw that Newport would get excited about. Cardiff at the Arms Park were nigh on invincible, three defeats in the last seventy three matches was a record that would stand comparison with anything in the game. On their last three visits Newport had come away empty handed - could have won, should have won - but at the end of the day Newport hadn't won and it was becoming a bit of a problem to one player in particular. Shane Howarth had taken the brunt of the criticism, largely as a result of some poor place kicking, the three matches had been closely contested and a few more points from the boot - well, no matter, this time it was going to be different.

Lose a game, no need to look for excuses, blame the referee. Easy, that's what he's there for surely? On a balmy Friday night at the end of March, referee David Davies produced one of those performances that will be talked about whenever these two famous old clubs meet. Mr Davies had first endeared himself to Newport supporters way back in 1993. The seventh round of the then Schweppes Challenge Cup had seen Newport drawn away to Bridgend. After falling behind in the early stages of the match the visitors had played themselves back into the game and were protecting a one point lead, 16-15, well into injury time. Then, in the game's final moments, at a scrum in front of their posts wing forward Chris Scott was penalised for not binding properly and Newport were out of the cup.

Now nine years later in Cardiff, while there was nothing to suggest any bias on behalf of the official, throughout the match the two factions of supporters on the terraces had equal opportunity to question Mr Davies' ancestry and they took them with a vengeance. Neither side could claim any advantage from the referee's decisions on the night; he was nothing if not consistent - consistently bad! Cardiff once again took the spoils and made it four consecutive wins and while all four matches had been closely contested, for the time being at least, Cardiff were holding the upper hand.

Therefore, by the end of March, Newport's dreams of retaining the Principality Cup had disappeared along with any aspirations of success in Europe. Add to this the defeat in the quarter final of the Celtic League and all that now remained of Newport's season was the Welsh Scottish League. Being crowned league champions was something the club had previously failed to achieve and it now had the chance to make up for the disappointments experienced in the other competitions.

By mid-April Newport had become favourites to take the title. The league standings showed the club to be heading the table one point clear of nearest rivals Llanelli and with a game in hand. Third placed Neath were a further three points behind having played the same number of games as the Scarlets and Cardiff were a further two points behind in fourth spot, but with two games in hand. Newport had an added advantage that may be brought into play in the event of clubs ending up on the same number of points, they had a considerably better try count than any of their rivals.

Despite failing in other competitions Newport had played well in the league and had lost only two of the first fourteen matches. Cardiff and Llanelli had both won their home matches and together with Edinburgh, where Newport were held to a draw, were the only blemishes on the league season to date. The highlights had been two away victories, at Pontypridd and Ebbw Vale. On a cold night at Sardis Road, the scene of so many humiliations, Newport inflicted on Pontypridd the club's most comprehensive home defeat in ten years and the Ponty supporters were more than generous with their appreciation of a Newport performance that few teams would have coped with on the night. 33-6 was the final score and Newport were looking good, very good. A wet, miserable night in March took Newport up the valley to Ebbw Vale. In atrocious conditions both sides produced a remarkable standard of play in a match that would be remembered for the off-the-field events more than those that took place on it. Newport won 32-22 and it was on the back of this victory that the club entered the final stages of the season in pole position.

At 7.30 pm on Wednesday 17 April, Newport were leading the table with 34 points and six remaining matches, four of them at home. At 7.30 pm on Saturday 20 April they were in third position, still with 34 points, Llanelli and Neath had both won two matches and were on 39 and 36 points respectively and Cardiff had closed the gap to three points, still had a game in hand and would be next up at Rodney Parade in seven days time. It was these three matches that turned Newport's bid for the title on its head. Neath, Swansea and Cardiff - home, away, home - all three were lost.

When scrum half Dale Burn broke his ankle in a friendly against Peebles on the eve of the Wales/Scotland international, Newport promptly recalled Llyr Lane who had been on loan to Ebbw Vale and the Under 21 player would have a big part to play in the run down to the end of the season. Ofisa Tonu'u picked up a leg injury against Neath and it was Lane who would have to see out the last five match-es in the most crucial of positions. Andy Marinos, at Swansea, and Jon Pritchard against Cardiff both had their seasons cut short by injury and all of a sudden there was a problem. Not only had Newport lost three important matches, but three players who had been prominent throughout the campaign were now side-lined. All that aside, it was the manner of the defeats that would give Ian MacIntosh most cause for concern.

Neath had played well, no complaints there, but Newport had failed to capitalise on a period of intense pressure early in the second half when a try could have changed the course of the match. At Swansea, against a side that had rarely performed in the season, they just folded. The bad old days were back - not quite as bad as a few years earlier, but bad by recent standards. The final result was 52-13 and pretty it certainly wasn't. MacIntosh may well have got his start-ing line-up wrong for this crucial game. With six quality front row for-wards at his disposal selection had never been easy but by this late stage of the season Rod Snow, James Richards and Adrian Garvey were probably first choice. Ceri Jones, Paul Young and Chris Anthony have never taken a backward step between them but the Swansea trio of Ben Evans, Garin Jenkins and Darren Morris each had a point to prove and they took the ascendancy immediately. It was on this foundation that Swansea set up their victory and by the time the Newport front row were replaced en bloc early in the second half, the match was way out of reach. With such a convincing defeat it seems unfair to suggest where the fault lay but all forwards will tell you that it is up front that games are won and lost and that certainly seemed to be true at St Helens.

Of particular concern to the marketing team at Rodney Parade would have been the early departure of supporters at both of these matches. Hundreds were seen heading for the gates with ten minutes left to play against Neath and the scene was repeated at Swansea. And Cardiff? Leading 14-0 going into the last quarter Newport lost 17-14, and a problem had become a crisis.

Crisis, what crisis? If A beats D and C beats B then A loses to C and D to B, if Newport beat E, F and G, score lots of tries and don't get David Davies they're home and dry, no problem. Well, it was something like that anyway.

In reality, come Friday 3 May, with nine days of the domestic season remaining, there were four clubs in with a chance of the league title - Cardiff, Llanelli, Neath and Newport. These clubs would feature in a total of ten matches and then, and only then, would the league positions be finalised. Neath had two matches to play while Cardiff, Llanelli and Newport all had three, and Newport, to be in with any hope of taking the title couldn't afford to slip up. Three wins, nothing less, and even then their fate would be in the hands of others.

Going into these last matches, Neath and Llanelli were on top with 39 points apiece, Neath having the advantage with a better try count. Cardiff were two points behind, with Newport a further three points adrift but comfortably boasting the best try count of the four clubs. If they were to tie for first place this would probably see them crowned champions.

Over the last weekend of April, Llanelli and Pontypridd had both played in the semi-finals of the two European competitions, Llanelli losing dramatically to Leicester in the Heineken Cup, a Tim

Stimpson late penalty deciding the match, while Pontypridd had won a thriller against London Irish to secure a place in the final of the Parker Pen Shield. Both Welsh clubs had very congested ends to their seasons having also progressed to the Principality Cup final and so the importance of each match had to be looked at carefully when team selection was made. With this in mind Pontypridd took an under strength side to the Gnoll where they were comfortably beaten by an ever improving Neath side. Meanwhile, Llanelli and Newport had travelled north of the border where results had always proved difficult to come by. Edinburgh made light of the Scarlets and ran out winners 40-8, a result that went in Newport's favour, but only if they could beat Glasgow.

The selected fifteen contained some surprises, Ian Gough was drafted into the back row, Matt Mostyn appeared at centre and on the right wing was Andrew Powell. Llyr Lane continued at scrum half and it would be left to him to score the match winning try in the fourth minute of injury time. Trailing 26-23 Newport were piling on the pressure and were awarded a penalty. Simon Raiwalui declined to kick for goal, preferring to go for a winning score. It came courtesy of Lane and Newport had pulled the match out of the fire winning 28-26. The next day saw Swansea continue their revival with a home victory over Cardiff and things were starting to look a little bit different. Neath were now in the driving seat with 42 points and Newport had leap-frogged Cardiff to go into third spot.

The matches played on the following Tuesday would see one of the contenders fall by the wayside. Llanelli won comfortably at Caerphilly and Cardiff, after some early scares, accounted for Bridgend but all eyes were on St Helens where Neath had a chance to virtually secure the title. The Welsh All Blacks not only had the weight of the Swansea support against them but also that of Cardiff, Llanelli and Newport, these three clubs' aspirations to the title pretty much dependent on a Swansea victory. It was all too much for Neath. They lost a titanic encounter 18-15 and saw their championship hopes bite the dust. Now it was a three horse race.

Newport entertained Pontypridd the following night and made

171

hard work of beating another under-strength selection. The side was falling apart behind the scrum and were only held together by all the experience and knowhow that Shane Howarth had garnered in his long career. The 34-23 final score flattered the home side, but it was a win and they were still in the hunt. Nobody was seen leaving early that night!

Now there were only two matches that would have any bearing on the final outcome. Cardiff and Llanelli at the Arms Park on Friday night and Newport against Bridgend at Rodney Parade the following day, and this only if Cardiff could win or draw. A Llanelli victory would secure the title. Television dictated the kick-off times, both matches being shown live, and never have so many Black and Amber supporters rooted for the Blue and Blacks. The Newport colours were prominent on the terraces in Cardiff, the club house at Rodney Parade was packed and thousands were glued to their television sets at home

The game was possibly the best the league produced in 2001-02 but this would be of no consolation to Newport. Cardiff surrendered a 25-8 advantage, Llanelli clawing themselves back into the game and it was 25-all approaching the final whistle. This could still work out all right, beat Bridgend and try count would see Newport win the title.

The tackle was pretty innocuous really. The referee didn't seem too concerned but his linesman had seen it differently. Iestyn Harris was penalised for a high tackle some forty yards out from the goal line and fifteen metres in from the left hand touchline; and up stepped Stephen Jones. In a perfect world he would have missed. In a perfect world he would have fallen over, sliced it, screwed it, topped it or any-thing that would have kept the ball away from the target, but he didn't. Stephen Jones is a fine kicker of a rugby ball, a skill he doesn't lose when under pressure. The contact was good, you always knew it would be, and the ball sailed high and true and with it went Newport's last hope of the title.

It was a huge anti-climax at Rodney Parade for the last match of the last Welsh-Scottish League season. Howarth kept control while all around him resembled something akin to the Keystone Cops. Allan Lewis would have loved his new charges to rub salt in Newport's wide open wounds but the home side hung on and picked up the three points that saw them end the season as runners-up.

But should Stephen Jones be held responsible for Newport's failure? Or could Cardiff be blamed for surrendering a 17 point lead at the ground where they had been all but invincible for over four years? No. To find the reason that Newport had failed was going to take a lot of soul searching, a lot of looking in the mirror and, most importantly, a lot of honesty.

The Architects

'A coach who suppresses natural instincts may find that he has lifted a poor player to a mediocre one but has reduced a potential genius to the rank and file.'

Sir Donald Bradman

In 1967 the WRU appointed David Nash as the first National Coach and at Rodney Parade former player Brian Jones together with Ian McJennett were appointed in similar roles at Newport RFC. The next thirty years saw a succession of coaches at the club, many of whom were ex-players. Adrian Hearn, Sid Jeffries, Roy Duggan, Charlie Faulkner, Roger Powell and John Ryan all took on the role, some more successfully than others but, as with all other aspects of the game, the position was unpaid: honorary.

By 1995 coaching had long been accepted as an essential among the composite factors that made up a rugby club and for anybody, ex-player or otherwise, there was a career beckoning for those with the unique gifts that the role demands. However, there would now be added pressures to go with the job. In the event of a team not reaching the level of success expected of it there would be somebody else to take the blame. Coaches would be hired and fired on a whim, the real problems swept under the carpet in the hope that a new face would sort them out. Once again the experiences of association football would show what lay ahead for those aspiring to be coaches at the big clubs and, even the not so big ones. The WRU repeatedly appointed and fired coaches of the National side until such time arrived that the only way serious contenders could be encouraged to take over the 'poisoned chalice' was by offering outrageous salaries to go with the job.

Two ex-players, Steve Jones and Paul Evans, were in charge of coaching at Newport in August 1995. Come the following season Evans had departed leaving Jones to carry on alone until the arrival of Steve Fenwick in 1997-98. This partnership didn't last the course either and at the start of the 1998-99 season Fenwick had left and a new position, Director of Rugby, was filled by Allan Lewis with Steve Jones continuing in a supporting role.

In January 2002 Allan Lewis became the first major casualty in Newport RFC's push to become one of the top clubs in Europe. In January 2002 there was still a long way to go but the first hurdles had been negotiated and things were slowly coming together. That's what Allan Lewis thought anyway. Events suggest that elsewhere within the club there were those who thought differently.

In three full seasons in charge of coaching at Rodney Parade, Lewis's record doesn't make bad reading. The first season was poor due to circumstances beyond his control, he had Premier Division rugby dropped on him at the eleventh hour and the season never got off the ground. Then the club were runners-up in the Welsh-Scottish League and the following year the cup was won. Not that bad; in fact many clubs would call it a period of great success. Indeed they did at Newport which makes subsequent events all the more strange.

The general opinion of what happened in 2001-02 was put down to the arrival at the club of Ian McIntosh. Contrary to this perception, Allan Lewis saw no problem and was quite happy to let McIntosh get on with the coaching while he developed his role as Director of Rugby. Lewis saw this as integral to the long-term success of the club and set about putting in place a structure that would ensure all matters pertaining to the on-field activities were addressed. Having already been instrumental in the appointment of Team Manager, Jim McCreedy, Fitness Advisor, Trystan Bevan, and Physiotherapist, Mike Delahay, the sort of structure he had in mind was starting to take shape and Lewis welcomed the opportunity to take this further.

Another to benefit from Lewis's all-encompassing vision of the future at Rodney Parade was Head Groundsman, Mark Jones. It had long been recognised that, in addition to preparing the best playing surface in Welsh rugby - a fact only once acknowledged by the media, and then in Welsh by the effervescent Ray Gravell - Jones was also highly thought of by the players. Lewis expanded his role to take in the responsibility of ensuring that the kit and other necessary matchday requirements were catered for and Jones responded by becoming an indispensable fringe member of the team on match days.

All this adds credence to the emphasis Lewis places on the difference between having a winning team and having a successful club; the difference being that a winning team is very much a short-term solution to a long-term programme, while a successful club will take the rough with the smooth and last the course longer. Patience is not seen as one of the virtues of those involved with the day to day running of most Welsh clubs and short-term success is obviously top of the agenda. But any team takes time to develop and short-term success may be limited while the foundations are being put into place which will form the basis for more long-term stability. This was Lewis's argument and he saw in his newly-defined role the opportunity to work towards this end.

Allan Lewis had a good coaching pedigree behind him when he arrived at Newport. After gaining the necessary WRU coaching qualifications while teaching in West Wales Allan Lewis's coaching career had started in earnest in 1982 when he and Gareth Jenkins took over at Llanelli. Both were ex-players at the club but whereas Jenkins had gone on to gain representative honours playing for Wales B, Lewis's playing career had been cut short when he suffered a particularly bad ankle break in a club match against Swansea in 1970. During his twelve year period as club coach at Llanelli the club won the Welsh Cup on four occasions and achieved the league and cup double in 1992-93.

Lewis had also gained valuable experience within the international arena. Firstly he'd coached Wales at Under 19 and Under 21 level, all fourteen matches played during his tenure were won including a 103-3 win over British Columbia, the first occasion on which a Welsh representative side at any level had scored more than a hundred points. He was assistant coach to Kevin Bowring during his period in charge of the Welsh team and more recently Lewis was a member of Graham Henry's administration where he filled the role of backs selector in the build-up to the 1999 RWC.

Immediately prior to joining Newport, Allan Lewis had been Director of Rugby at Moseley who were playing in Division Two of the Allied Dunbar League. Another club to fall victim of the financial demands of professional rugby, Moseley went into administration and this freed Lewis from his contract enabling him to make the move to Rodney Parade. One thing that stood out on his CV was that all the teams that he had been associated with had played attacking rugby and it was hoped that Newport would benefit from this approach.

When Allan Lewis met Tony Brown in January 2002 he had no idea what was about to happen to him. He was devastated. 'There's no other way to describe it; total devastation. I just could not believe it when I was told that my contract would not be renewed. This from a man who I thought the world of. I would never hear a bad word said about Tony Brown and I really felt that we had cemented a friendship that would last long after one or both of us finished at Newport. Why it all went wrong I honestly can't say. I still don't know if it was something I said or did, but there was a lot of backstabbing going on at the club and nothing would surprise me. I felt betrayed. I know I'll never trust anybody in business again.' These are not words coming from a bitter man, rather a man who feels very let down, a disappointed man who took some time to get his life back on track.

Ian McIntosh had visited Newport for a week in the 2000-01 season and had some input at Newport's training sessions. Prior to this visit Newport had lost four big games, two in the league and two in Europe and when they beat Pontypridd 33-13 at Rodney Parade the South African's input was credited with the improvement. These things happen all the time. A season in any sport resembles a roller coaster ride but a team doesn't automatically become either good or bad overnight on the basis of one result and all concerned at the club got rather carried away by that good performance. Mac returned to South Africa and Newport's season eventually came to its conclusion in winning the Principality Cup.

Was there a suggestion of player power? This seems possible when you look at the approach the team took onto the field subsequent to the South African's visit. The performance in the semi-final of the cup bore no resemblance to the original game plan with Teichmann preferring the 'stick it up your jumper' approach to the expansive game Lewis had prepared his team for. Perhaps it wasn't his team any more? The player-coach relationship is one that demands mutual respect and once this is in doubt then it becomes a problem. Ability doesn't always come into the equation; how many times has it been suggested that players aren't playing for the coach? Ridiculous as it seems this is quite possible - ask Graham Henry, John Plumtree, Lynn Howells and Bob Dwyer. All good coaches who experienced problems with their players, some of who made no secret of the fact. It may have taken twelve months from Mac's visit in January 2001 to Lewis's departure in January 2002, but the smart money was on that visit in 2001 kick-starting the end for Allan Lewis.

Nobody had ever suggested that Allan Lewis was the best coach in Welsh rugby, least of all the man himself. Sadly, there were many supporters at Rodney Parade who thought quite the opposite and were glad to see him leave, having quickly forgotten the Principality Cup win seven months earlier, but unfortunately that is something that now goes with the territory. Comparisons between coaches are almost impossible to make; squads are forever changing, the opposition likewise, with the clubs played also varying season to season. Having measured Lewis's last full season in charge by the results achieved in twelve of the biggest matches let us now take the same measurement on a year.

The 2000-01 season saw Newport win four of the twelve matches that would probably have been targeted as the most important. Using the same criteria for the following season under Mac little difference is seen. Of the six matches played in the group stages of the Heineken Cup there was an improvement with three won compared to two in the previous season. Staying with Cardiff, Llanelli and Swansea as the clubs most likely to be challenging for honours and the results are the same: Cardiff achieving the double and home advantage being the deciding factor against Llanelli and Swansea. For the coming season add Pontypridd, Neath and Lewis's Bridgend as clubs likely to be challenging for the silverware and the new coaching team at Rodney Parade are going to find it harder than either of their predecessors did.

In the last two seasons Newport had won a cup under Allan Lewis and been runners-up in the league under Ian McIntosh; the first left the club amid some controversy while the second was sent home a hero - what did he make of it all?

To sit face to face across a desk with Ian McIntosh is a sobering experience. Sobering because you quickly realise that when it comes to talking about the game of rugby, the actual playing of the game of rugby, you are out of your depth. The man has been around a long time, he's the top side of sixty and has acquired a lot of knowledge in that time. He doesn't throw this in your face, he's much too modest and polite, but get him on to a subject that he feels strongly about and the eyes light up, the accent gets stronger and the speed of speech quickens. To say Ian McIntosh is passionate about the game of rugby doesn't begin to describe his feeling for it. His family comes first in life followed by rugby and that's it. Maybe some golf but rugby, as he once said, 'is my drug'. He lives, breathes, eats and drinks the game but at the time of our meeting, Monday 27 May 2002, he was about to walk away from it; the sharp end of it anyway.

Ian McIntosh had walked away from the sharp end of rugby once before. He had chosen to end his coaching career after the Currie Cup final at the ABSA Stadium in 1999, little thinking that his services would once again be called upon and certainly never dreaming where that call would take him.

It had all started in Rhodesia in 1971. The young Ian McIntosh, like Allan Lewis, had suffered an injury that prematurely ended his playing days so he decided to compensate for this disappointment by pursuing a career in coaching. He had shown some revolutionary thinking during five years as a club coach and then, in 1971, he was offered the position as coach of the Rhodesian national team. Over six years he transformed the way the game was played in Rhodesia and it was during this time that he first encountered the club where he would end his career in rugby.

Mac's great interpretation, his vision of rugby, is first and foremost as an entertainment. He had observed two of South Africa's leading provinces play the game with vastly contrasting styles, the forward game of Transvaal and the more expansive game of Natal. Why shouldn't the two meet? When Cardiff toured Rhodesia in 1972, Mac saw put into practice the ideas that had been forming in his mind. During the next few years he changed the style of rugby played by the national side by adopting a much more flowing approach to the game and in 1973 he coached Rhodesia to a 37-7 victory over another side from Wales. This time the visitors showed little enterprise behind the scrum and the new methods taken on board by the hosts secured the comfortable win - the visiting Welsh club was Newport. Mac's first experience of the Black and Ambers was less than impressive and it would be many years before the paths of man and club would cross again.

Mac stepped down from his coaching position with the national side in 1977. There followed a few years where he sought a lower profile in the game and then in 1984 came the opportunity to move to Natal and take over as the province's coaching organiser. Two years later this led to the position of senior coach and over the next thirteen years he would take Natal to the very pinnacle of the game in South Africa. This period was broken in 1993 and 1994 when Ian McIntosh took on the highest coaching job in the country. After running the Springboks B side he was offered the opportunity that he had hoped would one day come his way; Mac was going to coach the 'Boks.

Politics within South African rugby appear to be as prominent as anywhere else and after two years in charge, a period that ended with a disappointing tour in New Zealand, the axe fell. There were many casualties. With the RWC due to take place in the country in twelve months' time rugby supremo Louis Luyt wanted change, and quick; nothing gentle in this man's approach. Mac received no credit for his contribution to what became a side that would win the World Cup. The appointment of François Pienaar had been made by McIntosh, players who would figure in the cup-winning squad had been introduced into the side by McIntosh but by the time Nelson Mandela presented Pienaar with the trophy he had become a forgotten man, all this was before the game turned professional. Seven years later would see a similar scenario played out, but this time Mac's role would be reversed.

Ian McIntosh returned to Natal and guided them to more success as the decade drew to a close. The province once again progressed to the final of the Currie Cup but his last match in charge failed to produce the fairy-tale ending.

So what was he doing sitting in an office at Newport RFC humouring somebody who was writing a book on the club's fortunes in the professional era? 'The club invited me to help with some training sessions in early 2001. A new voice and new ideas are sometimes worth listening to and I hoped my input would help. The team had lost a few important games and it was great to see them get the season back on the rails with a win over Pontypridd.' Thoughts of any further involvement with Newport were far from his mind when Ian McIntosh returned to Durban. Anyway, how can any sane person live in the climate South Wales has to offer?

When the chance came to join Allan Lewis and coach Newport in the coming season Mac had to think this one through long and hard. This was a club that had big plans and would be looking to achieve some major success in the season. There would be a lot of pressure, pressure that he thought was gone from his life. Did he need it ? Then there was the family, his wife, their three sons and their families - the grandchildren. What would his wife think about spending the best part of a year in the UK. Well, he came, and what had been viewed as a job shared became his own when Lewis departed in the new year.

Over the season Newport would regularly be featured in televised matches. There were plenty of them and this gave viewers opportunity to watch McIntosh closely as he went through the whole range of emotions, and this during eighty minutes' rugby. The cameras would zoom in on the face as the eyes stared at the on-field events. It would be the eyes that Mac would be remembered for by followers of the game, and not only in Newport; the eyes and the beanie hat. Here was an intensity that had rarely, if ever, been seen from a coach. Ian McIntosh certainly wore his heart on his sleeve when he watched his charges excel and disappoint.

Such emotions were not far from the surface in this normally radical man's makeup, and they weren't confined to the rugby ground. Sit across a desk from him and mention referees or Ebbw Vale. The eyes widen, the finger might start waving a bit and the room temperature starts to rise. These are not favourite topics but he has opinions that cannot be ignored and you can't help thinking that somebody somewhere should listen to them, but you know deep down that they won't, certainly not in Wales. 'I wouldn't go into a man's house and tell him how to organise it and I won't do that with rugby in Wales. But Ebbw Vale, that was staggering. You don't turn somebody away because that person sees things different to you. What sort of an attitude is that? Professional? No, it's not professional. It's as far from being professional as you can possibly get.'

And what about the referees? This is the big one, the eyes are larger than ever but at least Jean Evans has brought in the tea and biscuits so his hands are occupied. 'The Laws have taken over the game. The Laws are there to keep the game going not to stop the game. The referees in Wales blow the Law not the game. If a player falls over at a ruck but the ball isn't interfered with why blow? People criticise the referees in the Southern Hemisphere particularly in the Super 12s. For example, they only blow for crossing when there is definite interference, if the offence has no influence over the play then why blow? Here, the whistle would go and the game suffers. Then there's this fetish with the front rows. It ruins games. The cup match at Cardiff suffered because the referee didn't get to grips with the situation early on. When there's a good referee who stamps on any problem early on it tends to go away. Then the game has a chance to develop, entertain and excite, that's what people want to see.' Mac shows a certain sympathy with the men in the middle when he talks about assessors. 'I don't believe that assessors are there for the good of the game. The referee knows he is under scrutiny so what does he do? He lets the Laws take over the game. He refs the Laws; there is little if any empathy with the game and the players. Surely it's not meant to be like that?'

Welsh referees will be glad to see the back of Ian McIntosh. They have never seen his like before and it is unlikely that they will see his like again. On more than one occasion he needed to be restrained from confronting a referee with his anger, Jim McCreedy can certainly vouch for that. When Neath coach Lynn Jones was seen on television turning his finger on the side of his head and pointing a couple of rows in front of him viewers were left in no doubt what he meant and who it was aimed at. Mac was getting restless in his seat as his side were letting a big match slip away. Lynn Jones, in addition to being one of Wales's finest coaches, has a wicked sense of humour but make no mistake, he knows how good Mac was.

So how are we meant to interpret these comments? Coming from a South African, a man entrenched in the Southern Hemisphere approach to the game. Are they another sideways knock at the game north of the Equator or do they encompass a much wider perspective? There aren't many players or supporters who would not agree that the standard of refereeing in Wales leaves a lot to be desired. There are some who shine above the rest, Nigel Williams and Nigel Whitehouse certainly, but as a whole they are woeful. And it doesn't end there. Touch judges cannot be excused from the criticisms that follow every match. There have been many occasions when the man running the line has interfered when he shouldn't have and not got involved when he should. One high profile match at the end of the season saw both flags go up signalling a successful kick at goal when the ball was six feet wide of the posts. Fortunately the referee saw it differently and overruled the touch judges but instances such as this do pose questions about the officials' ability. No, it seems that Mac's thoughts on the way games are controlled need to be looked at. There will always be incidents picked up by the television cameras that identify decisions the officials get wrong or things they miss altogether, but the referee and his touch judges are only human, prone to error like everyone else. There will always be mistakes made and it is down to the IRB to ensure that everything possible is done to eliminate them by using the technology available but it is also down to the Unions and the referees in particular to allow the game to be played, to allow players the opportunity to express themselves and the crowd to be entertained.

Two days after the last match of the season and five days before he returned home seemed a good time to ask Ian McIntosh why Newport didn't win the league. 'Well it wasn't because Stephen Jones kicked that penalty. And it wasn't because of the injuries we picked up. All season there have been penalties converted and penalties missed. This one had a higher profile but at the end of the day it was just another penalty. Every side gets its injury problems during a season. Ours came late but most sides can probably blame a couple of defeats on injuries. No, we lost the championship with those three consecutive defeats near the end. Neath, Swansea and Cardiff. We took too long to pick ourselves up after the cup defeat at Cardiff and we lost three games that we should have won, or were at least optimistic about winning. Neath played well and we couldn't convert pressure into points early in the second half, Swansea was a disaster, no excuses there and Cardiff was another one that was thrown away. One of their tries shouldn't have been allowed but that happens. If Stephen Jones had missed it would have helped but we lost it, it was in our hands and we lost it.'

Nine months in charge of a rugby club puts severe constraints on a coach. He inherits a squad of players having had no input regarding their selection and he has to hand over to somebody else, a successor who will take the side forward and select players as he sees fit. Of course, Ian McIntosh knew when he came to Rodney Parade that this would probably be the case. At the end the ball was in his court, Tony Brown wanted him to stay, the players and supporters wanted him to stay, but he couldn't. 'If I was a younger man then I would have loved to stay and try and take the guys forward but the pressure is too great, it's a young man's job. Two days before every match it would start to build and the eighty minutes were becoming unbearable. You experience everything in those eighty minutes and it then takes time to come down, get back to normal. I've loved my time in Newport, I love the people, the place and the club but if I'm truthful I didn't enjoy the rugby. And before I came I knew this was likely to happen, I knew the pressure would take away the enjoyment. Working with the boys was great, I enjoyed all the training sessions, they're a great bunch, but when match day approached things changed and that I didn't like.'

At the end of the 2001-02 season Newport RFC are quite a distance from the finished article. There has been a cutting edge missing in the backs for the last three seasons and more, but it is the last three campaigns that bear the closest scrutiny, the seasons where the investment and the expectation have been greatest. 'The forwards are tremendous, I would rate their chances against any of the Super 12 sides but the backs need somebody who can provide that edge, someone who has the ability to create that gap, put players into space and has got the pace that can tear defences apart.' Realising this had led Mac to move away from his idea of rugby being an entertainment and adopt a more conservative approach, playing to the club's obvious strength in the forwards. However, at this point the eyes widen a bit and there is a definite twinkle, 'Somebody like Percy Montgomery would fit into this side, Percy would bring a lot to Newport's game.' Percy Montgomery, now there's a thought.

OK, so Newport sign another Springbok star, but if Mac were staying at the club for two or three years longer where would he look to strengthen the squad, how would he assemble a group of players that would take the club to the top? 'A squad of players is a living entity. It evolves through the seasons. You don't start with thirty players and end up three years later with the same thirty players, all three years older, there's more to it than that.' Now Mac starts talking about circles. Imagine three circles on a sheet of paper each overlapping the other a fraction. The circles are different sizes, there is a big one, a middle-sized one and a small one. 'The squad can be broken into three types of player. There is your experienced player, the one who has been at the club a while and is a regular first team selection. In an average club with thirty players on contract these probably account for twenty places in the squad and are represented by the big circle. Secondly, the development players. Those players who have come through the club's internal structure, the Youth and the Under 21s. These players fall into the middle circle and can be as many as six or seven strong. Finally, the small circle, the players that are brought into a squad, not only for their undoubted ability, but for their marketability. Players that will bring in casual supporters who the club will hope to turn into regular supporters.'

He keeps referring to rugby as an entertainment. Now, in the professional era, the game has to fight for its audience. The competition is strong, not only from other sports, though that in itself is a major problem, but from the way people live in the twenty-first century. 'The paying customer wants value for his money. It's essential that the game is seen to give this value. There is no room for sentiment or tradition in the modern game. When professionalism arrived it was time to wave goodbye to the traditions that had served rugby well over many years. For goodness sake I'm a traditionalist but that's not going to get my side anywhere when there's a big match to be won. When they renamed Kings Park there was uproar in Natal. The ABSA Stadium wasn't accepted by many people for a long time but the money put up by the corporation was essential to the development of rugby in the province. Neither did the concept of the Natal Sharks get the public support but now they can't get enough of it.'

There was less than a week left before Mac would wing his way back to South Africa. There was the small matter of the club's annual dinner which would take place at the prestigious Celtic Manor Hotel and see almost six hundred people applaud Newport's ex-coach, for that was what he now was. They would rise to acknowledge the commitment he had shown the club in his brief stay and they would listen when he spoke of rugby and the men that played the game, played the game for him and for the club. The beanie was donated to the club's museum where visitors in years to come will be left wondering what the hell it is. This time Ian McIntosh has probably left the sharp end of the game for good. There may be some television work and the lucrative after-dinner speaking circuit would love him but that will be where it all ends.

When he was prematurely dropped from the Springboks' coaching position a lot of work had been done that went unrecognised. Work that laid the foundation for the great achievements that lay round the corner. This won't happen at Rodney Parade. If Newport progress and move on to great things the input from Allan Lewis and the man with the wild eyes and the daft hat will not have been forgotten. As he said in his speech at the club dinner 'I've never enjoyed myself more with any group of people I've been involved with in the sport than I have with the people at Newport'. These are sentiments echoed by Allan Lewis and it is a great shame that these two great thinkers in the game did not have longer working together.

Allan Lewis and Ian McIntosh were Newport RFC's first two high profile coaches in the professional era. How they measure up in terms of success is fairly straightforward - Lewis, in three seasons won the Principality Cup and second and fourth spots in the league, which saw the club compete in the Heineken Cup for the first time, while McIntosh took the team to second position in the Welsh-Scottish League and ensured the club would continue to compete in the top European competition come the following season.

Because of their respective terms of office any comparison is not only difficult but extremely unfair. The beast that is a squad of rugby players is a living organism affected by many factors all pulling and pushing and not necessarily in the same direction. Stability is the prime requisite and time - time to put into place the foundations that the future can be built on. This hasn't been the case at Newport where, as has been explained, initially there was the need for an instant fix.

Lewis and McIntosh are like chalk and cheese. This isn't to suggest that they didn't get on; far from it. Speaking to them individually it is clear that a mutual respect exists. They are both aware of the tightrope coaches spend their careers walking, together with the many ups and downs that the job will bring. Not many of their kind are given the opportunity to put long-term strategies into place. Look around the clubs and ask how long the coach has been behind his desk. Not long in most cases, regardless of any silverware he may have brought to the club. The problem with the domestic game in Wales today is that the goal posts have been moved. Not in mid-season or anything as sophisticated; no, the goalposts have been moved as a result of the European competitions that now dominate the domestic game. The men behind the clubs want success in Europe and as a result of this change in attitude the importance placed on winning the domestic league or cup has diminished; until one or the other is won of course. But ask Tony Brown, Leighton Samuel, Peter Thomas et al if they would prefer to win the Welsh Cup or secure a place in the following season's Heineken Cup and you will see where the priorities lie.

This only adds strength to the argument that stability and long-term strategies are the most important factors to be considered by the Board of Directors now running each of the major clubs. Initially, Newport was the big anomaly - nowhere, way off the pace, it had to catch up quickly. Now, having made up lost ground, it needs to take stock and put realistic objectives into place. No club can expect to win Europe's biggest prize without having gone through some sort of apprenticeship. Brive took Leicester apart in 1997 and five years later the Tigers were celebrating their back-to-back victories on the same ground; well, if not the same ground, certainly in Cardiff.

If there are any lessons to be learnt from the last three seasons under Lewis and McIntosh the most important is possibly that the job needs two people working together. Not a simple case of one coaching the backs and the other the forwards more a case of one putting the bricks in place and the other designing the project - a builder and an architect.

Newport may well have been close to a perfect partnership with Allan Lewis and Ian McIntosh but the timing of their individual arrivals at the club was separated by three years making any realistic chance of a harmonious outcome non-existent. If two coaches are taken on by the club they should each be given clearly defined roles and objectives, for a predetermined length of time and then be left alone to get on with it. This is business management at its simplest but it is rarely seen in club rugby.

Knocking On the Door

'Therefore I summon age
To grant youth's heritage'

Robert Browning

If they're good enough they're old enough. This is a cliché that is now, unfortunately, rarely seen adopted when coaches are selecting their squads for the next big match, the trouble being that every match now played at senior club level is big. Be it in domestic cup, domestic league or European competition, the pressure is on the coach to get the right result and he rarely finds himself with any available latitude which would enable him to introduce one or two of the younger players at his disposal to the senior game.

This apparent lack of opportunity which young players are regularly coming face to face with is causing great concern among the game's administrators, the clubs and most importantly, among the young players themselves. What should be a straightforward exercise is proving to be anything but, and on this occasion it surely is the structure of the domestic game that is causing the problem. Where clubs once played anything between forty and fifty games in a season, this figure is now nearer thirty and, whereas before there would have been plenty of opportunity to blood the stars of tomorrow, this is no longer the case.

There is an excellent development programme in place that takes players through school, youth, Under 19 and Under 21 levels, but then the problem rears its head; there is nothing within the club structure that accommodates players too old to play in the Under 21s but not yet ready for regular first team rugby. There will be contracts offered to the very best among them but there will still be a huge imbalance in the senior squad between the established players and those hoping to break into it. The void that hundreds of young players enter every year sees many good prospects lost to the game, rugby

190

failing them at this crucial period in their development. There doesn't seem to be anything that can be done about it and it is difficult to know where to point the finger. The WRU aren't directly to blame, neither are the clubs who have invested heavily in their first team squads and obviously want their pound of flesh, it is the way the game has been allowed to develop that has resulted in this previously unidentified problem. It is an inherent part of a professional sport and after seven years it is starting to bite.

The structure of the club game has evolved during the professional era, more as a result of the demands put on it, than in response to the demands that have come from within it. Whatever is seen to offer the greatest financial benefit today is preferred to something that will not reap any immediate rewards. Better to contrive a Celtic League, that has no real purpose or interest other than to provide more of the same and in doing so, undermine many of the Heineken Cup fixtures that it will duplicate. This in preference to giving some serious thought and investment to the thorny problem of player development. Perhaps at this point in the argument it would be better to start talking about continued development rather than be accused of being critical of a system that caters well for players in their formative years. It is this continued development that is the essence of the problem and it is the players who are twenty-two and twenty-three years of age who are suffering as a result of it.

How much money clubs should invest in the development of young talent is a difficult question to answer but, as we shall see, there is every likelihood that in the not-too-distant future the clubs will become more reliant on the players they are bringing through their internal structures which could make such investment appear relatively cheap. Clubs can only measure their investment into player development against the results it produces - the number of players that make their mark in the first fifteen. Not many years ago Newport was on the point of disbanding its Youth team having identified that very few players actually made the grade and played for the first team, making it a far from cost effective enterprise. This met with great resistance, not least from the families of the players concerned who staged a peaceful protest on the night of the club's end-of-season dinner. The game was still amateur at the time but such cutbacks in the professional era are not an option.

The Working Party Report commissioned by the WRU identified this problem. It revealed that over the past three seasons, while three quarters of the Welsh Under 21 squad were contracted to Premier clubs, less than half played on a regular basis. Not a healthy situation for the long term good of both the club and national game in Wales, it being patently clear that players should not spend the better part of a season keeping the replacements' bench warm at the most important time in their career development. The Report correctly identified the problem presented by the number of overseas players now commanding first team places throughout the game in Wales, a problem not in any way unique to the Premier Division, and suggested that limitations on such representation should be put in place.

However, there may be a solution. Not one that has been instigated by the Union or the clubs but one that has come about as a result of the financial problems the game is experiencing, a solution that may well kill two birds with one stone.

Between 1999 and 2001 the total rugby costs at Newport - players' wages, associated staff wages and travelling expenses - almost trebled from £830,000 to £2.25 million. A similar increase would almost certainly have been experienced at most Premier Division clubs and these same clubs are slowly coming round to the fact that it is a situation which cannot be sustained and that one of the ways to address it is by bringing through more of the talent that their Under 21 squads produce. Far from suggesting that these players should be seen as cheap labour they will, however, give clubs the opportunity to introduce pay structures that are more in keeping with the realities of a professional game that is failing to pay its way.

Cardiff RFC has gradually been moving in this direction and the first team regularly includes players who have graduated through the clubs junior teams. Rhys Williams, Craig Morgan, Jamie and Nicky Robinson, Ryan Powell, Greg Woods, Adam Jones; all these players have come through the club structure and become regular first team players, some are first choice and already approaching senior status within the squad. At 23 years of age Craig Morgan is the oldest and it is clear that this youth policy is going to have to be taken on board by the other Premier Division clubs and whether they are initially prepared to gamble on such relative inexperience will have a huge bearing on where they will be in five years' time; still at the forefront of the club game in Wales or bankrupt.

At Rodney Parade in their last outing of the 2001-02 season Newport Under 21s were soundly beaten 51-17 by Llanelli. This brought to an end a season that had started full of promise but fallen apart in the closing months and, if results were the only criteria by which success was measured, then the Under 21s had failed to deliver. However, there are other factors that have to be taken into consideration before such judgements can be made, factors that are much more important when it comes to the bigger picture, much more important than winning or losing.

The previous night the first team played an important league fixture at Glasgow. Plagued by injury in the latter part of the season the squad of twenty-two, for a game that had to be won if Newport were to remain in contention for the league title, contained six Under 21 players. Perhaps it was fitting that it was scrum half Llyr Lane who had scored the match winning try well into injury time, but that aside, it was clear that some of these youngsters were ready for senior recognition and that the true measurement of success of the Under 21s was its contribution to the senior squad, the fact that players could comfortably make the step up, rather than one based solely on results. Newport are probably a season behind Cardiff in terms of youth development but Lane, centres Nathan Brew, Hal Luscombe and Scott Williams, together with forwards Rhys Jones, Gareth Gravelle and David Pattison will all be expected to challenge the first team incumbents in the near future.

Twelve months earlier Andrew Powell would have been viewed as a player who would soon challenge for a place in the senior team. Then fate took a hand and the opportunity came sooner than expected. Three seasons earlier another player had come through the system to lay claim to a regular first team place. Alix Popham, a back row forward from who much was expected, had gained representative honours at every level up to Under 21 and Newport were giving him plenty of matches to get acclimatised to Premier Division rugby. With the influx of high profile players at the start of the 1999-2000 season, Gary Teichmann among them, fewer opportunities came Popham's way but he was a young man and his time would surely come. Teichmann's departure left a gap in the back row that Alix Popham was earmarked to fill, then injury struck. Andrew Powell was drafted into the side, seized the chance to impress and after a handful of games had become a first team regular.

Andrew Powell was always going to make it to the top in his chosen sport. From his early days with Brecon Youth, playing rugby was all he had wanted to do and when the opportunity came to join high-flying Newport he grabbed it with both hands. Capped for Wales Youth Under 18 while still at Brecon, he progressed to the Under 19 squad as a Newport player and appeared in the FIRA Junior World Cup. A cameo appearance in the second row for Newport in a friendly against Pontypool went largely unnoticed and he had to wait until the pre season matches against Bristol and Aberavon before getting a chance in the back row. A couple of matches into the 2001-02 season saw Popham injured and the home league fixture against Edinburgh heralded the start of Powell's meteoric rise.

Such was his impact during this first season in the senior side he gained international recognition with Wales A and appeared for the Barbarians. But it was in the back row at Newport that his reputation was being made. Alongside Jason Forster and Peter Buxton, Powell made up one of the quickest units in the game. The balance was perfect and even if there are question marks over where in the back row he will finally settle, it was at number eight that he received the highest praise. Zinzan Brook rated Powell as one of the most promising players he had seen, high praise indeed, and it didn't stop there. BBC Wales featured him in its weekly magazine programme Scrum V and many respected pundits were forecasting an early appearance in the Welsh team. That didn't materialise and it was probably no bad thing when looking back at the poor performances the national side was producing. The 2002 Six Nations was not the place to kick start an international career in the red jersey of Wales. Scapegoats were in short supply and Powell was better off well away from it.

Powell is a raw talent. There is much work to be done before the finished article finds its way to the surface but the only way this player is now going to realise his enormous potential is by playing Premier Division rugby, European rugby; playing with the best against the best. His place in the team was probably not on the immediate agenda when fate took a hand. Whether Ian MacIntosh would have given him a game during the season if he had a fully fit squad at his disposal we shall never know, but events have subsequently proved that the talent is there and it can only be realised if it is given the opportunity.

Like many others his age, Andrew Powell is very concerned with the structure of the game which makes progress difficult and, unlikely as he is to be affected by it now, he can see many good young prospects slipping through the net. Powell signed a three-year contract with Newport which will carry him through to just short of his twenty-fourth birthday by which time he will have four seasons of Premier rugby under his belt and the best years of his career still ahead of him. Negotiating contracts with young, homegrown players is a particularly delicate procedure with the player understandably wanting as much as he can get while the club wants to see some return for its earlier investment. A balance has to be found and very often, the responsibility is going to rest with the players who will have to decide where their loyalties lie.

Andrew Powell would eventually have broken into the first team at Newport even if Alix Popham hadn't picked up his injury thereby speeding up the process. One opportunity was all it took but many players wont get the opportunities that are needed to make an impression in the senior side. Luck, or bad luck, played a part in

Powell's rapid rise but how many quality players are out there waiting for an opportunity that may never come? And when opportunity does come will they be used or abused?

Matthew J Watkins left Newport at the end of the 2001-02 season. At twenty three years of age he joined Llanelli after coming through Newport's Youth and Under 21 structure to become a regular first team player and, at the same time, gained representative honours through to Wales A. Why was a player who the club had invested much time and money in, who had been recognised by the international selectors, on his way to Llanelli? Many supporters at Rodney Parade were glad to see him leave and made no secret of the fact after some particularly poor performances by the player in the latter part of the season, but Watkins' is a case that needs to be looked at carefully before cries of good riddance should be heard.

Firstly, Matthew J Watkins didn't leave Newport to go to a lesser club. He left Newport to join Llanelli, current Welsh League champions, and a club where they certainly know a bit about three quarter play. Backs coach Nigel Davies is an astute observer of the game and one has to wonder where he sees Watkins' future in the game. It is difficult to imagine that money was the prime motive in the move, rather a case of the player's dissatisfaction at the way his career had been handled at Rodney Parade. Watkins found it difficult to stake his claim for a regular first team spot being selected in all four positions in the three quarter line, with rarely more than a few consecutive games in any position. There have been numerous players whose ability to play adequately in a number of positions has been to the detriment of their career and Watkins could find himself among them if Llanelli fail to bring out the best in what was once seen as a promising talent at Rodney Parade.

At twenty-three years of age Alix Popham is another prospect who could find himself in this unenviable position. His career as a number eight was definitely put on hold for the two seasons that saw Gary Teichmann at Newport and although this did not prevent him starting in twenty-nine matches and coming on as a substitute in a further fourteen, like Watkins, it didn't allow him to play more than three consecutive matches in the same position and with a third season largely spent struggling with injury his place in the first team is by no means guaranteed.

In the second half of the 2001-02 season Popham was put out on loan to Leeds, now, having lost Peter Buxton, there is a gap to be filled in the back row at Newport and Popham's chance may come again but the feeling is that a player needs to be recruited to fill the gap left by Buxton and if this proves to be so, then another young player will not be getting sufficient first team rugby. At a time when there are questions being asked about the number of quality players in Welsh rugby and the number of clubs that should compete at the top level as a result of this perceived scarceness, it seems ironic that there are many such players struggling to get regular first team rugby.

If financial pressures do result in less money being spent on players, then more opportunities will certainly come the way of the players of tomorrow, however, the gap between Under 21 and first team rugby will still exist. There is the obvious need for clubs to run a team that can be used to ease the transition and at Newport this will see the return of Newport United, traditionally the second team which had been dropped in 1998 but is due to be resurrected for the 2002-03 season. In addition to arranging fixtures with Welsh clubs that run a similar 'development' team there will be cross-border fixtures with leading English clubs, a move that can only be good for the future development of the game in both countries.

Where the Newport United team of 2002 will differ from its predecessor will be in the profile of players selected. Rugby clubs can no longer afford the luxury of players who, however loyal in the past, have nothing left to offer, which will mean that the United team will comprise of first team squad members who are not getting enough games or possibly returning from injury, and Under 21 players that the coaching staff are keen to see performing at a higher level. Exciting as this sounds there is the strong possibility that the Under

21 squad will be put under even greater pressure, a pressure that will see a knock-on effect through the club's junior squads with the demands from above being given priority, but the club as a whole should see improved player development and the long term benefits that it will produce.

Watching these developments with great interest, albeit from a distance, will be Steve 'Snickers' Jones, one of Newport's unsung heroes. Steve Jones has been responsible for the club's Youth team for the best part of ten years during which time he has coached many players that successfully progressed to the first fifteen. Newport Youth are distanced from the club in many ways. Firstly they play their home matches five miles away at Caerleon and beyond family and friends get no support to speak of and, being perfectly honest, there are not many followers of Newport RFC who know of their existence or, if they do, care about it.

If a team is to be measured by the silverware that it picks up then Newport Youth at the end of the 2001-02 season was without doubt the club's most successful squad. It boasted a host of players who had received international recognition and has over the years become a proven nursery for players who have represented Newport at senior level. Andrew Powell, Ian Gough, Dale Burn, Martyn Llewellyn, Alix Popham, Matthew J Watkins and many before them all started their careers with Newport Youth, coming under the watchful eye of Steve Jones.

From Youth to Under 21 and then the senior squad. Newport has a new Director of Rugby, Darryl Jones, and it is his responsibility to see that the quality players are guided through the system to the ultimate benefit of the club. For the 2002-03 season he will be joined by namesake, Steve, who will be helping to identify the players seen as those most likely to succeed and between them they will be making decisions that will reflect the likely needs of the first team squad, not only for today but more importantly those needs that will be pressing in three or four years time. There will be many that will fall by the wayside, lose interest, not be good enough, even be tempted to pastures new. Regardless of this the system will continue to produce the Powells, Pophams and Burns of the future and the ultimate responsibility will be with the club to recognise them and ensure that they are given the opportunity they all crave.

'Hi - I'm Simon Raiwalui'

'Children have never been very good at listening to their elders, but they have never failed to imitate them.'

James Baldwin

Shortly after agreeing to underwrite Newport RFC for a three-year period, Tony Brown identified four areas the club would have to prioritise if it were to reach its full potential. The major priority was the quality of player and coach recruited which in turn would lead to the second, the establishing of a commercial, marketing and merchandising department. He also prioritised the need to upgrade the stadium and finally, he wanted to see the club 'develop a comprehensive community development programme'. Community development programme - what exactly did that mean?

Later in the year Phil Davies was recruited by Brown and given the brief to get this fourth priority up and running. Davies had some previous experience in establishing community based projects having been instrumental in the hugely successful Rhondda Schools Initiative and the Capital Rugby project in Cardiff. He would become the club's first Community Development Director and twelve months later the initial fruits of his labour would see the light of day.

Gateway Rugby was officially launched on 28 September 2000 and nothing in the wildest imaginings of those present could possibly have prepared them for the impact this revolutionary project would have on Newport and the surrounding area. To best understand what Gateway Rugby means it is worth referring to the Objectives and Mission Statement published which outline the direction it wanted to take.

There were seven Objectives:

- To stimulate the participating students' general interest in and attitude to sport and to educate them to use their leisure time more positively.

- To provide a well-defined channel of progression that improves the likelihood that each student will fulfil their own personal potential.

- To use sport to engender 'team spirit' and to develop a realisation of the importance of respect for others.

- To promote desirable standards of behaviour and conduct.

- To promote the game of rugby football generally and to enhance and encourage the flow of young players into the mini-sections of rugby throughout the catchment area.

- To become part of the Welsh Rugby Union's player identification system, 'funnelling' promising young players into the WRU Regional and Elite programmes.

- To work with the Welsh Rugby Union in providing the opportunity of Coach Education for schools, ensuring continuity of the development work.

Summarising, the Mission Statement read:
'To act as a catalyst for bringing shared benefits to the rugby community of Newport and its surrounding areas by establishing working partnerships with the Education Authority, the Welsh Rugby Union, the local schools, the local rugby clubs and the community in general.'

Newport RFC was fully supported in Gateway Rugby by Newport County Borough Council, Monmouthshire County Council, The Welsh Rugby Union and Dragons Rugby Trust, Gwent Police, the Sports Council for Wales incorporating Sportsmatch Cymru, Newport Schools Rugby Union and the Prince's Trust Cymru.

With such high profile 'partners' involved Newport RFC had established the foundation from which Gateway Rugby could go forward. David Watkins became its first Chairman and President and speaking at the launch he made reference to his own formative years, both as a player and as a young man. 'As someone who benefited enormously from quality guidance as a youngster - guidance that helped shape and influence the rest of my sporting, social and working life - I am convinced of its benefits. Gateway Rugby provides the opportunity to influence our youngsters in a positive manner, not just in rugby terms but socially as well.'

Often referred to in the past two years, Tony Brown summed up the commitment of Newport RFC. 'Our goal is to help motivate our youngsters to be the best they can possibly be - not just from a sporting perspective, but in every area of their lives.' This saw the club assuming a huge responsibility to the community it serves, one probably greater than anything previously undertaken by any rugby club. But how was it all going to work?

The unitary areas that Gateway Rugby would initially target, Newport CBC and Monmouthshire CC, contain ninety schools. Comprising seventy six primary, twelve comprehensive and two private schools, it was the aim that all of them would eventually become involved in the project. The basic concept suggested that each school would receive visits from Gateway representatives at regular intervals throughout the academic year. Each visit would last for one hour and the frequency of the visits would be fortnightly, this frequency being a key requirement as it would enable ongoing relationships between the children and visiting representatives to develop.

To visit ninety schools once a fortnight throughout the three school terms was going to demand a lot of organisation and commitment. Gateway Rugby recruited three Community Development Officers whose main function would be the organising and supervising of the school visits. Mike Sage had been a WRU Dragons Development Officer, Gareth Mahoney had a background in teaching and Janice Chappell had long been involved in the development of Welsh women's rugby, both as a player and coach. All three were well qualified for the position of CDO and the first part of the jigsaw was now in place.

From the very first session, Gateway Rugby was a success. The teachers were impressed with the impact it was having on the pupils, it wasn't long before positive feedback from parents started arriving at the club and of course the children loved it. Certainly the sessions centred on a rugby ball but the principle could just as easily have accommodated a football, tennis ball... any type of ball, it didn't matter. The rugby ball became the focal point and the CDOs paid great attention to the development of skills which gradually saw improvements in coordination and reflexes while at the same time introducing the youngsters to the concept of being a team player. Boys and girls alike were involved and the highlight for many came when a session was attended by one of Newport's first team players. This had been the club's intention from the outset and over one third of all sessions held would see a high profile name in attendance.

However, this was not just about rugby. Referring back to the seven objectives set out by Gateway Rugby will show that while three had a definite association with the game, looking to both promote it and at the same time identify promising players, the other four were much wider reaching. Here we see reference to 'more positive use of leisure time', 'realising potential', the need and understanding of 'respect for others' and the importance of 'desirable standards of behaviour and conduct'. What should be seen as fundamental parts of character building unfortunately are largely neglected by modern society. This in turn leads to the problems so prevalent among today's young community and it is by addressing these issues through its coaching sessions that Gateway Rugby is doing its finest work. And it is the frequency of these sessions that enables the message to be put across. The CDOs gradually build up the all important relationship with the children that will see them accept more responsibility for their actions, see them reach a new found level of confidence and think more positively about everything they do.

All this was not going unnoticed in the local business community. Alan Williams, Managing Director of local company Chesilvale Electronics, had watched the rapid development of Gateway Rugby and was keen his company should become involved in it. He recognised a project that 'not only seeks to improve children's skills as sports-people, but also to lift their self esteem and confidence while at the same time building up their powers of communication and team work in every day life.' This led to Chesilvale becoming involved with a two year sponsorship deal for a substantial five figure sum.

The immediate success had surprised even the most optimistic observers and in January 2001 a fourth CDO was recruited, three months ahead of the original projection. Alun 'Archie' Evans was an old favourite at Rodney Parade in the late 1960s and 1970s and he would be taking responsibility for schools in the Abergavenny and Monmouth areas. From the start there had been provision made for five CDOs and it wasn't long before the complement was complete, another ex-Newport player, Andy Peacock joining the team in the summer.

At the end of twelve months all those associated with Gateway Rugby could rightly hold their heads up high. The statistics produced confirmed, if any such confirmation was needed, that the project had achieved astonishing results. Eighty schools were on board each receiving fortnightly visits. In total 1,119 coaching sessions had been held, regularly attended by 4,578 children. Newport Schools Rugby Union had benefited from coaching clinics conducted by Newport players and track suits for the squads had been funded by Gateway. The goodwill that was emanating from those directly involved with the project had, in truth, become immeasurable, but suffice to say there was rarely, if ever, a disparaging comment to be heard. Towards the end of this first year parents had been asked to complete a short questionnaire, their feedback seen as essential to how the project should move forward. Of the many that were returned to the club only one could be seen as negative. This commented on the 'thuggish' aspect of rugby and the parent concerned questioned the justification in exposing young children to the game.

When Gateway Rugby entered its second year it did not go unnoticed that many of the children it had been introduced to would have moved on to the next stage in their education. Those concerned felt it essential that contact should be maintained and as a result over two thousand children received letters from Simon Raiwalui in which he wished them every success in their new school and reminded them of their responsibilities to both their new friends and themselves.

This second year was going to be if anything more demanding than the first. Torfaen Borough Council had expressed an interest that schools in the Cwmbran unitary district be included and with one in Chepstow that actually fell under the jurisdiction of Gloucester Local Education Authority together with two private schools in the area, the number of education establishments now within the compass of Gateway Rugby stood at 110.

The original concept of what had become Gateway Rugby had also included a second project that would have a more educational bias. This would see pupils visiting Rodney Parade for what is known as an 'out of school learning experience' and it was viewed as essential that this should be launched in the coming year. During the close season Phil Davies had become the club's Communications Director and Mike Sage was now Operations Manager for Gateway Rugby giving him more responsibility for the day-to-day running of the scheme, which would in turn give Davies more time to devote to the next phase in the development.

Bringing pupils to Rodney Parade was going to be totally different to meeting them on their home patch so to speak. The club had already become involved in a work experience exercise which had seen ten students spend one or two weeks at the club working in tandem with a CDO. During this time they were introduced to many aspects of Gateway Rugby and at the end they received a performance report from their CDO which highlighted their attitude in the workplace together with any perceived strengths and weaknesses.

However, hosting groups of up to twenty, nine- and ten-year-olds Monday to Friday, with each visit lasting five hours, was something that was going to require a lot of preparation. The Key Stage 2 requirements of the National Curriculum would have to be adhered to, literacy, numeracy and information technology, and a full time Education Officer was going to have to be employed. Newport Local Education Authority became involved at this stage and funded the appointment of Phil James, a teacher who had first hand experience of Gateway Rugby and all it represented through the regular visits made to his school. Classroom facilities overlooking the pitch were made available, twelve lap tops were provided by the local authority and the Second Half was launched on 22 May 2002.

During a hectic summer term 860 children experienced the Second Half project. A typical visit starts with registration on arrival at 10.00 am followed by a tour of the stadium. This ends in Newport's changing room where the children watch a short promotional video followed by a brief talk from Phil James in which he draws attention to the lifestyle pointers that he wants the children to recognise: effort, achievement and success. Then comes the highlight of the Virtual Changing Room Experience, the screen comes back on and the children are face to face with an eight by six foot image of the Newport captain. 'Hi - I'm Simon Raiwalui'. The message so forcefully put across in the next few minutes is all about giving your best. 'Be confident and be ambitious, and be determined and brave enough to give your best to everything you do.' Then there is some work to do.

The VCRE is discussed and written up in 'Tommy the Tiger's Work-out book...' this needs explaining. Tommy the Tiger is Newport RFC's alter ego and if you are nine or ten years old, what Tommy says goes - no argument. In his work-out book he guides children through a series of well put together exercises which expand on their day at the club, in addition to which he encourages them to work through the remaining activities in the book back in the classroom or at home. These amount to a further forty hours of balanced educational exercises ranging from an introduction to the euro, diet and nutritional values and communication by email.

At every visit there is the opportunity to interview a player and, bearing in mind all these children would have been involved with Gateway Rugby, this invariably proves to be the second of the day's highlights. Not in any way inhibited by this situation the children ask their questions and then go away and write a report which they are encouraged to email direct to Tommy. Remember, these children are nine and ten years old!

With the Second Half up and running Newport were now beginning to see the full potential that was available through the club's innovative community project. Gateway Rugby had continued to go from strength to strength in its second year and all 110 schools in the unitary areas covered would be involved in the project from September 2002, and they would all send classes to Rodney Parade to listen to Simon and gain the many obvious benefits the Second Half has to offer.

During the second year Gateway Rugby had conducted a further 1,612 visits making the cumulative total 2,731. In total, 11,196 children had attended the coaching sessions and it seems highly probable that over a ten-year period, through its involvement with Gateway Rugby and the Second Half community programmes, Newport RFC will have reached into almost every home in its recognised catchment area.

Reference has already been made to the gap that exists between Newport's first team squad and the Under 21s. At junior level a much greater gap in terms of relevant age existed with only two groups being catered for: Under 11 and Under 15. While both groups have long been involved in national competitions there was a school of thought sharing the opinion that the intermediary years should be recognised. In response to this, Gateway Rugby, in partnership with the Newport Schools Rugby Union and the Cwmbran Schools Rugby Union, has been instrumental in the formation of development squads at Under 12, Under 13, and Under 14 levels thereby ensuring that the progress of young talent is not put on hold.

A competitive nature was introduced during the second year when HSBC Bank Plc sponsored the Gateway Challenge Trophy. The first stage of the tournament saw eight groups produce winners that progressed to two further groups of four schools that, in turn, saw two emerge as Monmouthshire champions and Newport & Torfaen champions. Undy Primary School and Ysgol Gymraeg Casnewydd then contested the grand final at Rodney Parade after Newport's last match of the season, with Undy duly becoming the inaugural winners of the Gateway Challenge Trophy bringing to a conclusion a further dimension to the project which seems certain to continue.

Beyond the parameters of Gateway Rugby and the Second Half,

Newport RFC has an active involvement in the Hartridge Rugby Academy. This is an educational foundation that encourages older students to continue their studies while at the same time giving them the opportunity to pursue their rugby development. Academy Director, Alex Lawrie prioritises 'development of the individual' which sees students encouraged to study for A levels and other vocational courses while at the same time working on rugby-related fitness and skill levels. The future is bright, with children aged nine through to students up to eighteen years of age all being given the opportunity to get involved with Newport RFC.

It came as no surprise when, at the end of year two, Gateway Rugby was awarded the prestigious Sports Council for Wales sponsored Sportsmatch Cymru, Scheme of the Year Trophy. In presenting the award, Chairman, Lynn Davies commented ' there is no doubt that the scheme is helping our young people to embrace sport as an integral part of their lifestyle, ultimately improving their health and well being in the future'

Many people have gone on record with their unreserved praise for what, in a ridiculously short period of time, has unquestionably fulfilled its 'aim to give south east Wales the best and most effective grass roots community sports project in world rugby.' On the basis of such huge success its seems likely that no matter what percentage of the children and students involved in these projects finally pursue the game of rugby, either as a player or spectator, the road will more than likely lead them to Rodney Parade and of the hundreds of messages of goodwill received by Phil Davies and his team, from teachers, parents and children, perhaps the following, from an anonymous pupil at Marshfield School is best representative of them all.

THE MARSHFIELD RAP !

Hey everybody, let's write a rap,

Let's be healthy and not get fat!

Gateway Rugby comes to our school,

Our CDO Mike, is extremely cool.

Let's start off by warming up,

We finish off by eating our tuck.

Mike comes to Marshfield on a Tuesday morn,

If it wasn't for him, we'd be weak as a prawn.

He's really fun and our number one!

He runs us round till we're hot as the sun.

We run, we dodge, we pass the ball,

We do all this in the hall,

We meet the players every other week,

To see Gary and Paul it's a real treat.

We play touch rugby and we touch the hip

To dodge around is a real great tip,

We've learnt a great deal from Mike Sage

He has taught us rugby from an early age

Postscript

'I have discovered the secret that after climbing a great hill, one only finds that there are many more hills to climb.'

Nelson Mandela

Rugby union has been a professional sport for seven years. Seven seasons completed during which players have received financial reward from the game without having to worry about the consequences. So much has happened in a relatively short space of time that those involved with the game in whatever capacity, be it as a player, administrator or supporter, have barely had time to catch breath. However, while some of the rugby-playing nations of the world took the change on board and introduced domestic structures that worked, others failed to do so and nowhere is this more true than in Wales where the game has been the subject of seven years of negligence. Seven seasons of professional rugby that have seen barely a week pass by without the headlines being dominated by off-the-field issues.

Envy, greed and sheer bloody-mindedness have prevented the game going forward for its betterment and there is no sign whatsoever that anything is about to change. The committee mentality that seems to be integral to every day life in Wales has refused to accept the changes that are so obviously necessary for rugby to succeed as a professional sport and, as a result, Welsh rugby has become the poor relation in the modern game. Believing international rugby to be the pinnacle of the game in Wales the WRU has shown how out of touch it has become with its domestic game. Ask any regular supporter of club rugby what their preference would be - Wales winning a Grand Slam or their club winning the Heineken Cup? Hypothetical in the extreme this may well be but the answer would almost certainly show a leaning toward club loyalty and it is this apparent unawareness that sees the WRU falling short in its responsibilities. This is not to suggest that the national game should be ignored or that the game's followers aren't concerned about its wellbeing, far from it, but it does show where priorities lie and if these were addressed by the Union then the benefits would be seen at the highest level. It is no matter of coincidence that when club rugby in Wales has been strong the national team has enjoyed periods of great success but the reverse is just as easily, and far more frequently, identified.

The brief synopsis on which this book was originally based had Newport RFC as its central 'character'. It was seen as a book that would chronicle the fortunes of the club over a seven year period and, rather naively, it was felt that this could be done to the exclusion of all else. Put the club in a goldfish bowl, look at it from the outside and tell the story from a very one dimensional viewpoint. After all, the club had come back from almost certain obscurity, it had seen the crowds return to Rodney Parade, a cup in the trophy cabinet and a lot of hard luck stories that would hopefully keep readers turning the pages. Surely this would be enough and, if not exactly providing a fairy tale ending, it had the next best thing.

Readers will have found out for themselves that this is nothing like a representative synopsis of the finished article. Certainly, Newport RFC was still the book's principal 'character', a hero even, but having created such a situation the book would now need a villain. What in fact happened was that instead of simply looking into the goldfish bowl and accepting everything seen inside as read, the finished article almost, it became obvious that there was a much stronger story to be told if it was viewed from inside the goldfish bowl looking out. This would provide a more complete picture of what had happened at Newport and would allow questions to be asked that would otherwise have been ignored. What may possibly have ended up being a very circumspect, even insular look at the professional game that rugby had become, could now encompass the wider picture and take on board the issues that were having an impact on clubs in the same position as Newport, but which were seemingly beyond their control. Unfortunately, accepting that this was the route to take it soon became obvious that what could have been viewed as a very positive book would now take on board many issues that would result in a more negative offering.

The villain of the piece will inevitably be seen as the WRU, which in many ways is correct as it is within its doors that the many issues that impacted on the game should have been initially addressed. Its failure to accept this responsibility will continue to hinder the games development at club level and until the personalities and structure within the Union are completely dismantled and replaced with something more suitable to a multi million pound business, then the problems are not likely to disappear.

Whether the arrival of an open game in 1995 can be blamed for the state of Welsh rugby in 2002 is debatable. Realistically there hadn't been a lot to get excited about for some years, but what is certain is the fact that Wales as a country was always going to struggle trying to support a professional game, even if that game was thought of as part of its national heritage. History had shown that the only area where the game had established itself at a highly competitive level was along the M4 corridor in South Wales. Even in this most densely populated part of the country one does not have to travel far off the major artery before it becomes clear that no professional sport could ever survive. The infrastructure just isn't there, whether the measurement be based on population, ground capacities or accessibility but, even after seven years of failing to cope with its demands, there are far too many clubs in Wales that are not prepared to accept the fact that they will never be in a position to embrace the professional game.

As a result of one man's commitment, Newport RFC has been able to drag itself from the brink of possible obscurity and is now seen as one of the leading clubs in the country. Money is a wonderful commodity and with a seemingly never-ending supply at their disposal, those at the sharp end of things at Rodney Parade have brought about a reversal in fortune. There is much more to it than that however, and this is the point that those watching from a distance fail to appreciate. Given the same amount of financial backing would every club in Wales have achieved all that Newport has in the last three seasons? The short answer to that is no. Why? Because there are many other factors in the equation that are equally as important as the availability of sufficient funds and it is these factors that would prove to be the downfall of most clubs. In simple terms, in estate agent jargon, the three most important factors are location, location, and location.

Ebbw Vale RFC are the latest club to go to the WRU in the hope that it will be able to see them through another crisis. This is the second time in four seasons that the valley club has experienced financial difficulty. In 1998-99 leading players Kingsley Jones and Byron Hayward were released in a commendable attempt to keep the club's overheads down but four years later and more of the same. This time three players would be removed from the squad and other employees would be made redundant. All part of a financial package put together by the Union and the club in an effort to keep Premier Division rugby at Eugene Cross Park. The club had rightly pointed to the paucity of home matches scheduled over a five month period during the coming season - only three were guaranteed - and the negative impact this would have on cash flow. This is a strong argument and one which the WRU had to listen to, similar examples had occurred in previous seasons but was this the real reason why Ebbw Vale were struggling financially? The club's main backer, Chairman, Marcus Russell, had already indicated that he would no longer financially support the club after some years of digging deep, the town had suffered a major economic setback with the decision to close the steel works and on the playing side Ebbw Vale were struggling. A culmination of events and circumstances which once again identified the tight rope being walked by Welsh clubs.

Still insisting that Premier Division rugby was wanted at Ebbw Vale, Russell referred to a wet Friday night in March that saw '8,000' turn out to watch the club play Newport, an exaggerated figure but one that could have been added to if everybody had been allowed in. Whatever the attendance, it had been largely made up of travelling supporters and to suggest that this was in any way the norm at Eugene Cross Park is ridiculous.

Nobody wants to see clubs with the great traditions the Ebbw Vales of the game can boast experiencing such difficulties, but when it is patently obvious that a professional game cannot be sustained in the town then sympathy will begin to wear thin. The WRU has a responsibility to Ebbw Vale and many other clubs like it, a responsibility that reaches much further than anything financial. The responsibility is to ensure that the game of rugby is played in the town at a level which will ensure public interest, quality rugby and a social focus. The only way this will be achieved is by the creation of a two tier structure within the game - a professional game at the top and an amateur one elsewhere.

So what of Newport, the club that Tony built? Well it isn't the club it was in August 1995, that's for sure. Writing a book charting a seven-year story that, from the outside at least, appeared to resemble something from the pen of Hans Christian Anderson, should be plain sailing. A marketing story to die for, some measure of success on the field of play, the return of the crowds - all the ingredients of a fairy tale with a happy ending. The problem is that while all these points are undoubtedly there to be applauded, Newport RFC is unable to extricate itself from the mess that is Welsh rugby and consequently faces the strong possibility that, like Ebbw Vale, it too could end up being a victim of circumstances that are beyond its control.

The first, and most important of the many problems the club has to face up to, is the fact that Tony Brown is unlikely to continue indefinitely with his financial backing. The day must surely come when even this most dedicated of men is going to have to say enough is enough, pack his bags and go. Where will that leave the club? At the outset Brown was optimistic that, after a period of heavy financial outlay, Newport RFC would eventually reach a position where it would be self-sufficient, be able to pay its way on a day-to-day, season-to-season basis, but this is clearly not going to happen in the foreseeable future and some form of contingency plan will have to be put in place to cover such a change in circumstances.

Likewise, Chief Executive, Keith Grainger, and Community Director, Phil Davies, are in positions that don't normally see a great degree of longevity. But these two men have contributed in no small way to the club's recent fortunes and they would not be easily replaced. Grainger in particular has not endeared himself to some of the people he has come into contact with but, while his aggressive manner made him unpopular in certain quarters, there are plenty of voices at the club who speak well of him. At the end of the day you can't make an omelette without breaking eggs. Some suggest that Newport RFC was a club just waiting to be marketed and that anybody could have pressed the button, a hypothetical argument that is difficult to rationalise, but at the same time one that carries little weight.

If the biggest problem likely to face Newport in the near future is something that only the Board of Directors will be able to address, the next serious threat is totally out of their control. The WRU have been a thorn in the club's side ever since it gained an element of independence. Appearing to view the club as a rival, the Union distanced itself from all that was happening at Rodney Parade, a situation that came to a head when Newport were due to stage a Wales A international against France. The WRU were reluctant to hand the marketing of the match over to Newport being particularly concerned that the pricing of tickets could under value the fixtures status. Newport could not work within the parameters being suggested by the Union and ended the matter by telling the WRU what it could do with the match. Many saw this as the club trying to upstage the Union while at the same time shooting itself in the foot - it will be a long time before the chance to stage an international match at any level comes Newport's way again - but the matter was viewed differently in the media.

In the Sunday Times, rugby correspondent Stephen Jones wrote 'If it were not so tragic for Welsh rugby, it would be hilarious. Last week two bodies argued about marketing rugby. About bringing in people to watch and lifeblood, commercial activity. They were Newport RFC, whose marketing, promotion and community operations cannot be bettered by another rugby club in Europe. And the Welsh Rugby Union, whose internal marketing ability is non-existent.

'The WRU has 'promoted' three A internationals this season, and all three were duly played in a funereal atmosphere, lacking spectators and serious sponsorship. The television producer must have cringed as his programme went out. The three games at Llanelli, Cardiff and Pontypridd, between them attracted about half the number of spectators that Newport drew to watch one match - their second string playing Uruguay on a dull Sunday at Rodney Parade. So which of the two institutions do you think has the superior marketing strategy? The terrifying thing about the WRU, you see, is that it thinks it is doing a good job for professional Welsh rugby.' One of the game's most astute commentators at his acerbic best, but unfortunately making a statement that few outside Newport would agree with. Another case of envy and tribalism getting in the way of simple common sense.

The match against Uruguay referred to by Jones attracted an attendance of 8,482. The fact that half the tickets had been given away, distributed through local schools, was never disputed by Newport, the club being quite open about the fact but even discounting this, an attendance of 4,000 for such an unimportant game played on a Sunday in the middle of November would have been more than most clubs could boast for important league matches. Which leads to the question - is the support base at Rodney Parade sufficient to take Newport forward, big enough to make the necessary contribution to revenue that the club must be looking for from this important source of income?

The latest Annual Report and Statement of Accounts published by Newport RFC Ltd is for the financial year ending 31 July 2001. At £3,382,822, turnover shows an increase of £2,048,835 on the previous year while the company reported a loss of £900,332, a reduction of £573,328 on 1999-2000. These two figures alone would suggest that Newport is starting to see a reversal in the trends of recent years however, included in the turnover figure is a donation from Tony Brown of £700,000. Taking this amount out of the equation would reduce turnover to £2,682,822, still a significant increase on the previous figure, but at the same time the loss would become £1,600,332, an increase of £126,672. What these revised figures now show is that an increase in actual operational turnover of 101% could not prevent the loss for the year increasing by 8.6%.

Taking these figures in isolation is obviously not the way to view a set of accounts but they do highlight the impact Tony Brown is having on the company and, more importantly, the impact that would be seen if he withdrew his support. The turnover figure must be increased, and it must be increased independent of any benefactor, before the future of Newport RFC Ltd can be viewed with any optimism. How? There are two obvious sources; firstly a significant increase in the support base, the attendances on match days and all the ancillary spin-offs this would generate, and secondly the WRU.

We have seen how the average attendances at Rodney Parade have escalated over the last three seasons and how, from an average gate of just under 8,000, the home support base of 6,400 was arrived at. What may well be criticised as a 'guesstimate' is surely not far off the mark and can be taken as a reflection of the current local interest the club is attracting. Rodney Parade is licensed to hold 11,676 spectators, therefore there is room for significant improvement on the average attendance seen in the 2001-02 season.

If the club could fill the ground for every home match during the coming season, and if the 3,676 additional paying customers were adults, on the basis that the majority would be restricted to the terraces - most seats being pre-sold - then it is a reasonable estimate that revenue would increase by some £35-£40,000 per match. With a maximum of fifteen home matches on the fixture list, and the extremely unlikely event of all the above criteria being met, there is a potential £5-£600,000 additional revenue available to the club. If each of the cumulative 51,000 extra spectators spent £3 at the club the maximum additional revenue Newport can possibly hope to generate from Rodney Parade on match days would be an optimistic £750,000. A mere £50,000 more than Tony Brown donated to the club in 2000-01. These figures have not been pulled out of thin air, neither are they based on any factual information, but they would not be found to be wildly inaccurate based on current prices, and with every assumption calculated in the club's favour, the reality of the situation should not be wasted on anybody.

The second option lies with the WRU. The governing body in Wales contributes funding to its member clubs but those at the sharp end of the game, those in the Premier Division, have long since felt that their share was not sufficient to help them sustain a professional game. This has led to much argument and conflict over the years which culminated with the 'Gang of Six' and all the turmoil that resulted from their proposals. Few informed parties would argue against the need to reduce the number of clubs in the Premier Division - the report by the Working Party came to this conclusion - the WRU, through its Chairman, Glanmor Griffiths, is on record as being of the same opinion and obviously the clubs most likely to feature in any restructuring are singing from the same hymn sheet. However, it will need more than a consensus of opinion from these three parties to implement the change. There is the small matter of the loyalty agreements signed by the clubs that guarantee a minimum of eight clubs in the Premier Division until 2008 and even then the proposal would have to be put before the member clubs of the Union, a sobering prospect. And there is the not so small problem that sees the WRU struggling with its own financial problems which emanate from the Millennium Stadium and all the borrowing that has to be both serviced and repaid. A question of title to the land the Stadium is built on has recently been raised, with the suggestion that BT have a vested interest in it, and this would have to be resolved before the possibility of selling the Stadium could be considered. This is a delicate subject that was raised at the WRU's AGM held in July 2002. There is no doubt that the Millennium Stadium would have a value well in excess of the liabilities that are currently outstanding and selling it could well be an instant fix to all the financial problems that are affecting the game. Why not lease the Stadium for the required number of days each season and let the responsibility for its upkeep over the rest of the year pass to another party? This is a proposal that the Union is preferring to ignore at the moment, being still of the opinion that the debt will be amortised over the coming years; time will tell. In the meantime, Newport cannot expect any further financial contribution from this source, over and above that which it currently receives, and the search for the fiscal control so desperately needed must continue elsewhere.

With these two possible sources of increased revenue faced by what appear to be insurmountable stumbling blocks, Newport is going to have to look at other ways of controlling its finances. Wages have escalated in recent years and the club is already showing signs of having taken this on board. There have been fewer summer signings in the last two years and there is every indication that the club is starting to look more and more to its development squads for first team players. The glaring exception to this policy is the 'signing' of South African star Percy Montgomery. This player will not come cheap but he will attract a new audience to Rodney Parade and this could be capitalised on in the future. After the van der Westhuizen debacle most supporters of the club will prefer to wait until Montgomery takes the field at Newport in a Black and Amber jersey before accepting this signing as a racing certainty, but this aside the club has been very modest in its pursuit of new players. With the departure of Ian

Macintosh, however, there was one area where the club had to recruit and Welshman, Leigh Jones together with ex England scrum half and captain, Richard Hill, were contracted to take over the coaching duties.

The policy of trying to control the wage bill could bear fruit in a couple of seasons when some of the highest paid players come to the end of their contracts or in some cases, their playing careers. Cardiff at the end of the 2001-02 season let Rob Howley, Neil Jenkins, Craig Quinnell and Jon Humphries move on, in addition to which they saw the departure of coach Rudi Joubert who returned to South Africa at the behest of SARFU while still under contract and therefore the subject of a compensation payment. These changes have probably reduced the club's overheads by as much as £500,000 and, like Newport, Cardiff has been relatively inactive in the signing of new players. The penny appears to have dropped and when one considers the wealth behind both Newport and Cardiff it is surely only a matter of time before the message is taken on board by other clubs currently paying their players far too much. There will always be the threat from English clubs wanting to take the cream but Welsh clubs are going to have to bite the bullet if they want a secure future.

Like any business recording regular annual losses, Newport RFC Ltd has to increase productivity and cut costs to be in with a chance of survival. This is not going to be easy for a club that is not in complete control of its own destiny. The areas that Newport has successfully exploited have been those where little or no outside input has been necessary; marketing and community projects and, of course, its on-the-field performance. Whether Newport was one of the 73% of the clubs polled by Rugby World that saw a brighter future in a professional sport is not known, but the club has certainly come a long way in the seven years and, after a slow start, has lasted the pace better than most.

Having got a firm footing on the bottom of the ladder Newport now has to start climbing and meet the new challenges that await. The support base has to be significantly increased, now is not the time to sit back and congratulate all concerned for a job well done. The marketing department have to look at what they have achieved to date and find ways of doing it again, twofold. The 'Sold Out' signs must be permanent at every entrance to Rodney Parade thereby creating a supply and demand situation where the demand outweighs the supply - that would deserve a pat on the back. There have been suggestions that the club could benefit from a move to an out of town location, a twenty thousand all-seater stadium. Fine, but not before one with an 11,676 capacity is failing to cope with demand.

And what of the team? The players who, in the eyes of many, stand for everything that Newport RFC represents. They must now deliver. Wonderful it surely was, but it must not be another twenty-four years before the Welsh Cup is won again. Neither must supporters have to get used to the disappointment of being runners-up in the league; for this to happen twice in three years isn't without merit but it mustn't become a habit. No matter how much kudos is placed on winning domestic competitions, Europe's glittering prize is the Heineken Cup and all else pales into insignificance when compared to it. Winning this most prestigious tournament brings huge financial rewards and clubs place qualification to compete in it above all else. This must be the real objective at Newport RFC, the one thing above all else that would confirm the return of the club to the big time.

There is no doubting the fact that Newport RFC has got it right. Regardless of the advantages it has over many of its rivals, ground ownership and wealthy benefactor, it has started to capitalise on the factors that are unique to it in an attempt to become a self sufficient rugby club. The population it serves, the history that it boasts and the message that it is putting across in the community will all stand it in good stead in the coming years but it will all be for nought if the problems that are outside its control are not addressed.

Tony Brown can feel particularly proud of the enormous part he has played in this great adventure and he must never be allowed to feel guilty at some not too distant future date when he takes that inevitable step back. Newport RFC will miss him when the time comes, not his money but the man who made it all happen. Having said that, it is time that clubs stopped relying on the likes of Brown to pay the bills because, while acting with all good intention, all they are really doing is camouflaging the brutal truth: the fact that the domestic game in Wales under its present structure cannot possibly sustain itself as a professional sport.

There really are 'many more hills to climb', but if any club in Wales is likely to negotiate them successfully it will be Newport RFC. Keep watching that bridge!

OTHER PUBLICATIONS BY

VERTICAL EDITIONS

Fast Lane to Shangri-La; The Story of a Rugby League Family
Author: Dave Sampson
ISBN: 1-904091-00-8
Price: £9.99

Dave Sampson's critically acclaimed autobiography captures the essence of Rugby League and mixes it with a good dose of Northern humour.

Salford City Reds; A Willows Century
Author: Graham Morris
ISBN: 1-904091-02-4
Price: £18.99

A century ago, over 16,000 Salford fans witnessed the first match at their brand new enclosure, a venue renowned throughout the Rugby League world as The Willows. This is the definitive story of that magnificent old ground - host to both Challenge Cup Finals and internationals - and the many wonderful players, legendary names like Jimmy Lomas, Gus Risman and David Watkins, who have proudly worn the red jersey of Salford.

Just Champion! Yorkshire's 33-Year Fight for their Cricketing Birthright
Author: David Bond
ISBN: 1-904091-03-2
Price: £14.99

Just Champion! recounts the story of 33 years of turmoil as Yorkshire County Cricket Club sought to regain what they regarded as their cricketing birthright.

Dean Sampson;
My Shangri-La
Authors: Dave Sampson and Dean Sampson
ISBN: 1-904091-04-0
Price: £10.99

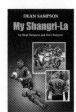

The follow-up to his father Dave's book, Fast Lane to Shangri-La. The book tells Dean's story of growing up in the Sampson household amongst other stars of Rugby League and his playing career with Castleford Tigers, England and the Great Britain touring party.

Vertical Editions titles can be purchased or ordered from your local bookshop, alternatively you can order direct. Send a cheque payable to Vertical Editions for the price of the book together with your name and delivery address to:

VERTICAL EDITIONS,
18-20 BLACKWOOD HALL LANE,
LUDDENDENFOOT, HALIFAX HX2 6HD
Free delivery in the UK